Apps

Digital Media and Society Series

Apps

From Mobile Phones to Digital Lives

GERARD GOGGIN

polity

First published in 2021 by Polity Press

Polity Press
65 Bridge Street
Cambridge CB2 1UR, UK

Polity Press
101 Station Landing
Suite 300
Medford, MA 02155, USA

ISBN-13: 978-1-5095-3848-5
ISBN-13: 978-1-5095-3849-2 (pb)

A catalogue record for this book is available from the British Library.

Library of Congress Cataloging-in-Publication Data

Names: Goggin, Gerard, 1964- author.
Title: Apps : from mobile phones to digital lives / Gerard Goggin.
Description: Cambridge, UK ; Medford, MA, USA : Polity, 2021. | Series: Digital media and society series | Includes bibliographical references and index. | Summary: "A trailblazing study of one of the most ubiquitous modern technologies"-- Provided by publisher.
Identifiers: LCCN 2020054803 (print) | LCCN 2020054804 (ebook) | ISBN 9781509538485 (hardback) | ISBN 9781509538492 (paperback) | ISBN 9781509538508 (epub)
Subjects: LCSH: Mobile computing--Social aspects. | Application software--Social aspects. | Smartphones--Social aspects. | Digital media.
Classification: LCC HM851 .G6448 2021 (print) | LCC HM851 (ebook) | DDC 302.23/1--dc23
LC record available at https://lccn.loc.gov/2020054803
LC ebook record available at https://lccn.loc.gov/2020054804

Typeset in 10.25 on 13pt Scala
by Fakenham Prepress Solutions, Fakenham, Norfolk NR21 8NL
Printed and bound by Short Run Press

For further information on Polity, visit our website:
politybooks.com

Contents

Abbreviations and Acronyms

1G	first-generation mobile network standard
2G	second-generation mobile network standard
3G	third-generation mobile network standard
4G	fourth-generation mobile network standard
5G	fifth-generation mobile network standard
AI	artificial intelligence
API	application programming interface
AR	augmented reality
ARC	Australian Research Council
BBS	bulletin board system
BoP	bottom of the pyramid
BRICS	Brazil, Russia, India, China, and South Africa
CDMA	code division multiple access
CEO	chief executive officer
CMOS	complementary metal oxide semiconductor
CPU	central processing unit
customer ID	customer identification number
dapps	distributed apps
DAU	daily active users
DVC	deputy vice-chancellor
EU	European Union
FCC	Federal Communications Commission
GPS	global positioning system
GSM	global system for mobile communications
HCI	human–computer interaction
HP	Hewlett-Packard
HTML	hypertext markup language

HUD	head-up display
IAMCR	International Association of Media Communications Research
ICT	information and communications technologies
IM	instant messaging
I-mode	Internet mode is a microbrowser technology that supports text, graphics, audio, and video for Web access
iOS	operating system for Apple mobile devices (originally iPhone operating system)
IoT	Internet of Things
IP	Internet protocol
IRC	Internet relay chat
ISDN	integrated services digital network
ITU	International Telecommunications Union
KaiOS	mobile operating system based on Linux
LED	light-emitting diode
LMIC	low- to middle-income countries
MMS	*module management system*
NFC	near field communication
NTT	Nippon Telegraph and Telephone Corporation
OCR	optical character recognition
OED	Oxford English Dictionary
OS	computer operating system
OTT	over-the-top
PDA	portable digital assistants
PPI	Progressive Policy Institute
QR code	quick response code
RFID	radio frequency identification
RL	real life
SDK	software developer kit
SME	social media entertainment
SMS	short message service
SoC	system-on-a-chip application processor

STS	science and technology studies
SSEAC	Sydney Southeast Asia Centre
UX	user experience
VPN	virtual private network
VR	virtual reality
WAP	wireless application protocol
WiFi	wireless fidelity
WML	wireless markup language

Tables

Acknowledgments

In this book I bring together ideas that I have garnered and mused upon since at least 2007–2008. That was the time when the smartphone took off, and subsequently apps have proliferated, spread, and become implacably installed at the center of contemporary digital infrastructures, which in turn now underpin many societies globally.

I am grateful for the rich body of work on mobile communication and media and for many conversations, exchanges, and critiques I have been fortunate to have from friends and colleagues in this field, which has come into existence in the early 00s. This book functions as the third volume in a series and takes up many of the concepts, technologies, and ideas I explored in *Cell Phone Culture* in 2006 and *Global Mobile Media* in 2011.

My thanks to Cherry Baylosis, Xu Wei Wei (apps in China), and Punit Jagasia (apps in India) for their research assistance. I am especially grateful to Rosemary Curtis for her peerless research advice and for the preparation and proofing of the manuscript.

I would like to acknowledge the support of the University of Sydney, especially through a Faculty of Arts and Social Sciences and DVC Research Compact Funding award for the project titled "Emerging Social Technology." Earlier funding from the Sydney Southeast Asia Centre (SSEAC) for the research workshop "Social and Mobile Media in Southeast Asia" (co-convened with Lim Sun Sun) proved germinal, and I am grateful to its director, Professor Michele Ford, for this award.

The book was written after I took up a position at the superb Wee Kim Wee School of Communication and Information at Nanyang Technological University, Singapore. In a practical and government-of-the-self sense, the COVID-19 circuit breaker left me no option but to finish the book. The angle afforded by Singapore, an entrepôt and a global crossroads, has proved enormously helpful. My thanks to various colleagues, especially Rich Ling, and to the thoughtful and engaged students in my courses, "Global Media Issues and Policy" and "Digital Media Governance," for many informative conversations.

It has been a pleasure to publish my first book with Polity. Sincere thanks to Mary Savigar for giving me the idea in the first place, for inviting me to consider it, for providing feedback, and for commissioning the project. I owe Ellen McDonald-Kramer a special debt of gratitude for her unstinting support and thoughtful advice through the process. Thanks to the reviewers for their helpful feedback.

Finally, thanks to my family, Bianca, Liam, and Jacqui, for their love, support, and interest especially during the close-quarter circuit breaker period of the COVID pandemic.

Gerard Goggin
Wee Kim Wee School of Information and Communication
Nanyang Technological University, Singapore
March 2021

CHAPTER ONE

Introduction

On Saturday, June 20, 2020, US President Donald Trump was looking forward to a campaign rally in Tulsa, Oklahoma, which he had been widely publicizing via his Twitter account. Only a disappointing 6,200 supporters turned up, leaving many empty seats conspicuously vacant in a stadium with a capacity of 19,000. The shortfall was credited to a prank by TikTok users and K-pop fans, who apparently booked half a million tickets for the rally, causing rally organizers to wildly overestimate attendance (Andrews, 2020). While the exact nature of this digital activism success is tricky to pin down (Madison & Klang, 2020), there's no doubt that this was an important moment of worldwide recognition of the influence of an app.

From mundane, everyday videos of teens idling and improvising, TikTok quickly established itself as major force in popular culture, especially during the COVID-19 pandemic, gaining a reputation for its signature abbreviated, hilarious, and whip-smart videos. Like YouTube before it, TikTok gained a following across many countries. Rajiv Rao, contributor to the Indian tech blog ZDNet, sung its praises: "TikTok introduced India to everyday stars from small towns and villages, and across genders, classes, and castes" (Rao, 2020). TikTok's vibrant base of users provided a platform to social activism, a high-water mark being the #BlackLivesMatter hashtag, which exceeded 12 billion views in mid-2020, before the prank on Trump's Tulsa event. Along the way, TikTok has been embroiled in considerable debate on its conservative and narrow norms of gender, race, class, and money—and hence on its contradictory role in reproducing and potentially supporting challenges to inequality and injustice (Kennedy, 2020).

Yet this flowering of cultural activity threatened to come juddering to a halt with India's June 2020 ban on TikTok and on 58 other Chinese apps over data security concerns. Hot on the heels was Trump, with his August 2020 executive orders that blocked TikTok and WeChat from US app stores and processed transactions of US citizens, then required TikTok to be sold to US interest (or face a ban).

The spectacular career of TikTok shows us only one facet of the omnipresent media and of the cultural phenomenon that is apps. Many people around the world use apps in a myriad of ways—to go to sleep, wake up, plan and manage their daily routines and unexpected events, track and guide their bodies, engage in relationships, or negotiate food, work, health, finances, pleasures, aversions, annoyances, and many other aspects of personal, public, and social life. During the COVID-19 pandemic in 2020–2021, apps have come even more to the fore, especially as a technology of choice, expectation, or—as with infectious disease—contact, tracking, and tracing and as a legal requirement and instrument of population and health surveillance and control.

The central argument of the book is that apps represent a pivotal sociotechnical development in a key phase of digital media development. You can see apps as the hinge between two stages of recent media and communication. On the one hand, there are the visions and realities of the mobile, cyber, and online societies, which people envisaged from the late 1980s through to the early 00s. On the other hand, there are the imaginaries and materialities of pervasive media and immersive digital societies, which emerged internationally in the 2010s and onwards, in all their different forms and inequalities.

Apps bring together mobile phones and the Internet; software, computational, data, and hardware developments;

web technologies, including the mobile web and what was briefly called Web 2.0; locative technologies; wearable devices; and connected cars, homes, and other environments. Great numbers of users access social media via mobile apps; but the two things are different. Apps provide bridges across the messy ecologies of media, technology, environments, and bodies. Yet apps also represent a litmus test for the shortcomings, limits, edges, and inequalities of digital media's diffusion and social functions. While apps can ease users' way into digital cultures, they also often fail or fall short; added to which, apps are often unavailable or too expensive. The apps system can be wasteful and amplify the environmental problems of smartphones and other digital technology. And apps can exacerbate digital exclusion and inequality just as much as they extend access and social participation.

As a guide to understanding the teeming and complex area of apps, the book is pitched at readers who would like a better understanding of apps as part of media, communication, culture, and society. It is aimed at university students of all levels, on programs from undergraduate through masters to doctoral. The book also provides a theoretically informed state-of-the-art account for researchers who study apps across a range of disciplines and fields. In the process, it seeks to lay out and discuss the pivotal role of apps in various contests over social futures in the emerging next-generation Internet, mobile technologies, the Internet of Things, AI and machine learning, automated technologies, platforms, and data cultures and infrastructures.

The Apps Pivot in Digital Media and Society

To make sense of the heady career of apps, I advance five key arguments in the chapters that follow.

First, as elaborated in chapter 2, I discuss the fundamental identity of apps as a kind of software. Like all software, apps have a relationship—and are in dialogue—with the hardware that their code operates as well as with the environments in which both the software and the hardware are situated. While apps have enormous variety and flexibility, they also operate within distinct constraints. Within these limits, apps offer an important bridging of digital media and society: they provide fabric for the sociotechnical systems and infrastructures that characterize many digital societies, as these have taken shape in recent years and are evolving toward the future.

Second, apps are often excitedly promoted as paving the way for wonderful kinds of innovation, woven together with new kinds of economics business models, which typically involve the catchall notion of entrepreneurship. Yet such apparently limitless potential is clearly offset by the fact that apps exist within systems of value, power, and control. At various levels, especially at the level of their construction, design, and affordances, apps constrain their users just as much as they enable them, if not more. Apps often channel their users, uses, and meanings into distinct social relations, economies, and politics. This is the argument I make in chapters 3 and 4, which trace the political and cultural economy of apps, their implication in geopolitical shifts, and the creation of new infrastructures and forms.

Third, in an extraordinarily creative way, apps are pivotal to a teeming field of media innovations; this is something I discuss in chapter 4. App media build on many of the aspects of computers, software, and code applications before the smartphone era. Since the early 00s at least, and indeed well before the turn of the century, apps as media have supported, framed, and mediated our contemporary developments centered on data, algorithms, machine learning, and AI. Taking a wider view still, it is remarkable how apps have been crystallized and have driven innovations across a very wide range of media. In part, these app media innovations have to do with interactions and development in social life and technology that center on the rise of various digital media forms—games, video sharing and streaming, camera, images, visuals, text, language, messages, sound, audio, music, voice, and so on. A reflex focus of many actors in these process as well as of commentators has often been on the app itself: its design, development, marketing, user acceptance, and viability. However, the app is often just the tip of the iceberg. The app helps create a new media form, but it does so as a portal, entry point, or strategic node in a larger system and assemblage.

Fourth, for better or worse, apps function as social laboratories; this is the subject of chapter 5. Apps are fabrics that help media stretch into new shapes, and they also expand our ideas of what functions media can perform. The myriad media of apps infiltrate everyday life in new ways. All around the world, apps have been seized or used to make do as resources for projects of social change. They can be pivotal in infrastructures that underpin political, social, and cultural change. The social laboratories of apps operate at a huge range of scales, which run from the small worlds of our ordinary lives through the meso levels of organizations, institutions, subcultures, communities, and publics to the macro levels of national, regional, and global settings.

Fifth, because of characteristics of apps outlined in these four arguments, we need to talk about apps and take their functions, implications, and potentials seriously, yet skeptically. There have been many anxieties raised by apps and their deleterious impacts on work–life balance, mental health, relationships and intimacies, misinformation and fake news, hate speech, extreme content, bias, discrimination, and inequalities, not to mention the future of cultural diversity, or accessible and affordable media. However, apps have been hard to pin down. They seem to be everywhere—"there's an app for that"—and yet they are kinda boring—just part of the digital and social furniture. Issues of values, politics, and policy associated with apps early on—such as the enclosure and control represented by the advent of app stores, the role of apps in the creeping commodification of culture and media, and then across swathes of social life—were slippery and hard to pin down.

Apps debates have changed dramatically in recent years. One obvious area of concern is the extension of data into many areas of human, built, and natural environments. Datafication has been widely discussed and critiqued. Apps are not just a bit player in the politics of data infrastructures, algorithms, and AI, as we can now see vividly from the wide and deep global and local issues raised by the entrenchment of what has been called "digital platforms." We don't have a clear sense so far of where apps fit into this global landscape, where media and communications offer enormous scope for advancing social progress, equality, justice, rights, and other important values and goals, yet the countervailing realities and future scenarios appear very bleak. By way of concluding the book, I look at the role of apps in the grand social project of putting media and communications firmly back in people's hands.

Thinking about Apps

In thinking about apps, we can start with work that focuses on the topic. The first dedicated book on apps was Paul D. Miller and Svitlana Matviyenko's 2014 multicontributor volume *The Imaginary App* (Miller & Matviyenko, 2014). Matviyenko was the lead editor of another landmark anthology of studies on apps, a 2015 special issue of the journal *Fibreculture* titled *Apps and Affect* (Matviyenko et al., 2015). This volume raised questions about the intense relationships that apps have with our bodies and on how we feel, perceive, and know things. The next milestone in app research was Jeremy Wade Morris and Sarah Murray's 2018 multicontributor volume *Appified*, which looked at the ways in which apps fit into and shape contemporary media and culture in general: "[A]pps represent not just a fashionable tech trend but a new way of accessing information, experiencing media, mediating commerce, and understanding the self and others" (Morris & Murray, 2018, p. 19). The fourth milestone is an ambitious effort to create methods for app studies; it comes from various researchers gathered under the banner of the App Studies Initiative who give us the following message:

> Apps are designed to perform as concrete software objects but are continually transformed ... the notion of apps as entirely self-contained also belies their involvement in the data flows of multi-sided platforms and their necessary entanglement with varying hardware devices and digital infrastructures that make their operations at once possible and, indeed, valuable. (Dieter et al., 2019, p. 2)

In addition to these four landmarks in app studies, extensive research on apps has been carried out and distributed across the reaches of many disciplines and fields, much of which I have consulted and drawn upon in the following chapters (insofar as space permitted).

It can be helpful to approach apps as a relatively recent development in the broader field of mobile communications and media. Scholars have theorized mobile communications and media as a new phase of communication technology and society (Katz & Aakhus, 2002; Ling, 2012). A range of cultural and media researchers have been especially interested in the way in which mobile communication unfolds, takes shape, and is imagined, used, and adapted in social and cultural contexts. Drawing on a wide range of traditions, and especially on cultural studies, researchers have contributed a rich body of work on the cultural dimensions of mobile media (Goggin, 2008). They have sought to understand the intensity and the reach of mobile media across social and individual life. There has been a symbiosis between smartphones and apps in their mass diffusion phase: "[S]martphones have changed the way we communicate ... smartphones are structured into the very way that we coordinate society ... The 'appification' of mobile communication is one of the key transitions in the development of the smartphone" (Rich et al., 2020, pp. 3, 9; see also Jin, 2017).

While apps have taken shape via other digital technologies such as smartphones, at the most fundamental level they are a form of software. They are constituted via programming and coding, which have materialities that shape the design, implementations, and effects of apps, as the case of news shows us (Weber & Kosterich, 2018). Since the emergence of software studies, theories and research around software have moved beyond grappling with the complexity of software and attempted especially to pinpoint its pivotal and catalytic role in the creation of digital media.

Apps have reshaped the Internet and how we experience it—especially because their emergence coincides with the rise of social media. Many of the most popular apps are social media apps such as the popular Facebook, Twitter, Weibo, or Instagram services. Social media apps foster what José van Dijck has called a "culture of connectivity" (van Dijck, 2013). They also make it hard for us to disconnect from digital networks (Hesselberth, 2018). Many social media services started as Internet services or as pre-smartphone mobile services. This includes Facebook, which many users experience and think of as a mobile app, not as an Internet-based software for a desktop or laptop computer. With mobile media, especially smartphones, come the kinds of affordances that offer different inventions and appropriations of social media, notably portability, availability, locatability, and multi-mediality, as Andrew Schrock argues (Schrock, 2015). The mix of connectivity and affordances is taken in new directions by messaging apps such as Line, WeChat, and WhatsApp, to mention but a few.

From the trajectory of apps, we can also return to funda-mental questions of media and communication. What kind of medium is an app? And what kind of communication does it enact or support? Apps are also a barometer and conduit for emerging directions in media of various sorts—such as sensory, haptic, audio, and sound media, as well as other kinds, less well recognized in high modernist media studies. Apps spurred new ways of thinking about media and media objects, for instance post-phenomenological approaches (Ash, 2018).

If nothing else, the rise of apps has been underpinned by an extraordinary growth in data and by the increasing role that smartphones and apps play in the new data infrastructures, economy, ecologies, and cultures. So here we find a range of critical work on data helpful for understanding apps. This work encompasses the part they play in surveillance (Thurman, 2018); the concept of data colonialism, including the compulsory nature of data enlistment, and the stakes in disconnection (Couldry & Mejias, 2019); the sociology of data selves and identities (Lupton, 2016, 2020); data sharing and social practices (Grundy et al., 2019); the leaky nature of data and the fragmented contexts of apps (Wilmott, 2016).

Apps have been significantly transformed and reconfigured by the rise of algorithms, AI, machine learning, and automation and by users' iterative interactions with these technologies. Apps themselves are shaped by algorithms: the ranking of apps by app stores, or the co-construction of social categories and relationships such as "friendship" or intimacy, are cases in point (see Chambers, 2017; Wang, 2020a). As for automation, it turns out that many apps, despite their intentions and design, are surprisingly unautomated—hence the ongoing issue of the relationship between human actions and automation has a strong purchase in relation to apps as well (Gervasio, 2019). Thus apps play an important role in understanding the nature and place of algorithms in contemporary media (Galloway, 2006; Gillespie, 2014; Neyland, 2019; Striphas, 2015) and in the conduct and governance of culture and of everyday life (Latzer & Festic, 2019). Scholars in critical algorithm studies have pointed to a range of problems caused by the growing dependence on, and indeed design premised upon, algorithms and apps. This aspect is captured in Sara Wachter-Boettcher's 2017 book *Technically Wrong: Sexist Apps, Biased Algorithms, and Other Threats of Toxic Tech* (Wachter-Boettcher, 2017). Various scholars have investigated the role of apps in reinforcing social inequalities and injustice, including those related to race (Benjamin, 2019; Poster, 2019).

A stumbling block here is the way in which apps are used, at least in much public discourse, to frame a familiar, welcoming user perspective on emerging technology developments. Also challenging is the way in which apps are conjoined with algorithms in promises of brighter, seductive social futures, and also in their dystopian, dark sides. An excellent example of this can be seen in imaginaries and in plans for future smart cities (Green, 2019), or in the area of digital government and service delivery—what Paul Henman dubs "digital social policy" (Henman, 2019).

An important shift in the nature of apps has occurred with the arrival of "digital platforms." Now in their ascendancy, digital platforms represent a new phase for apps. They have their origins in the different computer operating systems and software of the 1980s and 1990s, such as Windows and Apple. Games platforms also appeared; they represent another kind of "platform wars"—for instance, rivalries between Sony, Nintendo, and Microsoft and, later, between streaming providers such as Twitch (Taylor, 2018), Facebook Gaming, and YouTube Gaming. Games had a formative role in the invention of creative and computational aspects of digital platforms (Andreessen, 2007; Bogost & Monfort 2009).

Platforms are significant because they integrate various things that make them compelling for their users. While digital platforms take different forms, commonly they are corporately or privately owned infrastructure, enclosed or semi-closed systems, and offer new ways to connect the various sides of markets—consumers, producers, and intermediaries. Digital platforms involve systems that take advantage of the massive growth of data, using machine learning, algorithms, and AI. They also link new digital technologies: location tech, social media, mobile media, research, machine learning, AI, sensors, and the Internet of Things. Crucially, digital platforms create powerful network effects, which are gains that the network and other infrastructures offer to each new user, because she or he can access already existing users (Gillespie, 2010, 2018; Mansell & Steinmuller, 2020; Srnicek, 2019; van Dijck et al., 2018). Among other things, such digital platforms are often associated with new kinds of (digital) work and labor, as well as with intensive new roles for consumers and users (e.g. the roles involved in the ratings and rankings evident on many platforms such as Uber, Airbnb, or Airtasker).

Apps play an important role in many digital platforms. In the first place, they provide functionalities and benefits, including friendly and relatively familiar ways for users to access, negotiate, use, and participate in digital platforms (Ashlin et al., 2020). In addition, apps are vital in discourses of digital platforms (cf. Gillespie, 2010), mainly because they often are a prime selling point for these platforms. Consider, for instance, how smart cities developments—including what is called "platform urbanism" (Barns, 2020)—feature apps as a way to emphasize the seamless and beneficial incorpo- ration of citizens and consumers; or consider how digital government initiatives highlight apps.

The research, public, and policy debates on digital platforms also help us sharpen up our understanding of apps and their stakes. It has often been difficult to get a handle on the politics of apps, or on their social or design implications. This is especially the case because concern and inquiry have centered on individual apps or classes of apps, such as health, medical, and dating apps. The incorporation of apps into digital platforms has highlighted the underlying systems, digital ecologies, and economies they support and to which they belong.

Overview

In laying out the coordinates of apps, the book proceeds as follows.

In chapter 2, "What's an App?," I give a working definition of apps and look at the histories and important predecessors of apps that have shaped them today. I also outline the forms and functions of apps and their importance to contemporary media and society.

Chapter 3, "App Economy," lays out the fundamental elements we need if we wish to understand global app economies, industries, and systems of value and control. I seek to establish apps as eminently *international* media technologies in their economic, industrial, and power structures. While it often seems that the key players are Apple, Google, and others that are headquartered in North America, Europe, or the United Kingdom, apps are very much a global, regional, local, and international phenomenon. I follow the story of the economics, politics, and forms of apps by interrogating the striking transformations wrought in recent years by the rise of other regions and countries that challenge the dominance of the western app stores and tech companies. After exploring China's app stores and app market, I move to a discussion of how that country and various other Asian markets are innovating to create new forms and business models for apps in the form of mini apps and super apps— forms and models that promise to lessen consumer and business reliance on the "bottleneck" infrastructure of the app store.

In chapter 4, "App Media," we change the pace and focus on apps as media. In particular, I consider the ways in which apps reshape the boundaries of how we regard and experience media. With their flexibility, ductility, and indispensable role in the weaving of contemporary networked digital media, apps break new ground and open up new modes for us to make things, connect, create meaning, forge social action, engage in our cultures, and mediate. I look at apps as a multimedia and multimodal computational software, which operates as a kind of modern-day kaleidoscope. In relatively quick succession, I discuss app media as contributing to, being constituted by, and in various and often connected forms partaking in games media, locative media, realities media (virtual, augmented, mixed), photo and image apps and app visualities, moving image media, sound media, message media, and something I call "quotidian voice media."

In chapter 5, "Social Laboratories of Apps," I discuss the significant ways in which apps go well beyond the previous boundaries of media, spanning across the gamut of social realms. As I shall show, apps are framed and propelled by their actors to act as something of a laboratory of the social. They extend the qualities, the repertoire, and the immersive and catalytic role of digital media and communications, as this formerly specific and relatively enclosed area has scribbled over and redrawn the dividing lines between public and private spheres and has spurred new roles for and dependencies upon technology in our lives, other species, and our collective environments. The chapter focuses on four especially revealing areas, where apps have functioned as social laboratories of various kinds: health and well-being; money, especially payment systems, remittance and money transfer, banking, and FinTech apps; consumption, especially in the area of shopping apps; and relationships in the categories of dating and hookup apps.

In the concluding chapter 6, "After Apps," I move to ideas of the future and discuss how apps function as a resource and a prompt for the imagining, planning, and politics of the future. What, for instance, is the anticipated and emerging role of apps as a golden thread in visions and plans of the Internet of Things, 5G networks, and next-generation AI-supported infrastructures and technology and social systems? An overarching thread in this chapter is the need to critically evaluate the kinds of claims and discourses in which apps feature, especially in order to better ground, understand, and reimagine the social futures and values that are inscribed in and through apps. I bring together the key arguments of the book, discussing the place of apps on the wider scene of digital media and society. As the chapter suggests, apps are but one area in a sprawling set of digital transformations. Yet critical attention to apps is key to our understanding of digital societies.

CHAPTER TWO

What's an App?

What's an app, and what's an app store? As we have already seen, apps are obvious, but tricky to pin down. They are software, but depend on lots of other software, operating systems, hardware, and infrastructures. Then there are all the social conditions and dynamics that go into making apps possible—let alone useful and compelling, for their users and for social life. In this foundational chapter, then, I aim to provide a working definition of apps, to explain how they work and where they fit and bridge wider digital media and society.

In the first part I will give an anatomy of an app, looking at its main parts, what its functions are, and how apps fit into software, hardware, and other key technology systems. To understand the significance of apps as a social and technical accomplishment, it is useful to know a bit about their history and development. So, in the second part I look at predecessor technologies. I focus on histories of mobile technologies, especially handheld devices such as calculators, palm pilots, and portable digital assistants (PDAs), and then on mobile phones, but also on the network and software associated with these systems. This provides a context for understanding the smartphone moment in 2007–2009, which saw the launch of the iPhone, of Google's Android operating system, and of app stores and eventually an avalanche of apps and associated take-up and innovation across users, organizations, institutions, and developers.

Anatomy of an App

The word "app" is short for "application." The *Oxford English Dictionary* gives it this primary meaning:

> A piece of software designed to perform a specific function other than one relating to the operation of the computer itself; *esp.* (in later use) one designed specifically to run on a mobile phone or tablet computer. (OED, 2020)

The OED registers the earliest instances of the word "app" and its plural "apps"; these occurred in *Computerworld* magazine in the early 1980s. "Killer app" is a term recorded as appearing in the late 1980s. It was short for "killer application," meaning something indispensable or without a rival (OED). As software and computing historian Martin Campbell-Kelly explains, "[t]he 'killer app' hypothesis argues that a novel application, by enabling an activity that was previously impossible or too expensive, causes a new technology to become widely adopted" (Campbell-Kelly, 2003, p. 212). The moniker "killer app" was applied for instance to VisiCalc. VisiCalc was an application launched in 1979 that brought the spreadsheet to personal computing, paving the way for the PC to be taken seriously as a business tool (pp. 212–214). For some time, "apps" designated a diverse range of software applications for desktop or enterprises computers, handhelds (such as the Palm), Internet and web apps, and then, increasingly, mobile phones. For instance, applications for the mobile Internet wireless access protocol (WAP) were sometimes referred to as "WAP apps." At this stage, though, "mobile apps" could still refer mostly to applications and design solutions for mobile hardware and devices—not necessarily just to software.

This changes from roughly 2001 onwards. That year saw an increase in the frequency of references to mobile apps and handheld apps—or, in the US context, wireless apps—across a range of news and journalism outlets, especially in the trade and business press. This is not surprising, given the industry's growing focus on mobile applications development and the efforts to develop more content and services for emerging 2G and 3G mobile services. At the premier mobile industry event 3GSM World Congress in 2003 there were announcements of new commercial ventures designed to expand mobile app development and distribution. At this juncture, vendors were still seeking to link up mobile devices with software applications and data running on enterprise networks and services—the Canadian company Blackberry, for instance, was reported as aiming to "mobilise apps" (Moore, 2004).

As we shall see, apps really became a household word from 2008 onwards. To understand how this app moment came about, we'll shortly have a look at some of the kinds of technologies, social developments, and media cultures that created the conditions for apps to become a household word. In the meanwhile, let's see how apps work as a technology.

As software, apps cannot work without hardware. The key hardware for apps is the smartphone. The smartphone combines three previously separate functions: cellular mobile telecommunications; mobile Internet; and mobile computing. If you dismantle a smartphone, you will find a CPU (central processing unit). This is a computer chip that is typically integrated into a CMOS (complementary metal-oxide-semiconductor) SoC (system-on-a-chip) application processor. You will also find a power source in the form of a rechargeable battery. There will be one or more antennae (transducers) for receiving and transmitting data via electromagnetic waves in order to handle a range of different signals from cellular networks, Bluetooth, WiFi (wireless fidelity), the GPS (global positioning system), or NFC (near field communication). These may not all be housed in the same chip, but rather crammed into the device housings. Added to which, the antennae may be all in use at once, to help run apps across one, two, or all GPS, Bluetooth, WiFi, cellular mobile, and other networks (Hu & Tanner, 2018).

A smartphone usually contains a display. Layered over the screen is a touch screen. Typically this is a capacitive touchscreen, which senses a conductor such as the human finger, a stylus, or a glove with a conductive thread. Smartphones have notable audio capabilities in the form of small speakers used for input or output, music, speech, video, and other forms of audio. They have cameras, often very sophisticated ones—and, for some time, two cameras: a main one, rear-facing and of high resolution, and another, front-facing and of lower resolution, which is especially optimized for "selfies" and other kinds of mobile photography and video-making practice. Smartphones also have varying capacity to work with accessories such as headphones and with the different input options that accessories require. In addition to these capabilities, developed over the past forty or so years, smartphones incorporate a range of sensors that include gyroscopes, accelerometers, magnetometers, and promixity meters.

Smartphones have grown considerably in sophistication and capabilities, operating as they do at the frontiers of material science and technology, engineering, and computing, as well as interface, user experience, and other user-oriented disciplines. The hardware ensemble offered by smartphones provides a generative "base" or "matrix" for what apps can and cannot do. Apps have sent smartphones into the stratosphere as a consumer technology, so the software very much maketh the device. Conversely, for all their real and imaginary potential, apps remain anchored in the materialities of devices, their social contexts, and what users make of them.

Hence it is vital to understand that the proportion of people with access to smartphones varies significantly across different parts of the world, as well as across diverse groups and demographics. A survey carried out in 2018 by the US-based Pew Research Center found that, while there was an estimated 5 billion people in the world with mobile phones, only a little more than half of them had smartphones.

Specifically, its data showed that "a median of 76 percent across 18 advanced economies surveyed have smartphones, compared with a median of only 45 percent in emerging economies [9 surveyed]" (Taylor & Silver, 2019, p. 3). While comparable data are not available yet for 2021, it is highly likely that a large proportion of the world's mobile phone users will be using instead what is called "feature phones." Feature phone users may not be able to access apps, the operating systems that support them, or the features that smartphones offer—or at least not at the same level as the users of more fully featured smartphones. There are various reasons why people continue to use feature phones: cost saving, long battery life, ease of use, compactness, digital detoxing, simpler interfaces, lack of need or desire for additional features or apps (Nagpal & Lyytinen, 2013; Petrovčič et al., 2016). Feature phones support music players, radio, SMS, limited Internet connectivity and web browsing, and email. In recent years, there has been a burgeoning market in what Jeffrey James dubs the "smart feature phone revolution," especially in developing countries—which, he notes, is an important way in which the Internet is made available to many users at the bottom of the pyramid (James, 2020). Increasingly, there appear "hybrid" phones that incorporate as many smartphone features—especially in relation to mobile Internet, data, and apps—as is possible for a cheap and robust phone (Purnell, 2019). These hybrids include the JioPhone, provided by the Indian provider Jio, or phones using the KaiOs, such as those produced in partnership with Orange in Africa and the Middle East. Hence such feature phones do offer popular apps, for example Facebook, Twitter, YouTube, Google Search, Google Maps, as well as money transfer and other services. However, these apps can be difficult to use, given the constraints in computing power and hardware capability, as well as the challenges of connectivity and cost. We do not know very much about the nature and extent of app use in feature phones (James, 2020). This said, it is fair to say that the dialectic between the "have less" and the "have more" sections of the world's mobile communication users is ongoing. This tension casts the apps—their role, the place where we think they fit into our media—in a different light. It underscores that where the smartphone, the feature phone, and mobile communication in general will go in the coming years is an open question, but one that will be especially consequential for the future of apps.

While synonymous with mobile communication, apps are also used with a growing range of other hardware. Many mobile apps are adapted and deployed for desktop and laptop computer use, and vice-versa. Leading brands, from Microsoft through Apple to Google, make a virtue of the fact that their apps work across the ecosystem of devices—especially the troika of mobile, tablet, and desktops or laptops. Other hardware for which apps have been systematically developed and widely used are tablets, TV sets, and watches and other "wearables." Apps also feature in technologies such as cars, fridges, homes, gaming devices, VR headsets, and voice-activated devices such as Amazon's Alexa and Google Home. With the developments referred to as the Internet of Things, apps have acquired the potential to be designed for and installed in a range of low-power devices. They need to be customized for particular kinds of equipment and configurations, as each technology has different characteristics, architecture, affordances, contexts, and uses.

From understanding the nature and ecologies of the hardware, let's turn now to considering apps as software. Apps are programs written in code. They consist of a collection of files that are downloaded by users and installed on devices. Once installed, apps execute code to gather resources, initiate events, and make things happen. In doing so, they marshal the capabilities of smartphones and the power of computers. They do so via mediating layers of codes, services, application frameworks, application programming interfaces (APIs), and so on. Central to these software environments is the operating system (OS), which orchestrates the software, the code and its compilation, and the hardware.

We can grasp these OSs as a series or stack of layers that allow apps (and their developers and users) to best avail themselves of the capabilities and affordances of the smartphone and, through it, of the various devices, networks, software, things, data, and so on to which it is connected. Increasingly, smartphones are a critical and generative node in wider platforms. What we, as users, experience as apps is a veritable tip of the iceberg. The breakthrough in mobile apps was the creation of these platforms as powerful, supportive, easy-to-use app development environments, typically operated by companies that own or are custodians of an OS. As we shall explore further, especially in chapter 3, companies such as Google, Apple, and others allow developers to avail themselves of their software developer kits, their OS environment, and their services and then to offer apps via an app store (often associated with an OS owner, too). This is the kind of thing introduced in software and app development manuals that target the novice developer; these manuals typically set an exercise such as making a flashlight app or a "beer advisor" app.

The app development environments offered by OS providers have evolved, over the 15 or so years of their existence, to offer comprehensive support for a wide range of tedious, difficult, or costly aspects of developing, versioning, upgrading, and deploying apps across multiple device configurations. So much of the hard work of app development is "blackboxed"— especially for small developers, who can take many things off the shelf, as it were. There are many unrealized, largely invisible aspects of these hinterlands of app software and computing environments; and they are due to the growing complexity, scale, and yoking together of different technologies in the digital platforms. So a customer seeking to grow her or his business by developing her or his own app is reliant on an assemblage of digital media and communication. Thus the single app and its potential users and communities fit into a global picture, which is of course much larger. More on this later.

So far in this section I have been sketching an anatomy of an app. Apps are software that rests upon layers of other software, all ultimately written in code, and all collectively drive the machine of smartphones and other devices to undertake what Lucy Suchman famously called "situated actions" (Suchman, 2007). Among the many things that apps marshal, one that looms large is data. Data from smartphones have special links with personal and collective information.

If we recall the predecessor technology of the telephone, information about subscribers was most systematically known by the phone company, and it was gathered and made available in directories. The calling patterns were typically studied by engineers in telephone companies to inform their design and planning of network capacity and distribution. The content of conversations held during telephone calls and the calling parties themselves could either be overheard, on party wires or via the operator, or listened in through telephone interception or phone tapping (Goggin, 2006). Such interception was possible with mobile phones as well, although encryption made it more difficult. However, with mobile phones came the widespread sharing and collection of telephone numbers: the preciousness of this identifying personal information is underscored by its role in money transfer apps or in messaging apps such as WhatsApp or WeChat. As they evolved, mobile phones gathered and brought to maturation many other sources of data in the smartphone era.

Especially important are location data, which are obtained via technologies such as cellular network triangulation, GPS, and Bluetooth. Thanks to their portability and intimate relationship with their users, smartphones offer rich data for following these users' daily journeys and for approximating their locations. Many apps have been developed to take advantage of location data, the general arc moving from dedicated apps (e.g. check-in apps such as Foursquare, or map apps such as Waze) to incorporation of location data features in a wide range of other apps, especially social media ones.

Then there are data about people's bodies and bodily states. These are the kinds of data used by health and wellness apps. Such data are directly gathered from the sensors contained in smartphones, as we have just seen. Many of them are used inferentially—for instance in apps that monitor, gauge, and arbitrate sleeping patterns, the amounts and quality of exercise and physical activity, health, well-being, or any kind of behavior; and they often do so problematically (Barnett et al., 2018). During the COVID-19 pandemic, health researchers, medical practitioners, and developers sought to develop apps that would assist in the diagnosis of positive cases on the basis of data from sensors. Some apps encourage people to enter these data themselves, as in a diary or journal.

One of the major axes of smartphone data is the connection between the app that runs on the smartphone and what is accessed, transferred, and collected, be it via networks, via databases, or via people and other things. Apps have a communicative function, accessing data from elsewhere or sending their data to a server, a database, or a repository elsewhere—which is dramatized in the development and discussion of cloud computing. The rise of apps has been enabled by the rise of cloud computing. Many apps are designed for, and rely upon, the cloud (Sitaram & Manjunath, 2012). Key cloud-based apps include the Google suite of apps, Microsoft Office, and many health apps (Woodward, 2016). So the "appification" of mobile communication has been powered by the rise of the cloud (Stawski, 2015). There is a spectrum of such implementations, from the many apps running on mobile and other devices that draw data from and use the services and capabilities (e.g. machine learning, AI, virtual machines) of cloud-based platforms such as Amazon

Web Services (AWS) (Mishra, 2018), to cloud apps and cloud app marketplaces (Nguyen et al., 2016).

Another category of data is transactional data, which are generated when we make a purchase or book a ticket. There are also data on the activities we perform with apps. Watching a video via Netflix on a smartphone or tablet generates data that are held remotely as well as locally, and are "synced up" (i.e. updated) with one's account. More and more areas of everyday life require apps for participation: there is now, for example, check-in to places via quick response (QR) code, which is designed to enable infectious disease tracing in the COVID-19 pandemic through social media and search apps; and there can be requirements to book a swimming pool spot or do banking or money transfer via an app. Given such developments, many more data about people, their lives, and their environments are gathered by or pass through apps. This dataphilic quality of apps is not only defining, by now it is well nigh constitutional of apps.

Hence the constant struggle to staunch the flow of "leaky apps" (Ball, 2014; Cadwalladr & Graham-Harrison, 2014), and to put in place safeguards that can regulate the data gathering, data use, and data sharing done by people's main devices or by apps operated by better known brands and by companies with third-party apps or providers. This was (and remains) the nub of the problem with the 2018 revelations that exposed Facebook's sharing of user data with the Cambridge Analytica company. The Facebook scandal was but one of many instances of data breaches, poor practices, and lack of adequate legal and regulatory frameworks and redress that have made privacy and data governance a burning issue of our time. By turns, apps are at the frontline of concerns about both private companies' and the government's use of personal data for profiling, tracking, and surveillance.

Histories of Apps

So far I have provided a working definition of "app" and showed you what an app typically does and looks like. To gain a better appreciation of apps as a socio-technical system, it is useful to look at the processes by which they emerged.

The classic predecessors of smartphone apps can be found in the so-called handheld devices, which gained their markets in the 1980s and 1990s and persisted until the early oos. Handheld devices can be seen as part of the long history of the emergence of personal computing, with its debates on the kinds of control that users and developers may have over these tools and the software possibilities of their systems (Ceruzzi, 2003; Kelty, 2008). Such devices include handheld electronic calculators (Hamrick, 1996; McGovern, 2019), which attempted to replace the slide rule. For instance, Hewlett-Packard's HP-65 calculator of 1974 offered "full programmability," featuring "interchangeable magnetic cards as storage media for factory and user programs" (McGovern, 2019, p. 300).

A direct descendant of the smartphone is the family of devices variously called "handheld computers," "palmtop computers," and "portable digital assistants" (PDAs), the last term being one coined by Apple's CEO John Sculley (Sakakibara et al., 1995). The PDA was patented in 1975, and Toshiba is credited with bringing it to the market for the first time, in 1980 (Golder et al., 2009). The UK computer firm Amstrad introduced its PenPad in early 1993, just ahead of Apple's Newton MessagePad launched later that year, which featured built-in apps with web, email, calendar, and address book functions (Sakakibara et al., 1995). The Newton is claimed by some to have made a breakthrough; it had attributes that anticipated the smartphone OS and apps environment (Foley, 2000). It gained a strong following, and its brand community persisted in using it with quasi-religious fervor even after the device was abandoned (Muñiz & Schau, 2005).

Three electronics companies known for their calculators also launched PDAs: Hewlett Packard, Casio, and Sharp—which by the early 1990s dominated the personal organizer market in the United States (Glazer et al., 2017). In 1986 Psion launched its EPOC device, which featured the Symbian OS with basic applications such as a diary. Microsoft adapted its Windows 95 desktop OS, launching Windows CE for the PDA market (Foley, 2000). In this highly competitive market, the dominant provider was Jeff Hawkin's Palm Computing, famous for its Palm Pilot launched in 1996, which claimed 51 percent of the market in its first year (Chaston, 2016) and eventually 70 percent of the market and 10 million users worldwide (Foley, 2000). Pilloried as a "cult" (Brookshaw et al., 1997), the Palm Pilot also enjoyed a thriving applications ecosystem, boasting over 50,000 developers (Foley, 2000).

In many ways, PDAs referred to a range of different things that might be combined together: "palmtops," which were "'miniature' PCs ... which use keyboards and run versions of PC software like Lotus 1-2-3 and word processors"; "electronic organizers"; "mobile telephones which combine a portable telephone with computer capabilities," for example BellSouth and IBM's 1994 Simon product; and "pen-based computers" such as Motorola's Envoy (an early example of the persistence of stylus tools in mobile and portable devices) (Sakakibara et al., 1995, pp. 23–24). The applications had developed considerably in the intervening 15 or so years. Apart from their usefulness for office and home, PDAs were being considered and deployed around a range of specific settings: health, medical care, and nursing, diet and nutrition, education, disability support, safety inspections, and so on (Boudreau, 2010). One notable PDA app, for example, was a reader, not only for the Internet but also for newspaper and magazine content (Foley, 2000). On the cusp of the smart-phone moment, there were at least four different PDA OS and eco-systems: Symbian, Palm, Linux, and Microsoft PDA (Quirce García, 2011).

PDAs and handhelds are one obvious family of handheld devices, often associated with business and work uses. However, there is another set of handhelds that feeds into the artifact and media characteristics of the smartphone (Collins, 2014), as well as into the form, function, and dynamics of apps. These are game devices. Consider, for instance, Mattel's 1977 Auto Race, credited with being the "first fully electronic handheld game ever released" (Dillon, 2011, p. 162), and its top-selling 1978 Football Game (Collins, 2014). Or consider one of the most famous video games of all time—Tetris. Tetris started life as a board game, then was redesigned successively for early computers, TV consoles, and handheld devices such as the Nintendo's 1989 Game Boy (Ackerman, 2016). In 1994, Sony released its PlayStation in Japan, which entrenched the dominance of CD-based games (Dillon, 2011, p. xxi). Mass market commercial online games arrived within the decade, which was marked for instance by Microsoft's launch of its Xbox Live online gaming service in 2001 (Dillon, 2011, p. xxiv). An important milestone in mobile gaming is represented by Nokia's N-Gage phone, one of its range of devices dedicated to a different kind of media, beloved by aficionados—in this case gamers (Goggin, 2006, 2011).

Through the history of calculators, PDAs and palm pilots, and games devices we can recognize the importance of handhelds and their accompanying software as predecessors of present-day apps. Building on these insights, it is important to cast the net wider still and log the wide range of media affordances and cultures of use that crop up in later instances of smartphones, being creatively leveraged by apps—and this will be explored in greater depth in chapter 4. For the present, we will turn to the most obvious predecessors of apps after handhelds: application, data, and content services; and OSs associated with the first, second, and third generations of cellular mobile phones.

The first-generation analogue mobile phones that spanned the late 1970s to the mid-1990s were fairly rudimentary in terms of the programs and applications they could support. This is one key reason why during much of this period there remained a viable, burgeoning market for PDAs, palm tops, and the other handheld technologies we have just discussed. Operating system and software platform developments centered on 2G digital standard phones in their latter years and on their evolution to 3G networks and devices (Steinbock, 2007). In 1991 2G networks and phones were launched in Finland with the global system for mobile communications (GSM) standard (Hillebrand, 2002). Other 2G standards followed, such as the US code division multiple access (CDMA) standard, and also various standards in Japan, South Korea, and China. The 2G era was the decisive period for the diffusion of mobile phones, and one during which the technology was entrenched globally. It was an extended evolution, marked especially by a period of intense innovation associated with the mobile Internet, messaging, and data services, all under the 2.5G label (Noam & Steinbock, 2003). 3G was introduced first in Japan in 2001, then rolled out around the world. 3G featured significantly higher data transfer capabilities and video communication capabilities, but, owing to the high prices paid for spectrum and other issues, its take-up and diffusion were much slower than anticipated (Curwen & Whalley, 2009, 2010). It was followed by 4G, launching from 2012–2013 onwards—also a relatively convoluted affair, but one that entrenched mobile-Internet convergence (Curwen et al., 2019). 5G networks, with their close ties to the Internet of Things, commenced rollout in 2018–2019.

Despite the hype, these developments tended to be evolutionary in nature (Funk, 2002). As 2G developed, so too did networks, where digitization deepened. By the end of the 1990s, attention was increasingly focused on the phone as a zone for programming and applications. To underpin this situation, there were notable developments in OS for mobile phones. In 2000, for instance, Symbian released its first "fully integrated software platform for next generation mobile phones," especially offering "core compatibility for third-party applications, content, and services" (The Mobile Internet Community, 2000). The OS covered data management and synchronization, graphics, and multimedia, as well as browser engines for WAP and HTML, highlighting the focus on programming applications for mobile Internet. Microsoft Windows was another key player in the mobile programming area, as was Linux. Programming languages included Python, Java 2 Micro Edition, C++, and Open C. As mobile programming researchers put it, in this period "developers may start to see the mobile phone as a collection of capabilities that can be reassembled on demand for a given purpose" (Fitzek & Reichert, 2007, p. 8). These purposes are things such as the user interface (e.g. speaker, microphone, camera, display, keyboard, sensor), the communication interface (cellular; and short-range connectivity such as WiFi, Wireless local area networks, and Bluetooth), and built-in resources (e.g. storage, CPU, and battery) (p. 8). Increasing numbers of developers were engaging in the mobile applications area, building on the efforts in the predecessor handheld, games, and other personal technologies that we have already reviewed. A key difficulty, however, lay in the structure and control of the mobile applications and data environment, and this cautionary advice captures it:

> before going all alone, a new service provider [e.g. who has developed an app] should consider the options offered by 3rd parties. All network providers (operators) are open to new ideas ... Developers can either contact them directly or go through major handset manufacturers. (Fitzek & Reichert, 2007, p. 15)

While app developers are reliant on manufacturers and network providers, the threat lies in the fact that "[o]perators are large and powerful players" (p. 15).

There was mounting excitement about the potential for

programming and development of mobile applications. Developers and businesses were especially keen to take advantage of, and turbocharge, the enormous flexibility of mobile phones, as these were fast developing in power and sophistication. Mobile phones emerged from a set of industries, global and national policies, legal and regulatory frameworks, work arrangements, and user expectations that were quite different from the IT and software industries and were being reworked through the liberalization of markets and the privatization of key entities, especially telecommunication operators. The telecommunications operators, joined by some new players in the form of mobile carriers and various kinds of telecommunications service providers and resellers, were keen to maintain their vicelike grip on the content and services that were offered across their networks. For their part, the manufacturers had substantial control over the hardware on which mobile applications would run—a "first-mover" advantage of being able to integrate, or at least dictate, the terms in which applications would be offered to users of their devices.

The result was a dispensation that lasted for the best part of a decade, from the late 1990s until 2008, during which the environment for mobile applications was tightly controlled and contested. A wide range of new mobile data services and applications offered by developers, aggregators, or service providers rapidly emerged. The most profitable ones contained games, ringtones, graphics to customize a phone, video, or audio. Some of these services were offered as applications, others were offered via mobile web, SMS, or MMS. Often these services were called "mobile premium services" and offered by a dedicated telephone number range (outside the direct control of the operators), taking advantage of an earlier conceptualization of "valued added services"— that is, services that could be open to competition and that are over and above basic telecommunications ones (Goggin & Spurgeon, 2007).

To offer an app to a mobile phone user, the developer needed to make an arrangement with one of the following entities: a mobile phone operator (e.g. to offer it on its "portal" for download); a handset manufacturer (who might pre-install the application or make it available for download and purchase via his or her "catalog" or dedicated website); a reseller, who offers a range of applications for purchase; or an aggregator, who acts as an intermediary between an operator and a service provider (Goggin, 2011). Suffice it to say, from both the supply side and the demand side of the markets, this was a complicated and confused affair. Despite these challenges, the early oos offered great opportunities for app developers or service providers who could gain an audience and a following for their program and content, especially ringtones, screen backgrounds, and mobile games.

Contrast this glimpse into the chaotic world of mobile programs and data at the turn of the century with the one afforded by Japan's celebrated i-mode system and the innovative attempts of the country's industry pioneers. I-mode was introduced in February 1999 by dominant Japanese telecommunications carrier Nippon Telegraph and Telephone Corporation (NTT) DoCoMo. I-mode was an ecosystem of mobile Internet, mobile web, content, and services and, crucially, also an integrated billing system (Natsuno, 2003a). In technical terms, i-mode was underpinned by a version of the HTML web standard called c-HTML. The i-mode was tightly controlled by DoCoMo, allowing subscribers to access a wide range of mobile data services—these were forerunners to mobile premium services and to mobile apps and were offered by approved third-party providers—as well as the most popular services such as search, transportation information and maps, news, and weather; popular i-mode services included music, ringtones, and games (Ishii, 2004; Natsuno, 2003b). I-mode rapidly attracted users in Japan: their number rose to 33 million just three years after the launch (Ishii, 2004, p. 44).

I-mode was widely thought to be superior to the alternative offered by the mobile web in the form of WAP services, and Japan was celebrated for eclipsing its European counterparts in mobile Internet innovation (Funk, 2001). WAP was developed by Nokia, Ericsson, Motorola, and Phone.com in 1997 via their WAP forum. It aimed to unify the already diverse kinds of mobile and wireless technologies and networks that were available. WAP was invented before the smartphone, to run on the mobile phones available from the late 1990s to 2005 (Goggin, 2018). WAP is a protocol that allows mobile phones to display web pages. Over the next decade, a slowly growing number of website and web content providers fleshed out WAP mobile web offerings (Goggin, 2018). For the first few years of its life, WAP fell into disuse and was derided as a "failure" (Haas, 2006; Teo & Pok, 2003). However, it slowly gained momentum, especially in bandwidth-constrained countries. So WAP remains widely used today in browsing websites via mobile devices. Often nowadays mobile users switch fairly seamlessly between an app and a web link that, when they click on it, takes them outside the app, to a mobile website. In this way they encounter WAP.

In this section I have discussed the important immediate predecessors to apps: mobile programming, data, and services; the Japanese i-mode ecosystem; and the mobile web in the form of WAP services. They all anticipate important aspects of smartphones and apps. These histories also point to alternative visions and arrangements for apps that may be now in the background but remain active and could re-emerge down the track.

Apps in the Smartphone Moment

The pivotal moment for apps came in 2007–2008. The iconic figure here was Steve Jobs. Jobs heralded the paradigm shift from desktop computing to mobile computing when he first announced the iPhone. This occurred in one of his breathless signature product launch speeches, namely at the annual Macworld Conference and Expo in San Francisco in January 2007 (Jobs, 2010).

Jobs announced three new innovative products: a "widescreen iPod with touch controls"; an iPhone ("a revolutionary mobile phone"); and "a breakthrough Internet communications device" (Jobs, 2010, 01:30). He rhapsodized them as three in one, joined together in the iPhone (02:48). Jobs jokingly compared the new iPhone with the well-established iPod, introduced in 2001. He also critiqued the user interface experience of his main competitors at the time— Moto Q, Blackberry, Palm Treo, and Nokia E62. In particular, Jobs underlined that the rival devices did not allow buttons, controls, and keyboards to change dynamically with new applications. In his spiel, Jobs lauded the iPhone, claiming that it represented a catalytic shift and explaining that Apple will "build on top of that [the revolutionary user interface] with software" (08:15). To underscore what he saw as Apple's particular dedication to technology and design, Jobs quoted computer pioneer Alan Kay's oft-remarked adage: "People who are really serious about software should make their own hardware" (09:43; see Kay, 2008).

Initially Apple's iPhone was available only if a consumer took out a subscription with a particular mobile carrier. For Apple's mid-2007 US iPhone launch, the exclusive partner was AT&T (via its Singular, later renamed AT&T Mobility as part of the 2006 acquisition of BellSouth by AT&T). In announcing the iPhone, Apple emphasized that it was learning from iTunes and that the iPhone would "sync with iTunes" (Jobs, 2010). The "killer app is making calls," especially with advances in integrating contacts and visual voicemail (a collaboration between Apple and Cingular). In the January 2007 launch speech, Jobs demonstrated the boon of touch and swipe with iPhone with the help of a session of browsing the *New York Times*, but on a website: he was relying on the mobile web, not on an app (Goggin, 2018).

When they did eventuate, the first iPhone apps were all "native" to the device and all made by Apple. There were apps such as Apple mail, Safari web browser, phone, visual voicemail, calendar, camera, weather, clock, and so on. On this model, the software developers were forced to work with Apple to develop its own apps. At this initial stage, third-party apps were not permitted on the iPhone. Apple justified its tight control as a way of ensuring a superior user experience as well as delivering on its aesthetic, design, and security choices and thus safeguarding its emblematic brand (Isaacson, 2011; Ive & Zuckerman, 2016). However, criticism, backlash, and contest abounded, from user communities as well as from corporate competitors (Arthur, 2014). They all complained about Apple's signature moves to "own the consumer" (Montgomery & Roscoe, 2013).

There had already been a vociferous reaction to iPhone's locked-down ecosystem from tech communities, fans, hackers, and highly literate users, and it was publicized through practices and materials that encouraged the "jailbreaking" of iPhones—that is, the unauthorized removal of Apple's software restrictions (Goggin, 2009; Lee & Soon, 2017). Unlike PCs and most other mobile phones, Apple computers and then mobile devices, starting with iPods, had been deliberately engineered to allow official uses and servicing authorized by Apple—security by design, warranty and sales contracts, copyright, patents, and other forms of intellectual property protection (Miller, 2012; Swanson, 2010; Thiel, 2016). This gave rise to the creation of low-cost netbook computers that could run Apple software, such as the so-called MacBook nano. This "hackintosh" project was started around 2005 by software developers who paid attention first to Apple computers and then to iPhone (Magaudda, 2010), and it led to a phenomenon that Paolo Magaudda terms "the consumerization of hacking practices" (Magaudda, 2012, p. 4). In any case, the jailbreaking of iPhones in particular has been a newsworthy if risky pastime ever since (Timberg, 2013;

Hern, 2020c). At the very least, the jailbreaking of iPhones, especially as a way to circumvent the compulsory routing through the Apple App Store, raises significant competition policy, "net neutrality" (Selwyn & Golding, 2010, pp. 110–111), and digital rights issues (Cooke, 2020). Jailbreaking is a long-term issue for the users of many other smartphone and app ecosystems and for their manufacturers, who are often displeased with default or pre-installed software (this is sometimes termed "bloatware") (Cavusoglu et al., 2020). More on this shortly.

After months of considerable backlash from software developers, on July 10, 2008, Apple launched its App Store. It announced a software developer kit (SDK) for native iPhone apps in October 2007 and released it on March 6, 2008, claiming 100,000 downloads in the first four days and topping 250,000 by early June (Apple, 2008a, 2008b). Later that month Jobs unveiled "what we call the app store" (Jobs, 2008, 00:39). As an "exclusive way to distribute iPhone applications," Jobs suggested that most users would download apps "over the air, right to the iPhone" (2:25). He laid out a "business deal" whereby developers would pick a price, then Apple would take 30 percent of the revenue (for hosting the credit card and payment systems), and developers would take 70 percent (3:25). This is the basic structure of Apple's deal with developers, and it has held firm over the intervening years, though it's coming under increasing challenge. In August 2020, for instance, Apple kicked Epic Games, the owner of the popular game Fortnite, off its app store, on the grounds that it allowed players to purchase in-game items directly and hence avoided giving Apple its 30 percent cut. Epic responded with a blistering video and social media campaign.

So we can see that Apple has been remarkably successful at imprinting the basic idea, architecture, and business model of apps early in the day. Nevertheless, we can be rightfully skeptical of Apple's framing and design of apps and of its app store, as many have been. Let us look at the main alternative player to see how it sought to imagine and construct the universe of apps: Android, owned by Google.

Android is an open-source Linux-based software stack that includes a core set of system apps for email, SMS, calendars, contacts, Internet browsing, and other operations (Android, 2020a). Android Inc. began in 2003, in Palo Alto, as a startup led by Andy Rubin. Rubin was interested in developing an OS for digital cameras, but then diverted Android Inc. to focus on smartphones (de Looper, 2019). Google acquired Android in 2005 and announced the development of its Android OS in 2007, after partnering with handset manufacturers and carriers such as Samsung, LG, Sony Ericsson, HTC, and T-Mobile.

Google controls Android (Goggin, 2012), which it describes as "an open source operating system for mobile devices and a corresponding open source project led by Google" (Google, 2020). Android emphasizes that "apps included with the platform have no special status among the apps the user chooses to install" (Android, 2020a). Users can install and use third-party apps, and developers, for their part, can use the system's app capabilities as building blocks for their own apps. The early and continuing success of Android is often credited to this approach: "A significant factor in Android's rapid adoption is that Google freely licensed the operating system under open-source terms, enabling a wide range of handset makers to enter the high-end smartphone market without having to develop their own OS" (Pon et al., 2014, p. 982). To provide signature look, feel, and core functionality across the various devices from the wide range of manufacturers that rely upon Android, Google encourages the vendor to enroll in its compatibility program. If the device complies with the Android Compability Definition Document and passes the Compatibility Test Suite, it means that "Android apps in the ecosystem provide a consistent experience when running on your device" (Android, 2020b). Once they secure the Android compatibility of their device, firms are also encouraged to gain a separate license to run Google mobile services on top of the Android OS (Android, 2020b). Android has firmly established its global dominance and its place as the major alternative to Apple's view of the apps work. However, it is important to note that there do exist many other kinds of app stores. In chapter 3 we'll look at the teeming world of Chinese app stores, which have managed to relegate Apple and Google to minor positions. Before 2008, too, there were a wide range of mobile data and content portals, websites, services providers, and so on, as we have seen. Some of these, such as Nokia or Vodafone World, were leaders and were more well known. These mobile equipment vendors and network operators were especially in the ascendancy in a diverse and fragmented market. In the transition, Apple's App Store and Google's Android Market battled to establish themselves in the face of well-capitalized and savvy contenders. The companies that entered the list of the "app store wars" included Blackberry World (launched in April 2009), Nokia's Ovi, Windows Marketplace, Palm Catalog, Sony App Store, and Samsung Galaxy Store.

A notable new entrant from this period that has survived is Amazon. Amazon launched its app store in 2011, offering apps for Android devices and the Kindle Fire. When Amazon launched its app store, Apple filed a suit, alleging trademark infringement and other complaints. (Apple had applied to register "app store" as a trademark, seeking to gain exclusive use of the term, but this was opposed by Microsoft.) In January 2013, the District Court in California agreed with Amazon, determining that Apple had not provided evidence that consumers associated the name "app store" with any specific qualities of Apple as a company (Hudson, 2013). Rivalry between the two companies moved on to other fronts, centering on revenue splits and terms of use for Amazon's iOS app. In legal battles with Nokia in 2009, Apple again asserted patent rights over its app store, but this was a minor element in an extensive series of legal set pieces (Kolakowski, 2010) and of technology and business strategies that played out between these two companies (Cuthbertson et al., 2015; Tuunainen et al., 2011). By 2014, Apple and Google had largely cemented their dominance of app stores outside China. Because companies found it difficult to directly bypass app stores (though not for want of trying, as in Epic's Battle Royale of 2020), the main route—as followed by companies such as Spotify, Netflix, Uber, and many others—was building a market presence, integration of services, and take-up of the app itself (Fung, 2019).

Conclusion: "There's an App for That"

App stores mean little without the apps themselves. The sheer number of apps launched in the 2008–2013 period was extraordinary.

In the vanguard of apps, users were young users—a feature captured by the label "the app generation" (Gardner & Davis, 2013). While we need to be wary of the recurrent rhetoric of generations and technology (Goggin & Crawford, 2011) as well as of the diversity of the people gathered under the banner of "youth," it is evident that young users were key to the take-up of mobile Internet, and then to the development of mobile media cultures—apps being center stage in that process (Stald, 2008). Social media apps on smartphones were especially influential in the appification of digital media and society in this new phase (Goggin, 2014). In many ways, via young users, social media apps become "anchor" software for the explosion of app-centered smartphone cultures that extended to almost inconceivable lengths. The role of apps in youth cultures and in the lives of young people was quickly established as an important area for consideration, typically possessed of ambiguity and contradictions that could unfold quite differently across the borders and boundaries of different apps, subcultures, social locations, and local and transnational dynamics (Goodyear et al., 2019; Li et al., 2020; Jin & Yoon, 2016; Mihailidis, 2014).

Apps and their users are much younger than computer software previously had—or Internet or mobile phone applications, for that matter. Children figured prominently as mobile phone users, as the technology became more widespread. This trend accelerated with smartphones, but very young children became avid users of apps—and fast created a profitable market for app developers and app stores. Adults came to rely on apps to "babysit" children; thus apps displaced television from this role. Apps also became a byword for parental anxieties about the negative effects of overabsorption in digital media devices and cultures. It's fair to say that such anxieties are neither universal or general. As Shakuntala Banaji points out in her study of media-rich and media-deprived children in urban and rural settings in India, how we understand agency and cultural meaning depends on pivotal conditions such as class, responsibilities, labor, and knowledge (Banaji, 2015).

Once apps were domesticated by their child, adolescent, and young adult users (Haddon et al., 2005), typically in global North contexts, they became a staple of education— a linchpin of online and blended learning, pedagogy, and school as well as of further education, information education, and university education. Apps also became a new social and regulatory interface, stitching parents into the fabric of their children's schooling, as laid out by Lim Sun Sun in her 2020 book *Transcendental Parenting* (Lim, 2020). School apps allowed parents to follow the timetable and progress of lessons and homework at a minute level, eavesdropping on the incidental and consequential communication between pupils and their teachers. As children's media research shows us, the absorption of apps into the economies and relations of families and the roles of these technologies are themes that need careful unpicking (Clark, 2013; Livingstone & Blum-Ross, 2020).

Children and young people were only one group in an increasingly wide range of users who experimented with apps. Apps succeeded in delivering on many of the promises of earlier architects and promoters of technologies and imaginaries such as pervasive and ubiquitous computing, multimedia, and personalized media. They could deliver hypermedia to the person, engaging her or his identity, senses, and emotions in customized ways, which could be further refined via the reams of data that various apps were able to funnel and harvest. Along with smartphones, apps began to acquire status as a "go-to" zone where design was attractive, effective, and user-friendly, innovation brimmed over, and problems could be solved (or at least tackled). This techno-optimistic view of apps was summed up in a famous phrase. In early 2009, Apple and AT&T released a TV commercial that introduced the phrase "there's an app for that":

> What's great about the iPhone is that if you want to check snow conditions on the mountain, there's an app for that. If you want to check how many calories are in your lunch, there's an app for that. And if you want to check where exactly you parked the car, there's an app for that. Yup, there's an app for just about anything. (Apple & AT&T, 2009)

Hot on the heels of this advertisement were the parody ads, for example this mock ad from the US-based multicultural troupe the Latino Comedy Project, which imagines iPhone users crossing the Mexico–US border:

> Say you're not quite legal, but you need to get to El Norte without running into La Migra and or the drug cartels, there's an app for that. What if you need to find the biggest holes in the fence, not covered by 24-hour surveillance, well, there's an app for that too. Need to calculate a bribe for border guards, or coyotes? There's even an app for that. (Latino Comedy Project, 2009, 0:01–0:21)

With the official and popular meanings of apps crisscrossing, the word "apps" was well on its way to having an altered meaning, associated with mobile phone apps and the many kinds of things they could possibly do.

With an understanding of the fundamentals and emergence of apps, we will step back in chapter 3 to gain a macro view of the economies and industries of apps by looking at the systems and structures of ownership, control, and power that shape how apps are made and circulated, where they fit into social life, and what options they offer and allow their users.

CHAPTER THREE

App Economy

How do apps get made, by which industries and actors, what are they worth, and what are their implications for economy, society, and power?

As noted in chapter 2, when discussing apps, we often get the sense that they are invented in the bedrooms of teenagers and made through near heroic startups, through efforts of enterprise and entrepreneurship, and through microbusinesses inspired by the "economy of you" (Palmer, 2014; Gregg, 2015; Ehrenhard et al., 2017; Irani, 2015, 2019). Sure; yet, for all their apparent simplicity and DIY-ness, apps are the visible part of a much larger, deeper, and wider system and collection of things.

In this chapter I look at how apps are manufactured, produced, and circulated in the economy. The idea is to give you a working knowledge of the fundamentals of the global apps industries, production, and economies. I present data and indicative case studies on the key players in apps industries globally and regionally. I identify the features, size, and contribution of apps to media industries and to economies. This broad-brush, macro-level account of global apps leaves out many other parts of the story—parts related to work and labor in apps industries, production cultures, how design and innovation work at a detailed level across different settings, and so on. This is because my focus is on establishing the main contours of app economies and industries and on highlighting key issues of control and power—issues that extend deeply into culture and society.

What Are Apps Worth?

First, a caveat. Apps are many, and they come and go. However, systematic studies of apps, with solid information on them, are few and far between. App stores, if you can access them, provide lists of apps, number of downloads, and rankings. Market research fills the gap with "best endeavors" estimates on data. In many ways, apps are a bellwether in the fearsome complexity of doing theorization, data gathering, and analysis in order to understand the economies of digital technologies. For various reasons, it remains challenging to map and estimate the economic size and contribution of the app economy. As the International Telecommunications Union (ITU) noted in a 2017 report, "the app economy has emerged within and across multiple industries—the telecommunication industry, the software industry and the computing hardware industry—in a rapid evolutionary process that has quickly blurred the borderlines between them" (ITU, 2017a, p. 2).

The app economy stretches across ICT industries but, as "its disruptive influences reaches [sic] additional industries such as finance, transportation and accommodation, it increasingly incorporates economic activity that occurred within these traditional industry classifications" (p. 2). The ITU points out that national statistics are based on traditional industry classifications and, because "the app economy crosses so many of these traditional industry boundaries, it is difficult to collect information that would enable an accurate quantification of its economic size" (p. 2). Further, because apps operate across different kinds of infrastructure, devices, data sets, and contexts, there are definitional issues about how to allocate costs and revenue to apps versus, say, cloud computing (p. 2). That said, the available data indicate that apps are a reasonably big thing. The market research firm MarketLine estimated that the global mobile market for apps in 2018 had a value of US$443 billion—which means it increased by 8.3 percent from the previous year (*"Global mobile apps,"* 2019, p. 2). For all their aggregate revenue, apps involve a small purchase for most users. In May 2019 the average price for apps in the Apple App Store was US$1.01 globally (*"Mobile apps in Europe,"* 2019, p. 17).

The general pattern indicates that, globally, app revenue is concentrated in the markets of high- and middle-income countries. Consider, for instance, the 2018 figures for mobile app markets in North America. The United States accounts for 87.9 percent, Canada for 7.9 percent, and Mexico for only 4.1 percent of the North American market (*"Mobile apps in North America,"* 2019, p. 13). The revenue that derives from apps in Mexico is significantly smaller in proportion to the population than in Mexico's North American neighbors.

What Are the Most Popular and Profitable Apps?

Ranking and rating are two key structuring features and pastimes of digital technologies. App stores rate apps, so they provide a handy first port of call for looking at the diffusion of apps (see Tables 3.1, 3.2, and 3.3).

The lion's share of data concerning app download, revenue, and usage derives from the app stores, especially the likes of Apple and Google Play, which are integrated into the wider global field of data analytics and marketing. Large piles of data can be gleaned from app stores—witness the creative uses that academic researchers have made of these sources by scraping and analyzing the data in them, in order to measure app uses as well as a range of other phenomena; in these operations apps functioned as a proxy. This said, it remains true that Apple, Google, and other app stores jealously guard the bulk of their data; hence the most comprehensive figures are those made available via analytics and market research firms such as App Annie, MarketLine, and others—which have been used here as well. The app stores

Table 3.1   Top 10 apps of the 2010s, worldwide, by downloads and spend.

Source   App Annie. (2019). A look back at the top apps and games of the decade. App Annie Blog, December 16. https://www.appannie.com/en/insights/market-data/a-look-back-at-the-top-apps-games-of-the-decade.

	Top 10 By all-time downloads	Top 10 By all-time consumer spend
1.	Facebook (Facebook, US)	Netflix (Nexflix, US)
2.	Facebook Messenger (Facebook, US)	Tinder (Interactive Corp, US)
3.	WhatsApp Messenger (Facebook, US)	Pandora Music (Sirius XM Radio, US)
4.	Instagram (Facebook, US)	Tencent Video (Tencent, China)
5.	Snapchat (Snap, US)	LINE (LINE, Japan)
6.	Skype (Microsoft, US)	iQIYI (Baidu, China)
7.	TikTok (ByteDance, China)	Spotify (Spotify, Sweden)
8.	UC Browser (Alibabi Group, China)	YouTube (Google, US)
9.	YouTube (Google, US)	HBO Now (AT&T, US)
10.	Twitter (Twitter, US)	Kwai (OneSmile, China)

Notes   The data here cover the period 2010–2019. Combined iOS and Google Play data begin in January 2012. Data until December 31, 2011 are iOS only. The year 2019 is based on January–November data. Owner company and country of headquarters are included.

also offer developers, as an additional service, the detailed data on an app's take-up. Independent verification of and insight into these figures are things the companies could seek, as they have been, historically, features of ratings in other industries, notably television (O'Regan et al., 2002).

Table 3.2   Top 10 apps worldwide, by downloads, 2015 and 2020.
SOURCE   App Annie. (2021). App Store Rankings: Index. https://www.
appannie.com/indexes.

	2015		2020
1	Facebook Messenger (Facebook, US)	1	TikTok (ByteDance, China)
2	WhatsApp Messenger (Facebook, US)	2	ZOOM Cloud Meetings (Zoom Video Communications, US)
3	Facebook (Facebook, US)	3	WhatsApp Messenger (Facebook, US)
4	Instagram (Facebook, US)	4	My Talking Tom Friends (Jinke Culture, Outfit 7, China)
5	Clean Master (Cheetah Mobile, China)	5	Facebook (Facebook, US)
6	Subway Surfers (Sybo, Kiloo, Denmark; iDreamSky China)	6	Instagram (Facebook, US)
7	Google Photos (Google, US)	7	Facebook Messenger (Facebook, US)
8	Skype (Microsoft, US)	8	Google Meet (Google, US)
9	YouTube (Google, US)	9	Save The Girl (Lion Studios/AppLovin, US)
10	UC Browser (AliBaba, China)	10	FaceApp (FaceApp, Russia)

NOTES   June 2015 and June 2020 data for iOS & Google Play stores are
combined. Owner company and country of headquarters are included.

It is an interesting situation if we consider the long history
of ratings, consumption, and audiences in broadcast media,
books sales, or press and magazine sales and subscription to
begin with, and then the extended transition of these ratings
and audience measurement and analysis issues into the new
media areas, especially with the advent of Internet and social

Table 3.3 Top 10 apps worldwide, by revenue, 2015 and 2020.
Source   App Annie. (2021). App Store Rankings: Index. https://www.appannie.com/indexes.

	2015		2020
1	Clash of Clans (Supercell, Finland)	1	Honour of Kings (Tencent, China)
2	Monster Strike (Mixi, Japan; Tencent, China)	2	Pokémon GO (Niantic, US)
3	Puzzle & Dragons (Gungho Online, Japan; Tencent, China)	3	ROBLOX (Roblox, US)
4	Game of War – Fire Age (Machine Zone, US)	4	Monster Strike (Mixi, Japan)
5	Fantasy Westward Journey (NetEase, China; SEA, Singapore; 37games, China)	5	Coin Master (Moon Active, Israel)
6	Candy Crush Saga (King, UK; Tencent, China)	6	Gardenscapes – New Acres (Playrix, Ireland)
7	Boom Beach (Supercell, Finland)	7	TikTok (ByteDance, China)
8	Candy Crush Soda Saga (King, UK)	8	Brawl Stars (Supercell, Finland)
9	The White Cat Project (COLOPL, Sony, Japan; Morningtec, China)	9	Fate/Grand Order (Sony; Komoe; Netmarble; bilibili; China, Taiwan, Korea)
10	MU Miracle (KingNet, Kunlun, China; Hope Mobile, Vietnam; Webzen, South Korea)	10	Candy Crush Saga (US, Activision Blizzard)

Notes   June 2015 and June 2020 data for iOS & Google Play stores are combined. Owner company and country of headquarters are included.

media analytics (Bourdon & Méadel, 2014). To a certain extent, apps analytics has flown under the radar of these debates and merits much more attention, especially given the paucity of the available research.

One aspect of how apps are used and valued that is slippery when we try to pin it down is revenue. Broadly, we can divide this area into several categories:

1   FREE APPS   These are apps free to download and free to use.
2   PURCHASE OF APPS VIA A STORE   The revenue is split between the app owner and the app store on a 70/30 model. App stores typically charge a fee for a developer account, then take a percentage of the revenue for the purchase of a paid app or for an in-app purchase.
3   "FREEMIUM" APPS   These apps are free to download and free to use at the basic level of functionality and service. However, for the advanced tiers, the users need to pay extra to unlock the extra features and upgrade.
4   IN-APP PURCHASES   These are apps, typically games, where users are invited to purchase additional characters, points, currency, or features.
5   IN-APP ADVERTISING   These are apps supported (to varying degrees) through advertising. Often they are games, but increasingly also news and other apps.

Apps can be used to purchase services that bill the user, often via a credit card or a digital wallet. Also, as discussed in chapter 5, some apps, for instance WeChat Pay or Grab Wallet, have been developed as money and credit facilities that compete with stored-value cards, banks, credit providers, and other digital money and currency providers.

As we saw in chapter 2, the predecessor of apps was the mobile premium type of services, where mobile network operators "constructed a highly centralized model," dominated by the mobile portal business model (Roma & Ragaglia, 2016, p. 173). This model was breached by the Apple App Store's irruption onto the scene and by the quick follow-on from Google and many other providers. During the 2010s we witness a shift from the predominant app revenue models, which were based on the app store (free + paid = freemium), to purchasing from within the app itself (Roma & Ragaglia, 2016, p. 174), in a quest for the monetization of mobile apps (Appel et al., 2020). Via in-app purchasing, many of these apps can provide the kind of content previously offered by cinema and DVD, broadcasting, music stores and the recorded music industry, newspapers and magazines, and the like.

The shift to content provision via apps has increased the revenue associated with apps. A striking finding by a 2016 study predicted that, while paid and freemium apps did well in the Apple App Store, for Google Play "the revenue performance of the freemium model will be inferior to those of paid and free models" (Roma & Ragaglia, 2016, p. 187). Overall, the revenue yield for in-app purchase worked better in Apple App Store than in Google Play, where users were more reluctant to pay (pp. 187–189). These and other elements in the dynamics of the revenue model—for example pricing, store placement, and so on—also vary across product categories. For instance, offering a free app may be the best strategy for setting up and taking advantage of a revenue stream for a newspaper or a streaming video subscription. Contrast this with the games segment, where differentiation and price discrimination may be possible—indeed expected—across different groups of consumers and app stores (Roma & Ragaglia, 2016, p. 189). Things have changed with the diversification of platform ecosystems; in this area, research suggests that app developers need to pay careful attention to the platform they use and that the choice of product categories remains key (Roma & Vasi, 2019).

Thus, for app developers, investors, and owners as well as for suppliers who offer content and services via apps, there is a complex picture of what revenue strategy might work best in what situation. This creates a business opportunity in its own right. So, in the large space between app stores and app developers, we see the rise of intermediaries. There are firms such as AppLoving (the mobile games firm) that offer monetization platforms—for instance with "in-app bidding" for advertising to place ads in a game—in order to "maximize earning and grow your games" (AppLovin, 2020).

Apps now play an important part in the industry, economy, and audience experience of advertising. In the era of apps and smartphones, mobile advertising has moved to being a key part of the scene (Wilken & Sinclair, 2009, p. 441). Apps played a decisive role in bringing together various elements of mobile advertising that previously languished (e.g. location, personalization), along with new affordances offered by smartphones and app software. Thus in-app advertising has grown in visibility and significance and has improved its revenue strategies (Ji et al., 2019; Mojica Ruiz et al., 2016). We can gauge this, for instance, by users' irritation with the prevalence of in-app ads, especially interstitial ads (such as those overlaid on a mobile game or other app).

In-app advertising has two unique features: joint provision of the advertising by the platform owner and app developer; and agency pricing for apps sale (Hao et al., 2017). In-app advertising includes "app install" ads or ads that promote apps for users to install (Arora et al., 2017; Lee & Shin, 2016). It also includes "reward ads," where users "choose" to view ads in exchange for premium content (Guo et al., 2019). Reward ads have had a chequered track record across digital media innovation for many years; they were often perceived as a blight on video platforms, for instance. Given that mobiles are very young, children are exposed to advertising in ways that responsible industry practice and regulators have been slow to catch up with (Meyer et al., 2019).

A big part of advertising via apps has to do with the phenomenal growth of social media advertising, as this growth continues to be at the heart of the transformation of advertising. Many social media pivot on their use and access through mobile apps (Wilken, 2017). Advertising has become key, especially to all kinds of social media apps "born" mobile, such as Snapchat (Phua & Kim, 2018). Advertising follows the users and their usage, and much media innovation in advertising happens at the site of apps, by gathering new kinds of personal and non-personal data for the juggernaut of the new digital advertising platforms (Estrada-Jiménez et al., 2019; Desai, 2020).

The Global App Order

So far we have looked at which apps are most popular and high-grossing, and what revenue models underpin them. Now let's delve into the forces that control and shape apps. If we judge by political economy traditions, it is striking that many of the key players in apps are transnational, global media giants (Birkinbine et al., 2017). There are various big and powerful players that dominate the global app order, many of them also being instrumental in the wider political economy of information and communications technologies (ICTs) (see Table 3.4). The apps' titans are rooted in particular places and regions; these include the United States and East Asia, especially Japan, South Korea, and China (Chen et al., 2018; Hjorth & Arnold, 2013; Jin, 2017). It is difficult to directly construct a list of top app companies, because apps are often one part of a broad suite of products and services. So we would look for the digital platform companies that are at the top, given that these companies are closely associated with the fortunes of apps.

A number of these digital platform companies also feature among the top 100 companies in the world. From the various available indices, consider for instance *Forbes Magazine*'s popular annual listing of the world's 2,000 largest public companies (Murphy et al., 2020), where the following app players are listed amid serried ranks of banks, finance, insurance, petrochemical, car and transportation, retail, health, food, entertainment, electronics, and other corporations:

9. Apple
11. AT&T
13. Alphabet
16. Samsung Electronics
20. Verizon Communications
22. Amazon
28. China Mobile
31. Alibaba Group
39. Facebook
43. Nippon Telegraph & Tel
50. Tencent Holdings
69. Deutsche Telekom

In the top 100–200 places, there are a number of regional mobile technology companies such as the French carrier Orange (no. 156), the Mexican-based Latin American giant América Móvil (no. 157), and China Telecom (no. 174). Lower down on the list are companies that are significant players in app developments and whose business depends on their app, for example the Hong Kong-based CK Hutchison (no. 152), which counts mobiles among its property, infrastructure, and other interests, the Chinese online commerce leader JD.com (no. 238), Netflix (no. 284), and the Chinese smartphone firm Xiaomi (no. 384) (Murphy et al., 2020).

There are various other companies whose business models have been directly affected by the rise of apps, smartphones, and mobile Internet and that might also be mentioned, for example the US broadcast behemoth Comcast (no. 27), the entertainment icon Walt Disney (no. 36), the chip manufacturer Intel (no. 38), the Japanese electronics and entertainment conglomerate Sony (no. 58), the Japanese conglomerate holding company Softbank (no. 66), prominent in global app investments via its Vision Fund (the largest technology-focused venture fund in the world), or the US-based processor, graphics, gaming, and AI company Nvidia (no. 489).

Many influential players in apps are companies that have

Table 3.4 Top 20 digital platform companies by market capitalization, 2020.
Source Holger Schmidt. http://en.platform-fund.com.

Rank	Platform	Market capitalization (USD billions)	Region
1	Apple	1,840.0	America
2	Amazon	1,520.0	America
3	Microsoft	1,520.0	America
4	Alphabet	1,090.0	America
5	Alibaba	824.2	Asia–Pacific
6	Facebook	755.1	America
7	Tencent	730.4	Asia–Pacific
8	Samsung	334.6	Asia–Pacific
9	Ant Group	310.0	Asia–Pacific
10	PayPal	219.4	America
11	Meituan	218.6	Asia–Pacific
12	Salesforce	210.7	America
13	Netflix	209.9	America
14	Ping An	201.4	Asia–Pacific
15	Prosus	162.8	Africa
16	JD.com	130.0	Asia–Pacific
17	SAP	122.0	Europe
18	Pinduoduo	107.6	Asia–Pacific
19	ByteDance	100.0	Asia–Pacific
20	Naspers	84.2	Africa

established themselves in related technology areas, especially computers (e.g. Apple), electronics (e.g. Samsung), Internet search, software, and data (e.g. Google or Tencent), online commerce (e.g. Alibaba or Amazon), telecommunications (e.g. AT&T, Verizon, NTT, or Deutsche Telekom), mobile communication (e.g. China Mobile, Orange, América Móvil, or Vodafone), mobile phones (e.g. Xiaomi), social networking and social media (e.g. the pioneering Japanese firm Mixi, which launched its service around the same time as Facebook and boasts the all-time hit mobile game Monster Strike) (Nakamura & Furukawa, 2018; Takahashi, 2010).

There are many significant new interests, often more dispersed across the globe. Some of these come and go. Others maintain and extend their niche over time. Still others build scale and scope, often with complex investment, financing, share arrangements, mergers and acquisitions, and globe-hopping tax minimization. The most obvious players have been closely associated with the digital sector. Among these are the various firms that gained a foothold via their popular mobile games, for instance the British– Swedish firm King (acquired by the games giant Activision Blizzard), Finland's Supercell (in which Tencent acquired a 81.4 percent controlling stake in 2016), or United States' Niantic (a spin-off of Google). Then there are firms that are focused on particular media sectors and have a base in the innovation-rich, governance-stable, and financially trusted ecosystems of particular countries—as in the case of the Swedish music streaming company Spotify. Overall, we see that the international apps industry remains dominated by big transnational and regional players. These companies can typically leverage scale and scope; they also benefitted from ownership and control of key infrastructures, technologies, and customer bases. But, when it comes to the app developer industry, a different picture emerges.

In this industry there certainly are developers who strike it rich. This is the much loved news story around the world. Then there are app developers who become large or medium-size players. These are often associated with one app or a stable of apps—such as the blockbuster mobile games companies just mentioned. Another grouping is that of the app developers who seek to offer services especially to corporate, government, and other sectors. In many ways these form part of the software industry as well as of other design and digital industries.

As an illustration, the market size of the North American app development industry was estimated by the industry research source IBIS World (2020b) to have reached US$20.1 billion in 2020. This count includes names such as Appnovation, a company headquartered in Vancouver, Canada; Intellectsoft, an LA-based company with a focus on "smart enterprise" apps; WillowTree, a US-based mobile apps and web development; and Y Media Labs, an international, Silicon Valley-based "digital product and experiences" firm whose credits include the PayPay mobile app (IBIS World, 2020b). In the United Kingdom, the app developer industry was estimated as worth some £13 billion pounds in 2020 (IBIS World, 2020a). Two of the companies that loom large in app development are hedgehog lab, a global digital product consultancy based in Newcastle upon Tyne, and AKQA, an advertising and creative agency founded in London in 1994. In 2012 AKQA became a subsidiary of the WPP, which in turn is often regarded as the world's largest advertising company. In both the US and the UK smartphone app developer industries, no major player has a market share greater than five percent (IBIS World, 2020a, 2020b).

This snapshot of app development from North America and Britain belies what seems to be the larger global picture— namely one of app development unevenly distributed across the world. This is a public policy problem but also a social challenge, given the hopes vested in apps as a driver of innovation and good prospects across economy, society, and culture. An influential report authored by the consultancy firm Caribou and funded by the open web software company Mozilla sounded this warning, already in 2016: "despite its egalitarian appeal, developer participation in the app economy is heavily skewed toward the largest and richest economies." The report underscored that "95 percent of the estimated industry value is being captured by just the top 10 producing countries. For lower-income countries, the outlook is relatively bleak" (Pon, 2016, p. 6).

There have been some notable studies of the app economies and markets in particular industries, and they flesh out this picture. A 2016 study of Argentina and Bolivia found that, "in both countries, app distribution channels disconnected developers from users" (Wagner & Fernández-Ardèvol, 2016, p. 1781). In-country app users were neglected by the major global platform providers operating in these markets, and "commercial developers were not distributing apps to the public by any other method" (pp. 1781–1782). A more upbeat study, also published in 2016, of the app economy in a Latin American country focused on Colombia. This is one of the policy reports issued by the US-based Progressive Policy Institute (PPI) in a series on the app economy. The PPI itself was founded in 1989, as an "intellectual home for the new Democrats," for whom the digital economy was clearly a signature theme, and was very much associated with President Bill Clinton (Progressive Policy Institute, 2020). The PPI's Colombia study estimated that, as of September 2016, Colombia had over 83,100 app economy jobs and a "rapidly growing number of app developers," but also various local jobs associated with this specific sector and many more, in the wide range of Internet and digital sectors now dependent on apps (Di Ionno & Mandel, 2016, pp. 1–2). The authors underscore the need to continue "with the types of policies that facilitate app economy growth" and point out that doing so "will allow Colombia to participate in the global mobile revolution as a producer rather than a consumer" (Di Ionno & Mandel, 2016, p. 9).

A similarly optimistic picture emerges from various app economy studies undertaken by the PPI. Its study of the quite different Canadian market, for instance, finds that "Canada has a vibrant app economy that spans the iOS, Android, and Blackberry ecosystems" (Long, 2019, p. 8). Such prescriptions are familiar third-way frameworks of a pro-market and liberal democratic character. But another piece of research offers a different perspective and alternative policy measures. A study of the Canadian game app economy carried out in 2019 by David Nieborg, Chris Young, and Daniel Joseph also points to significant issues about dominant app platforms and the absence of distribution channels and effective policy settings that could offer viable alternates—for instance, the lack of support for "local cultural intermediaries" such as informal not-for-profit cultural organizations, which could amplify the visibility and reach of local games developers (Nieborg et al., 2019, p. 61). As Nieborg and colleagues bluntly put it, "Canadian content developers active in the platform economy face an economic deck that is heavily stacked against them" (p. 59).

We certainly need more research of this ilk to fill out the global and local picture on app development. However, the work available so far does suggest that, when it comes to apps, there are real and ongoing global concerns about political and cultural economies, politics, and policies.

Apps remain embedded in the larger structures, dynamics, and geopolitics of the convergent Internet, mobile, and ICT industries, a complicated set of relationships and forces (Mansell, 2012; Winseck, 2017). The big picture here, as Dwayne Winseck describes it, is that the US hegemony of global communications—a palpable concern since the middle of the twentieth century—is being challenged and displaced in crucial areas of Internet, mobile, server, and ICT infrastructures (Winseck, 2019, p. 229). This dismantling of the myth of US hegemony is relevant to apps too. It certainly is the case that the US still exercises dominance in particular fields such as operating systems and software and in important areas of computers, engineering, and frontier technologies where apps have been located or that fuel innovation and systems that apps increasingly rely upon. However, clamorous global rivalry is afoot.

Accordingly, tracing the tangled path of app economies

through a range of international locations is a crucial task. App economies outside major international metropoles are unclear and disputed. These centers are themselves expanding, and their relationships are transforming and being displaced. One indication of these processes can be found in recent claims that India would assume pole position as the largest base of app developers by 2024 (Mandel & Long, 2019). But we need to be skeptical of such claims, given the growing evidence about the unevenness of the digital economy, labor, value, and circuits that emerge around the world, especially in low- and middle-income countries, and about the clear inequalities associated with these developments (Graham, 2019).

These are recurring questions, but let's zero in on something that still remains a bottleneck or a choke point for apps when it comes to access and distribution: the app store.

The App Store: Ruling the Roost

If, in most cases, an app is a software application that users activate and use on their personal device, how do they gain access to this app? Typically, users download their app via an app store.

We saw in chapter 2 how the app store concept came into existence and how it works. In many ways, the app store is an early instance of what is now widely referred to as a digital platform. Earlier versions of app stores tended to bring together two sides of a market: app developers and app users. However, as app stores evolved—especially in conjunction with their associated technologies and the media and digital environments in which they were made sense of, communicated about, and marketed—apps started to look and feel very much like the kinds of arrangements talked about and conceptualized as digital platforms.

Many app stores bring together the various sides of the market interested in apps. In the technical terms of economics, finance, and business disciplines, they are multi-sided markets, as is emphasized in the digital platforms literatures (Campbell-Kelly et al., 2015; Trabucchi & Buganza, 2020). Developers, large and small, can offer their apps via an app store. Potential users can browse an app store, or can arrive at it via a link. As noted, Apple's App Store and Google Play dominate globally. A big competitive advantage of both is their alignment with their respective mobile operating systems.

Building on its own app store, iOS, and distribution of consumer products, Apple has a set of strategies for retaining and expanding its customer base and for entrenching the dominance of its ecosystem. One important aspect of this activity is how Apple works the software–hardware continuum through its tight vertical and horizontal integration of supply line elements. Like other smartphone manufacturers, Apple progressively incorporates features of popular apps into its operating system and devices, or showcases its own pre-installed apps with such features.

Take for instance the flashlight or torch feature of smart-phones, now taken for granted by users. This feature first developed through the design of flashlight apps. Flashlight apps commandeered the light-emitting diode (LED) flash of the iPhone's built-in camera, becoming popular downloads: "iPhone owners bracing for possible power outages from the 'storm of the century' can make sure a flashlight is handy by downloading a virtual one onto their devices" (Whitney, 2012). In 2013 Apple introduced its iOS7, adding a flashlight feature in its control center and making it accessible with a swipe and a tap (later the flashlight was activated via Siri). This innovation led one tech commentator to declare that "Apple essentially just mass-exterminated every flashlight app in the App Store" (Tsotsis, 2013). Other formerly standalone apps have endured the same fate. Among them, to mention just a few, are weather apps, measure apps, emojis, and fertility and period prediction for women. This last function, previously offered by apps like Clue, was incorporated into Apple's own 2019 Health App (Albergotti, 2019). The movement has gone the other way too. Apple has unbundled core apps that were pre-installed, offering them via the Apple App Store, just as larger app developers such as Google often unbundled or disaggregated their omnibus apps from 2015 onwards, turning them into single-function ones.

Evident here is the centrality of intellectual property to apps as much as to smartphones. This area of software and technological innovation is rife with self-protection measures from developers and corporations—measures such as patent and other copyright, trademark, and intellectual property safeguards, which have featured in the furious legal and extra-legal rivalry over smartphone innovation (Fröhlich, 2014; Galetovic et al., 2018). Apps are the tip of long and often obscure histories of technology innovation, especially proximate histories of hardware and software that clearly anticipate the popularity of smartphones. Not for nothing did Steve Jobs remark, sounding comical just as much as imperious, that Apple was going to "reinvent the phone"—but "boy, have we patented it!" (Jobs, 2010). A legion of smartphone technologies and companies begged to differ, whence the many years of litigation that ensued (Nam et al., 2015; Paik & Zhu, 2016).

In the area of competition and trade rules and policy, debate over app stores continues unabated across many jurisdictions. Apple has been subject to various legal proceedings. A consumer device owner who was heard in the US Supreme Court case *Apple Inc. v. Pepper et al.* in 2019 alleged that the corporation acted as a monopoly when it required iPhone and iPad users to download apps only from its portal, while at the same time charging a 30 percent commission on each app sale (Albergotti, 2019; "Clayton Antitrust Act and Sherman Antitrust Act," 2019). A rising tide of app developers across the United Kingdom and Europe, especially after the latter's successful efforts to curtail Apple's anti-competitive conduct, have focused international attention on how Apple takes advantage of its app store (Smith, 2020)—much to the delight of its competitors.

The second dominant app store is Google Play—formerly Android Market. With Android, Google aims to strike a balance between on the one hand maintaining and driving a core of functional elements that should ensure recognizable features and user experience across a range of different mobile and other devices, and on the other hand allowing developers and businesses to customize and create their own distinctive services and products (Google, 2020). Reflecting on the recent Android experience, Google engineers contend that "giving more freedom to all ecosystem entities and creating an equilibrium are a transformation necessary to further scale the world's largest open source ecosystem with over two billion active devices" (Yim et al., 2019, p. 1).

At various times in the early days of its entry into the mobiles market, Google sought to develop its own phone, fanning many rumors (Arthur, 2014; Claburn, 2007; Moutinho, 2016; Vogelstein, 2013). But, after Apple's launch of the iPhone, Google choose to prioritize developing the Android OS and its own app store rather than competing head to head with smartphone vendors (Goggin, 2012; Pogue, 2014). This has paid off through the creation and maintenance of a major alternative to Apple iOS apps. With the entrenchment of the smartphone and tablets as default devices in the contemporary digital media environment, Google's strategy has ensured that users would continue to purchase Android devices. This said, Google has dabbled in bringing various devices to market in partnership with vendors, hoping to gain acceptance for a signature device. This long-running project has not really taken root; and in the laptop market, too, Google has been a niche player at best—for instance with its Chromebook and the Chrome OS. For the most part, Google's equipment development has functioned as a way for the company to experiment and showcase the capabilities of the Android OS and its apps. In addition, Google has increasingly gained a market share and sought to develop, promote, and secure allegiance to its own apps. So, like Apple, Google too juggles its split loyalties.

Google is the custodian and owner of an OS. It also operates and controls its own app store, while having a strong commercial interest in its own apps. Google's suite of apps include an expanding range of software, the most popular being Gmail, Google maps, Google (search), Chrome browser, Calendar, Drive, Docs, Photos, Duo (voice chat), and Hangout. For business customers, Google offers G Suite, which brings together these kind of apps and others, such as Forms, Sites, and Scripts, as well as back-end tools for managing users in an enterprise and for analyzing the data they generate (what Google calls Work Insights).

Underpinning Google's apps is its unrivalled store of user, apps, device, location, and other data (Hyunjin & Matthew, 2011). In this sense, with its "empire of data centers" (Gilder, 2018), Google is, by turns, ideal paradigm and *bête noire* (Rushkoff, 2016; Vaidhyanathan, 2011) of the data turn and algorithmic turn (Berry, 2019), as these have shaped apps and positioned them at a crucial node in the wider digital media environment (Gehl, 2014; Rogers, 2018). Google data have been a phenomenon in its own right, given the Google Trends website of publicly available data (Jun et al., 2018) that a wide range of research and policy draw upon to understand all sorts of issues, from French youth unemployment (Fondeur & Karame, 2013) and German car sales (Fantazzini & Toktamysova, 2015) through marijuana use (Cavazos-Rehg et al., 2015) and tourist arrivals (Bangwayo-Skeete & Skeete, 2015), to influenza epidemics (Lazer et al., 2014). Google data have been drawn upon across the globe to map and model the spread of COVID-19 (Strzelecki, 2020).

For its part, Google is putting particular emphasis on its ability to cover a broad and integrated range of apps, across as many technology landscapes as possible. Google explains that

Android "runs on devices of all shapes and sizes, providing you a vast opportunity for continued user engagement" (Android, 2020a). Apart from the mature area of web browsers (used via Google Chrome OS devices such as Chromebooks), Google features Android potential for product areas such as smart watches (the Wear OS by Google app), television ("Build apps that let users experience your app's immersive content on the big screen"), auto ("Write your apps for an in-car experience without having to worry about vehicle-specific hardware differences"), or things ("Experiment with building apps for smart, connected devices that integrate with custom hardware peripherals") (Android, 2020a).

Building a viable, ubiquitous, cross-app platform is of increasing importance, since users owned or accessed multiple devices—at least those with the means and incentives to do so. The lure of Apple's and Android's app platforms is that they are, to a large extent, ecosystems that allow users to move relatively easily across devices and environments while still using the same apps.

The idea of apps, like that of spanning platforms, has migrated into a range of technology-intensive environments. Here the app is no longer associated with individual users or family or household members, who may own and operate devices severally or collectively. Rather apps figure also in public, institutional, or organizational settings, or at least they are called "apps"—because calling "app" a piece of software gives its users a sense of familiarity. This can be seen in smart city planning. Here apps feature increasingly in the digital platforms and approaches that proliferate as public–private partnerships between local and regional government and technology companies. The best known are IBM's Smarter Cities Framework (Alizadeh, 2017) and the mosaic of bottom-up apps that offer aspects of smart city technology.

Two events in 2020 secured the dominance of Google and Apple in app stores and app markets, and also their interdependence in the long run.

First, in March 2020 Google and Apple announced that they would partner on COVID-19 tracing technology by releasing application programming interfaces (APIs) that should "enable interoperability between Android and iOS devices using apps from public health authorities" (Apple, 2020a). The two companies pledged to join their data-gathering efforts. This meant that users of either Apple or Android apps could download the contact-tracing app without the public health authority having to develop an app for each platform. The next step saw Apple and Google creating a "broader Bluetooth-based contact-tracing platform by building this functionality into the underlying platforms" (Apple, 2020a). In their announcement, the companies suggest that this would allow more people to participate and would support "interaction with a broader ecosystem of apps and government health authorities" (Apple, 2020a). This unprecedented cooperation of the two perhaps most iconic tech companies at the time brought a wave of response and concern.

Second, in October 2020, news broke of a US Department of Justice anti-trust suit against Google. Eleven US states joined, and others were to follow, all alleging that Google protected its monopoly on search by illegal means advertising (Kang et al., 2020). At the heart of the case was the allegation that Google paid Apple up to US$11 billion for top-billing on its iPhone, with the result that as much as a half of Google's search volume derived from Apple devices (Copland & Higgins, 2020).

Like many aspects of apps, their economics—as an important element of the so-called digital economy, as a minor but crucial part of the ICT sector, and as a rich vein of the wider economy—is substantial. The picture presented so far shows the app economy to be highly concentrated, and the markets to be dominated by a few large and wealthy transnational companies. It is, however, a complex picture, which looks quite different depending on region and country location. The app economy contains a diverse range of large actors, as well as the much vaunted multitude of small apps. Shaping these new economic landscapes, their capabilities, and their opportunities are strategic infrastructures, socio-technical systems, and ecosystems. While the arena for apps changes, Apple and Google have an oversized influence on how we access, use, profit from, and gain value from apps. Yet this dispensation is more fragile and contestable than it looks. The order of the world's apps is changing dramatically for a numbers of reasons, as we shall now explore.

China's App Store Exceptionalism

While dominated by influential commercial actors, the power relations of apps are not monolithic. There still exist many app stores operated mostly by device vendors or covering specific categories of apps or markets. These app stores tend to coexist alongside Apple and Google, in their interstices, as it were. This cues us to consider a major exception to the app store hegemony rule: China.

China has a long set of histories of ICTs, Internet, mobile communication, social media, digital economy, and software that have shaped the emergence of the world's biggest single national market for apps. Consider the outpouring of user innovation and creativity with apps in China and its diaspora—for instance the way in which popular Internet-based messaging software such as QQ has been remediated in the era of apps, or cultures and early forms of online and mobile news and journalism, citizen activism, or political commentary. Digital public spheres and practices such as microblogging and photo sharing have shaped the emergence of apps such as Weibo, and forms of entertainment, media, and popular culture have shaped a massive, diverse range of highly profitable and influential apps and accompanying digital cultures. The rise of livestreaming is a case in point.

China saw an explosion of interest in app stores shortly

after the launch of the Apple iPhone (Perez, 2010). By 2010, the Apple App Store was introduced to China, and this marked a new beginning for Chinese iOS apps. Over time, in the face of stiff competition from the many Chinese mobile phone vendors, Apple shifted its strategic emphasis to services, including apps and its app store business (Qin, 2017). In the process, Apple carried out delicate negotiations with and accepted online regulation from the Chinese government. Despite these challenges, by late 2016 news broke that China had outstripped the United States as the biggest source of Apple App Store revenue. In early 2017, however, as part of its efforts to extend Internet control to the burgeoning mobile Internet, the Chinese government introduced new rules, which required app stores to register and update any changes (Lucas, 2017). Also that year, tensions over Apple's success and market influence came into the open. Apple faced actions by disgruntled local developers who requested that authorities investigate possible breaches of price and anti-monopoly laws (Qin, 2017). The eventual upshot was the March 2020 takedown of the game Plague. This came as a blow, given that Plague had been the most popular game in China for the previous eight years, both in the Apple App Store and in the global game store and community platform Steam (NDEMIC Creations, 2020).

In 2010 Android devices were also introduced to the Chinese market. One year later, in 2011, China was proclaimed the world's largest smartphone market (Chen & Hu, 2013). Other Chinese communities, notably Taiwan through the HTC Corporation, had earlier played a pioneering role in the first handsets developed with Android (HTC made the first Android handset, T-Mobile G1, in 2008, then its own branded phones from 2009 on). These advances brought with them considerable app-related opportunities for local IT companies and software developers.

While in the West Google Play may be the major Android app store, on the Chinese mobile app scene local Android app markets reign supreme. What paved the way to their success is the 2010 ban on direct access to Google Play, when Google pulled out of mainland China as a result of mounting public concerns in the western world over human rights, freedom of expression, and censorship. At the time, Google redirected its search engine to a Hong Kong Internet domain address (Gaudin, 2010), occasioning creative, if convoluted work-arounds. Consider, for instance, the case of the much celebrated Google Translate app. Google maintained a web-based version of Translate, and Chinese users could use Translate when connected to a virtual private network (VPN). In 2017 Google reintroduced Translate with support and maintenance from Google's Chinese joint venture. It made available an iOS version, which was available in Apple's App Store, and an Android version available via direct download (Russell, 2017).

Although still significant in size, Apple and Google apps and their app stores are a side show in China. Their exclusion from full market operation has left the field wide open for the flourishing of many other app stores. In 2018, there were an estimated 400 plus Android app stores in China, each with its own policies and standards (see Table 3.5). The Chinese apps fall into three broad groups: app stores run by Internet and mobile technology companies; vendor-specific app markets; and dedicated app stores, often serving specialized markets (Wang et al., 2018). Chinese Internet and mobile technology giants are a significant force among the app stores. Their app stores include Tencent Myapp, Baidu Market, 360 Market, PP Assistant (Alibaba's app store), the state-owned telecommunication company China Mobile's MM Store, established in 2009, Wandouija (also owned by Alibaba), China Unicom Wo Store, and China Telecom 189 Store (Wang et al., 2018). The three Chinese tech giants Tencent, Alibaba, and Baidu are front and center. Their leading positions are underpinned via their own app stores, via their acquisitions and cross-platform app store ownership, and via their market-leading, signature apps.

Table 3.5 Top 10 Android app stores in China, by monthly average users, 2020.

S<small>OURCE</small> AppInChina. (2020). The AppInChina app store index. July 8. https://www.appinchina.co/market/app-stores.

Rank	App Store	Market Share (%)	MAU
1	Tencent My App	25.99	281,488,000
2	Huawei App Market	15.09	163,428,000
3	Oppo Software Store	10.22	110,664,000
4	360 Mobile Assistant (Qihoo 360 Company)	9.73	105,368,000
5	VIVO App Store	8.68	93,981,000
6	MIUI App Store (Xiaomi)	8.47	91,716,000
7	Baidu Mobile Assistant	7.98	86,428,000
8	Anzhi Market	2.65	28,748,000
9	PP Assistant (Alibaba's App Store)	2.24	24,295,000
10	China Mobile MM Store	2.16	23,390,000

N<small>OTES</small> The AppInChina App Store Index is the index of China's largest Android app stores. The market share is based on the top 29 ranking app stores. MAU (monthly average users) is the aggregate of daily active users over a month (typically, users who have viewed or used an app at least once in the month).

Tencent owns and operates Myapp, and the company is of course best known for its pervasive WeChat app (see the important discussion in Li, 2020). Tencent is also a majority-owner of Sogou. Sougou is known for its Sogou Pinyin, the "dominant input platform in China for both desktop and mobile systems" (AppInChina, 2020), which has seen its mobile keyboard app figure as China's third largest app (Sogou, 2020). Sogou is China's second largest search engine (Sogou, 2020), and it is boosted by the fact that it is the default search engine for WeChat accounts (leaving others such as Baidu at a disadvantage). Sogou has billed its mobile keyboard as China's "largest voice app," and has invested heavily in AI and other technologies to leverage data and sustain its advantage over Baidu in voice search (Dai & Chau, 2018; Sun, 2019).

Baidu is well known as China's largest and most popular search engine, gaining from Google's exit from the market in 2010. Its app store, Baidu Mobile Assistant, benefits from prominent placement in search results when users look for apps on baidu.com. Baidu also acquired HiMarket in 2013 for a record US$1.85 billion. The package containd the HiMarket app store, available in English and Chinese versions, and the 91Wireless app store, with its 91 Assistant (AppInChina, 2020; Pfanner, 2013).

For its part, the e-commerce and online services corporation Alibaba, operator of Taobao, has its own app store, PP Assistant. In addition to offering Android apps, PP Assistant features two app stores for iOS—one app store for official Apple devices and another for devices that have been "jailbroken" (AppInChina, 2020). In addition, Alibaba owns Wandoujia, an app store that specializes in multimedia and mobile entertainment and that it purchased in 2016 (Jing, 2016). Alibaba is also an investment partner in Meizu (AppInChina, 2020), having purchased a minority stake in early 2015 (Haiyan & Yuan, 2015).

In the area of vendor app markets, China has a large smartphone industry, and each vendor typically has its own app store, which comes pre-installed on the device. These vendors are Huawei App Market, OPPO Software Store, VIVO App Store, MIUI App Store (Xiaomi), Lenovo Le Store, Cool Pad, ZTE App Store, MeiZu Flyme, and Gionee (AppInChina, 2020; Wang et al., 2018, p. 3). The only prominent foreign vendor is the Samsung App Store.

A third group of Chinese app stores focus on providing apps, often to specialized markets. Apart from the app stores already listed that have been acquired by Alibaba, Baidu, or Tencent, this group contains Anzhi, a longstanding app store; Safe Market, priding itself on listing only secure apps; App China; Kuan, owned by Coolapk; and the mobile games provider Shouji (AppInChina, 2020). Here it is worth returning to the story of Google apps and their vicissitudes in the Chinese market. In 2018 Google Play did finally arrive in the Chinese consumer market as part of the Google Mobile Service (GMS). However, many observers regarded this move as being already too late. This was because China's domestic app stores were already fully developed by that time, which made it difficult for Google Play to be competitive. Despite the challenges it has faced, Google Play has been able to provide a window for Chinese app developers and smartphone makers to reach out to global users. Developers can release international versions of their apps via this system, and Android phone manufacturers can install Google Play on their gadgets to sell them in the West. So, while Google Play is still not an official app store in China, it maintains a presence in the market, claiming the 23rd spot, with a 0.04 percent share of the top 29 ranking app stores and 467,000 monthly average users (AppInChina, 2020).

Beyond the App Store: Stand-Alone Apps

The kinds of controls that have been put in place and maintained by the app store have fueled considerable rivalry—most consequentially in China, where Apple and Google have been banned or stymied, and a thriving clutch of app stores have sustained themselves. In other places it has proven financially difficult for competitor app stores to gain much of a toehold, let alone sustain themselves. Instead, for players with deep pockets as well as for ones seeking to scale up promising startup app ventures, one avenue has been building services and functionality within the app itself. In this area, Asian apps have been in the spotlight.

There are many apps with a particular niche; but, unsurprisingly given the sheer number of apps, finding, downloading, using, and continuing to use apps are non-trivial issues to which developers, researchers, and app promoters and businesses have devoted considerable effort. We will return to this topic from a different angle, in the discussion of everyday life and apps in chapter 5. For the present, we might see it as a version of the problem of the "long tail," which has been discussed in relation to a range of other goods and services available by digital means.

The Internet, mobile and social media, and digital distribution channels allow access to a bewildering range of goods and services, where items that potentially generate a relatively small revenue can still be economically viable. For the long tail to operate in a crowded digital environment and for relatively niche or small apps to be viable, many technologies and techniques of search, discovery, personalization, and recommendation (Oestreicher-Singer & Sundararajan, 2012) have emerged during the nearly two decades since the British–American business technology journalist Chris Anderson, editor-in-chief of *Wired Magazine* and head of TED Talks, popularized the term in 2004 (Anderson, 2004, 2006). The long tail is an especially interesting issue for the sharing economy, in which apps play an important part (Geissinger et al., 2020). However, with apps, there is a key issue for their backers to address: the ongoing need for software upgrades and development, to ensure compatibility and interoperability across the ICT systems in which such apps need to operate. So there are significant problems faced by app developers: obsolescence, waste, and recycling. For users, there is the ongoing burden of maintaining and updating app software and mobile devices (Chun, 2016).

It takes a lot of work, still ongoing, to make apps discoverable, downloadable, and sustainable over time for users. So there is a set of reinforcing reasons that underpin recent developments toward the integration of apps. Let's explore this through a discussion of two related trends in apps, dubbed respectively "mini" apps and "super" apps.

Mini apps

One emerging trend in the area of mobile apps that China has pioneered is the idea of mini programs—subapplications of a mobile app, or apps within an app. WeChat first released a mini program on January 9, 2017. The date also marks the 10th anniversary of iPhone, which shows Tencent's ambition to take "evolutionary" action. Also called "lite" apps, these mini programs allowed users to quickly access or open things without having to download them or leave the parent app. Also, such lite apps can be accessed via the parent app without having to be separately downloaded from an app store (Liao, 2019). Initially, WeChat developed mini programs with the aim of expanding its existing mobile ecosystem by linking the online with the offline scenarios. Mini programs would allow users to engage in more activities via the messaging app, for example for making payments. Being simpler and more compact than mobile apps, the mini programs would occupy no more than, say, 10 megabytes, while still performing basic functions. Thus far, there are more than 200 categories of mini programs on WeChat that offer gaming, transportation, bill paying, e-commerce, travel, and entertainment services.

Mini programs came into the spotlight in 2018, when one gaming app, Tiao yi tiao ("Jump Jump"), became a hit; user growth subsequently accelerated. Other major tech companies in China soon followed suit in catching the wave. Many of the popular apps and each of the eight leading apps— WeChat, QQ, Baidu, Alipay, Taobao, Toutiao, Douyin, and Quick Apps—developed their own mini program systems; hence local competition for any new opportunity provided by these innovations has greatly increased. The use of these mini apps is significant. To give an example, in 2019 the number of daily active users (DAU) of Alipay's more than 120,000 mini programs reached more than 230 million, while the DAU of WeChat's 1 million mini programs hit 200 million (Liao, 2019). Indeed in China mini apps have become mainstream to a fair extent. This is signaled for instance by China's General Office of the State Counsel, which in 2018 launched a digital government services app (in particular, citizen feedback and suggestions on both WeChat and Alipay: see Xi, 2018). Another example is the popularity of travel and tourism mini apps on WeChat (Cheng et al., 2019).

In the heat of the mini app moment, questions were raised as to whether this development represented the "app store killer" (Ma, 2019) or augured a "post-app era" (Cheng et al., 2020). Importantly, mini programs can bring ease and convenience to both users and the app developers, which means that users no longer have to install a variety of apps on their phones but can just use the most essential ones instead. Among other potential advantages, mini programs are lightweight, low cost, and easily integrated into WeChat's infrastructure (Cheng et al., 2020). This is a great benefit to many Chinese users, especially since their cheaper smartphone brands do not have a great deal of storage space. In addition, the program developers can make them on a much more limited budget and in a shorter timespan than is the case with more complicated apps. However, these lite apps often do not have the functionality of larger, more fully featured and powerful apps, which work in their own right inside an app platform.

In addition, this proliferation of mini programs brings some concerns with it: one view has it that Chinese app developers, in dealing with mini program function risks, sacrifice the chance to have an open working environment. We can use WeChat as an illustration of what this means. WeChat is a semi-closed platform, which implies that the web developers have to master its exclusive coding language (Sohu.com, 2018). Another issue is raised by the low production costs and low entry threshold of a mini program: this feature might pave the way for the production of fake goods and other illegal behavior (Qian, 2018). As a cautionary response, in February

2018 WeChat suspended around 2,000 mini programs on its platform for violation of rules.

Interestingly, the idea of a mini app has a history dating back at least to web-based social networking systems associated with "widgets." Because MySpace and Facebook had the capability for profile customizing but did not extend this functionality to their users, providers popped up, offering mini apps—or "music-related widgets mini-applications" (Bruno, 2008)— before the social networking service providers stepped in to do so. Google also offered Google Gadgets, mini applications that would work within Google's homepage and that developers could add to a portal (Krill, 2007). Mini apps are one notable development in the struggle of app companies to consolidate and extend their customer base, revenues, and profitability. Other developments with a similar aim took a different tack. Here again China has figured prominently, as a much acclaimed pioneer for a trend in apps that includes mini apps but has much wider implications—namely the idea of "super apps."

Super apps

At a certain moment in the evolution of apps and digital platforms, around 2019, some apps were dubbed "super apps," in an attempt to capture the spread of their service, product, and experience offerings. These super apps were discussed with enthusiasm and their prospects promoted as exemplars of a next phase in the digital economy. While the super app concept does not really pass muster analytically, it is useful to explore and unpack it, as it offers insights into the economic and industrial trajectories of apps. It is not just the next level up for apps, but rather conveys the dominance of some digital platform companies, globally and regionally.

"Super apps" is a term with at least 25 years' currency. In 1995 an article in the industry magazine *Network Computing* proposed electronic (e-) messaging as one of the super apps of tomorrow (Gerber, 1995). As apps gained in popularity, they were often seen as super apps, on account of their potential to solve everyday, practical challenges (Gase, 2014). With the advent of smartphones, the formula "the right apps can give you super powers" took off; this was the super apps' way of singling out some apps as essential must-haves (Rodriguez, 2012). In 2019 the term took on a different meaning. In many ways, super apps resembled mini apps—rather like an "ecosystem play," as suggested in *Forbes* report: "This 'Super App' creates an ecosystem where the users' time is monopolized and there is no need for them to use a variety of apps" (Atkins, 2019). The discourse is very much about super apps being a strategy in emerging markets in the Southeast and elsewhere in Asia, as well as in South America; and companies that take the strategy of "aggressively expanding horizontally and dominating a specific geography" are compared to the "US/Silicon Valley model," which seeks to "grow vertically and go global" (Atkins, 2019).

In particular, it was proposed that Asian super apps show the way for western counterparts in the digital platform realm such as Uber, which were perceived as struggling to retain, consolidate, and expand their hold on markets (McGee, 2019). Leading Asian super apps mentioned at this juncture were Tencent's WeChat (Xue & Yu, 2017), Alibaba Pay, and the Indonesian Gojek app. Here the argument tended to be that the Asian apps have become more effectively integrated, offering more comprehensive services and managing more successfully the new "back end" demands of the systems that underpin digital platforms—especially payment, digital, mobile money, and fin tech systems. Exhibit A in the super app discourse is an app we have already encountered, WeChat. As we have seen, WeChat has managed to pivot from its mass user base, which it gained as a messaging app, to covering a range of other services. This prompted its being dubbed a "mega app" (Zheng et al., 2019).

The different kinds of global Internets and how they

are imagined have long histories (Goggin & McLelland, 2017). The language of super apps is a way to talk about the international enclosure of the Internet into commodified platforms, especially mobile devices and networking. Consider, for instance, the proposition advanced in a late 2019 *Financial Times* story that looked at the contrasting Internet worlds (as they were seen) of China and the West (Liu & Shepherd, 2019). In the United States, the journalists suggest, users still use desktop or laptop devices and web browsers, as well as mobile apps, to access goods, services, and service. By contrast, in China "almost all Internet access is mobile ... and mostly takes place within 'super apps' such as WeChat, which have their own self-contained shopping, messaging, and search functions" (Liu & Shepherd, 2019). As a result, China is depicted as a stark example of how search engines like Baidu (or Google, for that matter) helped struggle, in the web era, to gain access, typically via smartphones, to the kind of content centered on message, video content, audio, and so on that occurs within the mobile apps and digital platforms. Baidu and Google do not have direct access to this content in the way in which a particular app company would. Instead, a company like ByteDance, progenitor of the hugely popular TikTok, develops its own search engine strategies—to search both its own content and content from other sources, such as the web. In doing so, ByteDance, Tencent, and others are short-circuiting the step from user "search" to customer "recommendation" (or "product or service") (Liu & Shepherd, 2019). The contrasting history of Google is perhaps the most sustained longitudinal case of how to commercialize search. Through products such as Google AdWords and Facebook, with its dominance in digital advertising, this history shows us that what is key is the area of "recommendation ad technology," underpinned by algorithms that take best advantage of proprietary customer data (Liu & Shepherd, 2019).

Through Uber Eats, Uber was also an early mover in food

delivery. However, this was originally established as a separate app; this was before Uber went for the "one stop shop" strategy, following Chinese apps such as Alipay and WeChat. If WeChat emerges from the digital media landscape of messaging apps, Gojek, Grab, and Uber are seeking to build on their foundations and core business in ride hailing. What the discourse of super apps reveals is about the potential, but also the complexity of doing integration across digital markets. Along with bringing together different services and products under the same shingle of the super app, what appears to distinguish WeChat, Gojek, and Grab is the fact they have successfully devised and rolled out digital money and payment platforms. The long dream of e-commerce and mobile money has reached a highly profitable junction, opening up vistas of riches for the coming decade and beyond, as I will discuss further in chapter 5.

As much as anything, talking of super apps is a way to continue war—or rather business rivalry—by other means. A super app is in principle an integrative technical, user, and business approach to leverage existing customer bases and to expand into other product and service opportunities. Another, more standard approach is one that we have already seen: choosing varieties, blends, and admixtures of merger and acquisition, partnership, and strategic alliance.

Facebook is a leading instance of a company that has been successful in reimagining and reconfiguring its affordances and its reach (Brugger, 2015) by acquiring various competitor firms and their technologies (Goggin, 2014) and by interacting with various stakeholders and partners. This is best explained by Anne Helmond and her co-authors, whose argument emphasizes Facebook's ability to forge and dissolve corporate partnerships over time and presents it as a major factor in the company's wielding of techno-economic weaponry, as it has forged "a constantly changing platform that derives power from its ability to create institutional dependencies among its vast network of partners" (Helmond et al., 2019, p. 124). At the level of platform architecture, and especially of its *programmability*, Helmond and colleagues show the ways in which Facebook has worked to ensure its evolution and to accommodate the many stakeholder groups and customers it needed to address as it massively expanded. Secondly, the authors make the case that Facebook's focus on and cultivation of partners such as Developer Marketing and others was crucial during its development, as it help it maintain an ecosystem that allowed it over time to sustain an infrastructure (Helmond et al., 2019).

Earning its reputation as a social networking service, at that stage alongside competitors such as MySpace, Orkut, and Friendster, Facebook rapidly developed culturally and materially (Miller, 2013) and became one of the first social media giants (van Dijck, 2013). In its expansion, it acquired the social gaming concern Zynga, itself a successful messaging platform, even more widely used in its shift to being centered on its app and supported by smartphone technology (Ceruzzi, 2012), cultures (Haddon & Vincent, 2018), and Facebook's construction of digital participation (Lovink, 2011). Facebook then acquired WhatsApp in 2014. The obvious reason for the WhatsApp takeover was that "Zuckerberg needed a dog in the messaging fight" (Hoefflinger, 2017, p. 159).

Among other benefits, WhatsApp helped amass users from emerging markets, where messaging apps became more popular than Facebook. This was dramatized by the April 2020 announcement that Facebook would pay US$5.7 billion to acquire 10 percent of the Indian cheap mobile and Internet giant Jio, owned by the conglomerate Reliance Industries (Fischer, 2020; Telecom Regulatory Authority of India, 2020). For Facebook, the investment and alliance offered a way to finally consolidate its customer base in the quickly growing Indian market. In 2016, Facebook had launched its Free Basics app, which met with a storm of criticism in India, especially for the violation of net neutrality policy (Prasad, 2018). There were also other concerns that it raised around the world, for instance in Africa (Nothias, 2020). In the intervening four years, Facebook had gained approximately 400 million users via WhatsApp—up from 36 million in 2014, when it was just one of many competing messaging apps (Phadnis, 2014). The hookup with Reliance Jio was targeted at e-commerce expansion and timed for a period when digital participation and consumption had arisen as a result of India's COVID-19 nationwide lockdown. In 2020 Reliance had launched JioMart, connecting customers with local neighborhood shops and businesses and competing with Amazon and Walmart's Flipkart. WhatsApp was slated as a platform to help JioMart in its expansion. A *Financial Times* report characterized the move thus: "Facebook and Jio creates [*sic*] huge lake of Indian data" (Parkin & Murphy, 2020). The irony is unmistakable: the report picks up the fact that, in speeches of late 2018 and early 2019, the Reliance Chairman Mukesh Ambani, India's richest man, warned Prime Minister Narendra Modi of the threat posed by foreign companies (*Economic Times*, 2018) at a time when India had reached the top worldwide in mobile data (Ambani, 2018). Ambani suggested that "necessary steps will have to be taken to migrate the control and ownership of Indian data back to India—in other words, Indian wealth back to India." "Data colonization is as bad as the previous forms of colonization," he said, adding that "data freedom is as precious as the freedom we won in 1947." In this context, the new partnership with Reliance Jio offered WhatsApp a way forward: it could now address longstanding issues with data localization and protection (Mishra, 2019). Such issues had been highlighted in a 2016–2017 Indian Supreme Court judgment in a case where two law students challenged WhatsApp's privacy policy over its sharing user data with Facebook ("SC issues notice," 2017).

Conclusion

In this chapter we have explored the new world order of apps as they have developed in recent years. Apps have been prominent in the transnational shifts in information, communication, and technology entailed by displacements of the capital, infrastructure, technical, and cultural capabilities of leading countries in the global North—displacement caused in turn by challenges from other countries and regions. In the wake of earlier ICT and mobile innovations in East Asian countries such as Japan and South Korea, China has established itself as a new reference point for digital media transformations—an especially interesting case when it comes to apps. As we saw, India and a number of other Southeast Asian countries are sites for important developments in, and struggles over, the economics and the politics of apps.

All in all, apps have played an influential role in the broader reshaping of media economies and industries and in the relationships of the media with audiences, users, and their own social and cultural contexts. As we shall see in the next two chapters, it can be hard to pin down the exact nature, significance, and contribution of apps, but they reappear as crucial items in the reinvention of the media as well as in contemporary change and innovation in digital societies.

CHAPTER FOUR

App Media

Structures, dynamics, and power relations, as we have seen, play a big role in how apps are made and emerge. In the next two chapters we will look at the important aspects of the use and consumption of apps and the practices, rituals, meanings, and values that are associated with them. Here in chapter 4 we explore apps as media and what is distinctive about apps by comparison to other kinds of media.

The twin questions of what a medium is and what media are have a long pedigree. During the protracted digital transition, we have witnessed a debate under way across different traditions and theoretical positions (Couldry, 2012; McQuail & Deuze, 2020; Peters, 1999, 2015). In this chapter I draw on the theorization of digital media in general, and especially on theories of kinds of media most cognate to apps: computers, software, telecommunications, Internet, human–machine communication. Particularly germane is work that theorizes mobile media, locative media, and social media, such as outlined in chapter 1. I relied on this kind of work for the broader account of apps developed across this book as a whole.

Leaving the abundant theories of media aside, there are many kinds of media relevant to or remediated by apps that I will not be able to discuss in detail. Mail and epistolary media, for instance, of which email apps are an obvious legatee, have long and dense histories (Brunton, 2013; Milne, 2010). Books and print culture are another field that I will be able to cover only in passing (Farman, 2014; Snickars & Vonderau, 2012). All these are significant parts of what has made apps what they are. They also highlight significant factors to consider in relation to thinking about apps as media. If I were writing this book in the early 2010s, I would have probably focused on these dimensions of apps, as they became media. In the intervening years, multistranded arcs of app media innovations have broadened and other elements have come into view. So, in order to illustrate leading aspects of the dynamics at play, I have chosen to focus on the following aspects of app media: games; location; realities; images; moving images; sound; voice; messages.

Game Apps

Consistently, games figure prominently as one of the most downloaded, used, and profitable categories of apps. Game apps build on long histories of play and games and on how these histories are picked up, reconfigured, and added to by digital games—computer, video, online, and especially mobile games.

Mobile games really emerged as a force in the 1990s. They ranged from games built in or included as standard in handsets, such as the iconic Nokia Snake game or poker, through to games developed for various generations of mobile phones, especially 2G and 3G mobiles (Goggin, 2006). Many apps recapitulate the popular, enduring aspects of games that these early mobile games latch onto (Johnson, 2018). For too long, mobile games did not garner the kudos that console-based or PC-based games attracted among dedicated gamers. Mobile games were regarded as time fillers, "snack entertainment," or casual games by comparison to "hardcore" gaming (Chess & Paul, 2018, pp. 108–111). Important scholarship in mobile games has challenged the picture. The work of Larissa Hjorth drew attention to and theorized the pioneering East Asia games scene, which is characterized by the dovetailing of gaming cultures with the wider mobile social media cultures that emerge in places such as Japan and

South Korea—user-generated content, social practices, and digital practices associated with social networking systems such as Mixi, Cyworld, Line, and Kakao Talk (Hjorth, 2009; Hjorth & Arnold, 2013). Scholars such as Adriana de Souza e Silva showed the unfolding of mobile games and play at the intersections of public space, location, and urbanism at various sites in the Americas and elsewhere around the world (de Souza e Silva, 2009; Shklovski & de Souza e Silva, 2013). Ingrid Richardson drew attention to the embodied, sensory, and hybrid dynamics of mobile gaming, as they developed in a long and complex evolution into and through the smartphone era (Hjorth & Richardson, 2014; Richardson, 2020).

Once apps had taken off, the pejorative, gendered way of dismissing mobile games really looked pretty implausible. Apps became the face of the "casual revolution," as Jesper Juul (2010) put it. Juul noted that the rise of casual games was aided by a "perfect storm of combining factors" that included "changing demographics"—successive generations of video game players with different needs through their life course— as well as the "widespread presence of personal computers in the industrialised world" (Juul, 2010, p. 147). The rise of apps went hand in hand with the expansion of gaming across previous demographics, especially genders, as Tama Leaver and Michele Willson explain:

> As online social networks such as Facebook facilitate social games played with a user's social network, and mobile devices such as phones and tablets mean almost anyone can take a suite of game apps, wherever they go, games have become increasingly ubiquitous. (Leaver & Willson, 2016, p. 1)

In relation to the global diffusion of games, it is evident that mobile games, and especially game apps, were a notable factor in the great international expansion and diversification of games markets, digital games cultures, and social practices. Apps certainly take mobile gaming well beyond their early associations with locative play and experimental, art movements. Location, and especially location data, are important to games in their app phase. As Hjorth and Richardson argue, this fact requires us to rethink "small game practices" well beyond the "casual"; we need to consider "ambient," "cultural," and other kinds of play—how such play is constituted, for instance, through "temporal, social, emotional, and affective" kinds of labor (Hjorth & Richardson, 2014, p. 159). Game apps are also at the cutting edge of haptics and the extension of the senses into contemporary media (this is discussed further down).

One of the first blockbuster game apps was Angry Birds, the work of the Swedish developer firm Rovio (Chih-Wen, 2012). This was one of most successful game apps, spawning versions for the web as well as for PCs. Celebrated for its clever immersive and evocative design (Chow, 2013), profitability, and skill in belying its complexity, Angry Birds has retained its popularity, which generates specialist uses, too: for instance, Angry Birds is the chosen terrain for the AI community's annual competition to build intelligent agents, in other words it is the place where researchers vie to design AI that can play at novel levels in the game and be better than the top human counterparts (Stephenson et al., 2020). Angry Birds was the most prominent in a galaxy of mobile games that achieved their reach, influence, and participation as apps. Alongside millions of minor, niche, and evanescent games, such apps contained top-grossing marquee titles such as Candy Crush, described by David Nieborg as an exemplary "connective commodity" on account of its leveraging of network effects designed to make the free-to-play model lucrative (Nieborg, 2015), or Clash of Clans, which set off alarms for consumer protection thanks to its in-game purchasing systems, which take "games as a service" (Lehdonvirta, 2009) to a new level (King et al., 2019).

These compelling, commodified aspects of games pivot on new affordances and temporalities of media. Consider, for instance, the way in which players devote attention across long spans of time to games such as Clash of Clans, which require significant player engagement and labor, and constant switching between the "foreground" and the "background" of the player's perception and smartphone screen. These game mechanics have prompted a genre of "background games"—the likes of Tiny Tower, Simpsons: Tapped Out, or Pocket Planes—which require the player to set up tasks that are accomplished by the game over a period of days. Players can put in the "hard yards," and accumulate the rewards, or short circuit the process by paying, and thus dispense with the labor of waiting (Keogh & Richardson, 2018).

The reach of digital games vaulted far beyond their previous roles, when apps took on a starring role in the gamification turn. As it emerged in the early 2010s, gamification is the idea that the principles, mechanics, and elements of video and computer games, especially game design, can be applied widely across information, communication, and media—and, better still, across whole swathes of real life (Goethe, 2019). Proponents of gamification and its mindset have ported it across a preposterously broad range of areas, very often as a lever to enhance motivation, adherence, and buying into the desired behaviors. Gamification in web and mobile apps is widely promoted as a strategy by which digital media companies can "deliver a sticky, viral, and engaging experience to their customers" (Zichermann, 2011, p. iv). Gamification features across a wide field of technologies, but its deployment, its adoption, and, where useful, its productiveness have often been supported by apps. As Ole Goethe explains, "a good percentage of the apps installed in your smartphones use gamification as a technique to keep you always hooked" (Goethe, 2019, p. 43). So gamification is deployed to retain app users, especially in games based on freemium—that is, in free-to-play games (p. 97). Gamified apps have been developed and deployed to address an array of challenges across contexts not usually associated with leisure or digital entertainment (Dubbels, 2017): health and well-being (smoking addiction, non-communicable diseases, food and nutrition) (Miller et al., 2016); education and support for learning across a range of settings and institutions, especially ones in transition, for instance universities (Almeida & Simoes, 2019; Bell, 2018); workplace learning, adherence to organizational goals and strategies, and meeting requirements (or just plain and simple "following orders"); business (Reiners & Wood, 2015); sales and marketing; cultural heritage (Ioannides et al., 2017); social inclusion, equality, and empowerment (Stewart & Misuraca, 2013); and law enforcement (Akhgar, 2019).

In a leap beyond the insight that play is central to digital media cultures (Frissen, 2015) and that we live in a "gameful world" (Walz & Deterding, 2014), gamification via apps produces schemes for tackling grand social, civil, and economic challenges, as well as concerns related to the care of the self. Gamification has been deployed as part of "serious games" (Stieglitz et al., 2017), and "persuasive games" approaches, but in many ways it has wider ambitions, despite its obvious limits. The results of gamification are mixed at best. There's a growing acceptance that gamification may well have its place but, just by itself, stands little chance of solving deeper issues related to the meaningfulness of a task or an endeavor, or to people's free will in accepting a challenge and in persisting with it (Brühlmann, 2016). What is more, app-enabled gamification has significant elements of politics built in (Nolan & McBride, 2014; Tulloch & Randell-Moon, 2018). Games scholar James Ash picks up on this feature in his suggestive argument that the logics of what he calls "interface envelopes" have spread from video games and digital media environments to other kinds of social and material interfaces and social settings, all of which were previously non-game (Ash, 2015). For Ash, these problematic situations involve new issues, especially in the case of the overfreighting of "affective design" as a way to address major social or psychological issues. On an affirmative note, the incursions of gamification can surely be offset by the larger publics and higher stakes in the great participatory expansion of gaming via apps. This amounts to a new accountability, such as proposed by Adrienne Shaw and Shira Chess:

> What once belonged to a community that was specific, specialized and lacking in diversity can now belong to nearly everyone. And when it belongs to everyone, more people get to have a say in what games, and perhaps game cultures, look like. (Shaw & Chess, 2016, p. 285)

From apps as games media we move now to locative media.

Locative Media

Location-based gaming in urban settings was a distinctive site for early experimentation in mobile games in the late 1990s and early 00s. A decade or so later, location-based gaming apps became an important thread in the broader take-up, acceptance, and commercialization of locative media and smartphones. This is an argument made by Dale Leorke in his discussion of Red Robot Lab's 2013 game app Life Is Magic: "the entrance of location-based games into the app economy represents a shift away from their roots in the locative art movement, one which illustrates the growing capture of digital play by the increasingly competitive mobile gaming market" (Leorke, 2015, p. 133). As Leorke chronicles, the shift of experimental locative games into game apps offered via Android and Apple's app stores was pivotal to these new kinds of digital games being taken seriously by videogame and technology industries, commentators, and users (p. 140).

Scholars of mobile locative media have charted the sociotechnical ways in which the evolution of mobile communication and media shifted our perceptions, our emotions and affects, our embodiment, senses, and cultural practices in relation to locating and re-embedding ourselves digitally in spaces and places (Farman, 2012, 2014; Sheller & de Souza e Silva, 2015; de Souza e Silva & Frith, 2012; Frith, 2015b). App developments have been deeply bound up with these intricate patterns, affordances, and social relations. If early location-based social media apps such as Foursquare and Yelp, with the check-in to location features they developed and popularized (Wilken & Humphreys, 2019), have declined, then these features have certainly been absorbed into the fabric of social and mobile media technologies like Facebook (Wilken, 2014; see Wilken, 2019), as a "form of zombie media that animates and haunts other media platforms" (Evans & Saker, 2017, p. 88; Frith & Wilken, 2019). Such apps underscore the dawning recognition that mobile communication—or indeed the Internet before it (e.g. in the 1990s and 00s)—was placeful as much as it was placeless (Frith, 2014). In their remediation of place, locative mobile apps showed a new phase of communication and placemaking—replacement, perhaps—that is under way (Evans, 2015; Wilken & Goggin, 2012).

A wave of location information in the apps era has come from sensors, as we have seen. Sensors convert stimuli or property from an environment such as heat, mass, light, motion, sound, pressure, and so on into an electrical signal. In essence, a sensor detects a change or an event in an environment and transmits the information to other devices. Thanks to advances in material sciences and engineering, instruments and measures have undergone a period of miniaturization with the help of microelectronic and microelectromechanical systems; then, with the help of nanotechnology, they shrank still further, to work at the nanoscale. Smartphones also incorporate and rely upon a range of sensors: motion sensors, image sensors, light detection and ranging (LiDAR) scanners, and 3D time-of-flight sensors. Such sensors support technologies such as augmented reality (AR), discussed in what follows. Sensor data from the increasingly sophisticated smartphones are used for a wide range of apps, including smart city parking (Krieg et al., 2018). Well under way, with the Internet of Things and 5G, is a process of hybridization of sensors, mobile devices, environments, and networks and of decentering and reconfiguring the smartphone as we have come to know it (Pau et al., 2019). We can glimpse the logics at play in the career of one early sensor technology, widely relied upon for consumer transactions as well as for supply logistics: radio frequency identification (RFID) technology. RFID is the successor to barcodes and centers on tags that can be read when in range of RFID readers (Frith, 2015a). Near-field communication (NFC) is a kind of RFID with a range of only a few centimeters that is incorporated into most smartphones, having featured in the 2004 Nokia 3200 GSM phone (Want, 2006). As Jordan Frith points out, NFC "democratizes RFID" by "turning smartphones into both RFID tags and readers" (Frith, 2019, p. 84). It is NFC that underpins everyday purchasing through contactless pay systems pioneered by Google Wallet in 2011 (now Google Pay), credit card providers such as Mastercard and Visa, Foursquare's Square application, and then Apple Pay, Samsung Pay, and so on (p. 85). All these are discussed in chapter 5. Such a system is likely only a harbinger of things to come. As Jordan Frith suggests, RFID tags are a form of mobile technology that works in the background but constitutes an important "infrastructure of identification," key to IoT.

App developers have been availing themselves of such location and activity information since apps were first designed for and installed on smartphones. It has developed as a very busy two-way street, so to speak. Apps harvest, analyze, and curate location information available on smartphones. Users have some control over the settings—in that they allow apps to access such information—but not as much as many of them desire; and even the bias toward "opting in" for users has masked and perpetuated an incessant gathering of device information. Then smartphones support an app ecology where apps can have access to other apps. So information gathered by, and underpinning, some apps—say, social media apps like Facebook, or the Google suite of apps—can be combined with information or algorithms and processing power from other apps. Further, such aggregative or multiplicative app information can be combined with the device information or, indeed, with multiple device information, as one app can often be used across different devices. The complex information ecology of apps provides key software fabric to hardware digital environments.

Realities Media: Virtual, Augmented, (Re)Mixed

We witness a movement, reminiscent of the cultural and technical trajectories of locative media, from a refusal of offline space and desire to "replace" it to a recognition and embrace of the ways in which digital media weave into and redouble space—but also, at times, to a resistance to and disavowal of these ways. I am thinking here of the emergence of virtual reality (Chan, 2014; Rheingold, 1991) and the kind of reception it received in its early years. I also have in mind the scholarly and popular distinction between the virtual world of cyberspace in the 1990s and real life (RL). AR is a way of combining these worlds at a time when digital technologies are widely and frequently used across many more areas of daily life, and hence are immersive. In a mobile Internet world that turns into a smartphone world, it steadily made little sense to draw untenable and unproductive distinctions between online and offline states. Apps ushered in AR—first as a test bed, then as a mass medium. After that, apps gave the green light for virtual reality (VR) to come back in style.

The definition and boundaries of AR are an interesting topic in its own right (Liao, 2016). As Geoffrey Rhodes puts it, in relation to discussing Pokémon GO and the long wait for the AR "killer app," "what is AR again?" (Rhodes, 2019, p. 8). The emergence of AR is often traced back to TV broadcasts in the late 1990s and early 00s, notably the 1st & Ten system offered by the company Sportvision, which depicts virtual lines in its broadcasts of American football—layering of games statistics, other information, and advertising for broadcasting sporting events (Liao, 2016; Wassom, 2014). Antecedents of AR were developed for head-mounted equipment in the 1980s and 1990s. AR also made its way to portable digital assistants (PDAs) (Anders et al., 2007, p. 107).

Apps turbo-charged the adoption of AR. As Tony Liao and Lee Humphreys note in their study of the popular AR app Layar, "mobile AR is made possible by a convergence of several enabling technologies, which are important to consider for emergent practices surrounding AR" (Liao & Humphreys, 2015, p. 1420). Craig notes that, by "using mobile technology, the AR application can be experienced at the location where it makes the most sense" (Craig, 2013, p. 212). In addition to technology constraints, usability, and user acceptance and preference, there are also environmental and contextual challenges and issues around AR (pp. 215–217). A deep problem at play is the one signaled early on by Liao and Humphreys in their warning that, "[a]s AR's potential for tactical reproduction and reinterpretation of space is realized, it is possible that strategic forces will seek to reclaim, limit, and possibly censor some of that tactical production" (Liao & Humphreys, 2015, p. 1432). This clarion call was timely, given the controversial Google Glass and the incandescent public reception it sometimes received for its perceived intrusion into social norms of public space.

Google Glass was a wearable technology in the shape of a pair of eyeglasses without lenses; it was announced in 2012. Glass featured a head-up display (HUD) just above the right eye—as well as camera, microphone, and GPS. The technology was matched with its own Glass OS. It was also backward compatible with a Bluetooth-equipped smartphone using the MyGlass companion app. Google Glass prototypes attracted a great deal of scientific, engineering, design, and human–computer interaction (HCI) attention—and, courtesy of Google's global marketing, considerable publicity worldwide. Google triggered something of a backlash, a kind of moral panic that the latest intrusive mobile technology was blurring the boundaries between public and private space. Promoted inside the Tech for Good community, Google Glass was also the catalyst for various collaborations between Google and other partners, such as disability organizations and accessibility and inclusive design practitioners interested for instance in the potential of Glass to "read" signage and public information so as to help blind people and those with vision impairments in navigation and wayfinding. Google Glass established a "partners" program that saw various leading-edge users vetted and enlisted to beta-test, experiment with, and spread the word about Google Glass (Ellis & Goggin, 2016). Early on in 2015, Google decided to let it ride and not move to full commercialization. Instead Google released its Glass Enterprise Edition in 2017 (with a version 2 in 2019). In the washup, what Google Glass achieved was to educate the public on the possibilities of AR devices and media.

Development of wearables and their accompanying AR app innovation continued relatively unabated in the years immediately after the Google Glass experiment. The consumer take-up remained largely with smartphones. In this regard, Pokémon GO can be fairly regarded as the first mass global AR app (Athique, 2016). Pokémon GO was developed by a Google internal startup, Niantic. Niantic's first product was the Field Trip app (2012–2019), developed for Google Glass, Android, and iOs devices (Niantic Team, 2019). Dubbed an "Internet connected guidebook," Field Trip offered users "facts about the places around them—unprompted, without the need to even ask for the information," as the *New York Times* put it (Alison & Co., 2015). According to John Hanke, Niantic's founder and the former head of Google Maps, "[t]he idea behind the app was to build something that would help people connect with the real, physical world around them" (quoted in Miller, 2012). The *Atlantic* staff writer Alexis C. Madrigal suggested that "the app is Google's probe into the soft side of augmented reality" (Madrigal, 2012). In April 2015, Niantic launched "a new version of Field Trip with full support for Android Wear devices such as the Moto 360 smartwatch" (Alison & Co., 2015). As it turned out, Niantic earnt its AR stripes for another product: the cult mobile location game Ingress (Hodson, 2012; Leorke, 2015).

Launched in late 2012, Ingress is a mobile AR "capture the flag" style of game associated, as Kyle Moore (2008) has suggested, with a new kind of "situated play" in urban environments. Ingress commanded a dedicated international following (Leaver & Willson, 2016), not least as a form of geomedia that pivoted on new kinds of interplay among the regional and global instances, as Shira Chess (2014) suggests: this is what she dubs "augmented regionalism." Ingress also provided the opportunity for Google to experiment with AR technology in mobile gaming (Hodson, 2012). Famously controversial and also acclaimed as an app that propelled people to enter parks and other public places (Suellentrop, 2014), Ingress was also critiqued for its incursions into privacy and data surveillance (Hulsey & Reeves, 2014).

Ingress commanded the loyalties of a keen band of gamers over a number of years, but its big hit as a course was the wildly successful Pokémon GO. Pokémon GO was launched in the same week in August 2015 in which Google reorganized itself as a corporation, relaunched its business as Alphabet, and spun off Niantic Labs. Niantic's Pokémon GO builds directly on the player community, features, reputation, and especially database of Ingress. In a masterstroke, the game draws from the visual grammar, narrative, and audience resources of the Pokémon franchise as much as it does from the sociospatial practices associated with earlier mobile technologies and locative mobile gaming we've just discussed (Humphreys,

2017). Pokémon GO took the world by storm, drawing large crowds into public places to play the game (Geroimenko, 2019; Hjorth & Richardson, 2017), attracting plaudits and generating criticism by turns (Feldman, 2018; Humphreys, 2017). It was praised for its reanimation of social participation, face-to-face interaction, and physical exercise (Ma et al., 2018); alternatively, it was decried for the disruption of quiet neighborhoods, for the players' insensitivity to culturally significant heritage and to other sites (Henthorn et al., 2019), for geographic and socioeconomic bias to its datasets, which skewed the distribution of PokéStops, Pokémon gyms, and spawn points (Juhász & Hochmair, 2017), and for potential risk to limb and life (Pourmand et al., 2017). Ultimately Pokémon GO experienced a meteoric rise followed by sharp decline, not least owing to its pricing structure and business model, which required continual usage through in-app purchases and sponsorship (Butcher et al., 2020); then its use was discontinued by a long tail of dedicated players—many of them older players, too.

The story of Pokémon GO highlights the mass market appeal of AR apps: the technology captures its audience's imagination, intersects with the practices of audience members, and is well designed and implemented. From 2010 to the early 2020s, we can point to many examples of AR experiments and take-up across areas such as education and edtech (Mundy et al., 2019), the galleries, libraries, art galleries, and museum sector and other types of cultural heritage (Luna et al., 2019), memory work, local information (Forsyth, 2011), tourism and travel, medicine and health, social and community services and support, for instance digital visualization for aging people (Fernandez et al., 2017), and social and consumer behavior change (Javornik, 2016). Mobile AR also combines with 3D printing (Daly, 2016), and then it can generate, for example, patient models in medical and healthcare settings (Wake et al., 2019). It can be used in the advertising and marketing of brands (Wafa & Hashim,

2016), as well as in the obvious areas of interior design and real estate.

App-based mobile AR has proven a lightweight and flexible alternative to hard-based mobile AR platforms. This take-up and use has grown in spite of obstacles of downloading and cross-platform compatibility apps. This environment is changing, as various network, device, and platform developments are under way when it comes to AR. An option with strong feasibility is the web-based mobile AR, especially with the advent of mobile-edge computing with 5G networks (Qiao et al., 2019). In a more speculative vein, there is some discussion of a next-generation AR. In December 2019, for instance, Niantic and Qualcomm announced a partnership intended to develop "next-gen augmented reality headsets" that "could bring games like Pokémon GO and Harry Potter: Wizards Unite to a much more immersive environment through augmented reality glasses," by using Qualcomm's Snapdragon XR2 5G AR platform (Qualcomm, 2020). In these visions, we see that AR is referenced together with VR, the two being envisaged to combine different kinds of "realities."

Apps and Digital Visualities

The invention of the camera phone and its launch in 2001 has been at the heart of the constellation of changes in image, in photo taking, in sharing, collecting, and curating practices, and in visual cultures. Many aspects of the story of the rise of mobile images—the development of everyday practices of imagery via camera phones, the gendering of such practices, their forms and meanings in different regions and cultures, and how self-presentational phenomena such as selfies gained a centrality in many societies globally— have been told elsewhere (Senft & Baym, 2015). Apps have played a crucial role in this phenomenon.

Apps have offered a way to bring together the different parts of camera, photo, and image culture that were coevolving but still needed bridges between their elements. A user could take a photo with a mobile phone, but it was difficult to share it widely using just *module management system* (MMS), storage media, or Bluetooth. Over time, the improvements in mobile Internet, networks, and connectivity and falls in the price of data meant that sharing photos from Internet-enabled mobile phones became much easier and more affordable.

For instance, photo-sharing services included Flickr, which was launched in 2004 by the Vancouver-based Ludicorp, then acquired by Yahoo! in 2005. Flickr was the service of choice for many keen photographers, amateur as well as professional; in Jean Burgess's (2010) words, it hosted the cultural practice of "vernacular creativity." Key to the success of Flickr's service was the use of website technology, including storage (interestingly, in 2019 Flickr's data were migrated to Amazon Web Services by their owner, SmugMug, which had acquired them in 2018). Although Flickr's service did evolve with the development of apps, the companies associated with mobile devices, OSs, and apps easily outstripped them. Apple developed a highly successful approach to photos and image management via its iPhoto software, offering storage, organization, curation, and sharing integrated with iOS and devices. Google launched its photos and storage option, popular with Android OS phone users. In many ways, though, the action in photo apps was elsewhere.

The enormous growth of social media platforms globally and their centrality to everyday media meant that they were given a box seat for capitalizing on the growth of photo media. The advent of apps for social media brought with it image capture, processing, and display capabilities. These were integrated in most of the leading social media apps and were quickly taken for granted—indeed they became defining features of platforms such as Facebook or Twitter. Apps offered the ability to immediately post photos to one's social media account, and also to collect photos in albums.

A considerable amount of software, database programming, network capabilities, and hardware engineering, design, and refinement went into these functionalities, which are core to digital cultures and on which billions of social media app users rely.

The most celebrated breakthrough in images wrought by apps is due to one single app. Originally developed as a convenient, easy, and mobile-centric way to manipulate, tweak, and enhance photos by applying a stylized pre-set filter, Instagram propelled developments in image-based social and mobile media, building on earlier visual cultures of the Internet and web (Senft, 2008). It underpins many digital features that have exerted a major influence across contemporary social life. Instagram was one of the various apps that Facebook acquired in its ongoing efforts to horizontally integrate emerging elements of the social media landscape and experience (just as it did with social games); and the Instagram merger has been one of Facebook's major pillars ever since. As Tama Leaver, Tim Highfield, and Crystal Abidin remark in a definitive study, "Instagram is more than an app, more than a platform, and more than a jewel in the Facebook 'family.' Rather, Instagram is an icon and avatar for understanding and mapping visual social media cultures" (Leaver et al., 2020, p. 4). Notably, Instagram is key to the various changes seen across social and digital media in relation to celebrity (Abidin, 2018; Marwick, 2013), especially micro celebrity (Senft, 2013); but its reach and significance stretch much wider. Different genres of pictures, for example, have became common across apps and platforms and are especially important in the pursuit of securing followers in the new "attention economy," some genres being more in the mainstream than others (Paasonen, Jarrett, et al., 2019). Photo apps have become pivotal to the conduct and negotiation of many aspects of daily life, as is evident in workplace cultures and sociabilities (Paasonen, Light, et al., 2019). The rise of apps in visual digital cultures also underscores the new, mediated kinds of work and labor that social life presupposes, be it the work of participation or of non-participation, or even the frustrating quest for viable modalities of disconnection. In the mix are also new kinds of value, work, and industrial practices, all laid out by Crystal Abidin and others in studies on influencers (Abidin & Brown, 2019; Marwick, 2019).

Through improvements in mobile cameras interlaced with advances in computation, the photo and imaging capabilities of apps have been used well beyond the contexts of leisure, entertainment, and personal media and communication. In medicine and health, apps are now often used for disease detection ("App spots signs of disease in photos," 2019). Apps have also been devised to further stretch the transmedia and transcoding potential of the visual—for instance, with apps that read text in an image out aloud (say, if a user snaps a photo of a printed page or sign) (Rutkin, 2016). Apps also automate the process of manipulating photos, stitching them together into composites or combining them with other materials. Other apps that use machine learning and AI to draw on a database of images can generate photo-like images or virtual worlds (Reynolds, 2017).

All in all, apps play a crucial role in the user and system experimentation and entrenchment of algorithms, as a visual cultural gateway to engaging, experiencing, and ordering social media cultures. This, too, is a striking feature of video apps.

Moving Image Media

Communication at a distance via moving images is a long-held dream. It became possible with telecommunications standards such as integrated services digital network (ISDN) and with expensive videoconferencing. It was popularized and brought to the masses with the advent of interactive video applications on the Internet, famously Skype. With 3G mobile networks, video calling was a heavily marketed feature; however, it gained little take-up. Mobile handsets were shipped with video capabilities. This trend was propelled by Apple's iPhone, which featured FaceTime, a video over Internet protocol (IP) application that displaced Skype as the market leader. Various other video over IP applications were brought to market and attracted users such as Viber. By the early 2020s, video conversational apps were widespread. Capabilities were embedded across pre-installed apps like FaceTime, well supported by operating systems. Many users preferred to use the video communication features of their social media or messaging apps, especially Facebook, WeChat, or WhatsApp. Corporate and workplace video communication apps gained traction, and with the COVID pandemic quickly became widespread via the phenomenon of Zoom. Zoom and similar video apps crossing over from corporate and enterprise communications into households and everyday contexts drew on the layered affordances described above. Video apps came into their own, as key elements in new media for recording, creating, editing, and circulating content.

Video recording and communication via mobile phones and broadcasting via the Internet were especially popularized by the video-sharing service YouTube. There were many other platforms before and afterwards, but YouTube struck a chord in participatory culture (Burgess & Green, 2009) that still resonates. While web access figures prominently, YouTube is very often accessed via its app. YouTube consistently ranks as one of the most popular apps and is part of the essential toolkit of most users. In its mobile app career especially, YouTube has played an enormously important role in the development of user-generated content and digital cultures in many countries (Burgess, 2015).

Various efforts were made to develop other kinds of video apps and digital practices, especially ones that center on very short video. Vine, for instance, was a video-hosting service featuring short-form looping videos of six or so seconds. Twitter purchased Vine in October 2012, as a fitting complement to its short-text medium. Vine achieved a following for some years, gaining a reputation for humorous videos and comedy (Kunze, 2014) and paving the way to fame and influence for many of its proponents (Duguay, 2016). Vine was ultimately sidelined by the rise of Instagram, which introduced a short video feature as a competitive move (Marwick, 2015, p. 145), and of Snapchat (Newton, 2016); similar functionality was then incorporated into other platforms. Vine closed down in 2019. In January 2020, one of the creators of Vine, Dom Hoffman, launched a new app, Byte, which was immediately beset by bots and spam, but then attracted an early following in the United States (Brown, 2020; Savov, 2020) and was boosted in mid-July 2020, over rumors of a US ban on TikTok.

TikTok, dubbed by some the "new Vine," has for its part eclipsed its predecessors in short and quirky video and supported a creative ferment of video social media cultures across the world, establishing it, as we have already seen, as one of the most profitable app companies. The government of India's ban on it along with other Chinese apps, followed by attempts by the former US president Trump to pressure ByteDance to divest itself of TikTok's US operations in favor of Microsoft, has vividly demonstrated the range, diversity, and influence of TikTok among different cultural, language, and social settings. It has also shown us how, much like Instagram and various other apps, TikTok supports new moneymaking, cultural production, visibility, and celebrity opportunities, often for those who have not previously enjoyed access to or participation in media or digital platforms.

While it is in video that some of the most interesting media innovations concerning apps have occurred, significant and lucrative developments have also transpired in cinema and television. It could be said that the advent of apps finally unfurled the promise of mobile movies and movie television (Goggin, 2006, 2011). It is through apps that movies and television have gained mass audiences on mobile devices;

this was something of a game changer for the industries. An early development was the rise of "companion" apps to television that fed into the phenomenon of "second screen" viewing: audiences watching the TV screen while communicating via their mobile phones, Internet, and social media. Such apps have been largely absorbed into the fabric of TV consumption, kicking off major developments in technology, industry, and media cultures. To make sense of the situation, scholars, following Amanda Lotz's (2017) lead, distinguish between open-access platforms, which include now Netflix and others such as Youku Tudou, Facebook, Weibo, and Twitter; and game-play and streaming platforms such as Twitch or Duoyu; portals such as Netflix, Amazon Prime Video, and HBO (Lotz, 2019); and hybrids such as iQiyi, which combines user-generated content with professional film and TV (Wang & Lobato, 2019, pp. 358–360).

Apps clearly built on the affordances and systems of previous forms, especially Internet movie distribution, and rental or purchase models such as Apple's highly successful iTunes. Yet the more recent epicenter of cultural and technology innovation has been in subscription services— especially streaming services. This is exemplified in the case of Netflix, a household name in many parts of the world. What is distinctive about Netflix is its recommendation system, personalized via algorithms, which draws upon its customer data to keep the customer watching its content. This interface, backend technology, and massive network and infrastructure investment helps Netflix maintain a customer-friendly focus and façade, relegating to the background the obvious issues of IP and licensing that mean that its catalogue, like that of other TV subscription and streaming services, is limited— and also is jurisdiction-specific. The reality for most users is that no one TV or video service can provide everything they need, especially when traditional television broadcasters struggle to maintain their relevance and offerings in the face of the pay-for-television market or informal media economies of video sharing, downloading, user-generated content, and so on.

Netflix has radiated out from its US stronghold, pursuing market share in a range of other countries. As well as sourcing and curating content for local and regional communities, language groups, and taste cultures, Netflix has also invested in and coproduced TV series, shows, and movies in order to establish its presence in geo-linguistic markets. This has been discussed by scholars such as Ramon Lobato and Wilfred Yang Wang, who chart the "effects of multi-territory streaming services on national screen markets" (Wang & Lobato, 2019, p. 359; see also Lobato, 2019). There is heated and continuing debate over the implications of Netflix and other streaming services on cultural and media diversity and on specific kinds of audiences and territories (such as national ones). Scholars such as Evan Elkins raise questions about the "algorithmic cosmopolitanism" of global players' strategies (Elkins, 2019), echoing earlier critiques of the globalization of culture. Others, such as Stuart Cunningham and David Craig, who stand in an equally long line of theories of accenting the complex and surprising productive dynamics of globalization (see García Canclini, 1989, 2014; Morley, 2000), look at social media entertainment platforms that offer pathways for cultural diversity and find them to be "communicated through formalized conventions (such as youth-oriented genres) that are increasingly global," with differential implications for "cultural power and influence"— depending on the engagement of locally situated and relevant institutions and actors (Cunningham & Craig, 2019, p. 262).

The app is often referenced in these analyses, but its role is often hard to pin down. As recent research on the contours of new television and video ecologies has indicated, apps play a significant role within particular positionings and constraints. Consider, for a start, that affordances of TV apps can vary widely. One can download programs for offline viewing via the iOS or Android OS Netflix apps, for instance, but not yet for viewing on the laptop or computer. Or we can parse the struggle among many players for the positioning of apps for viewing on household television devices and subscription services. The overlooked set-top box and the crucial "real estate" of the smart screen television interfaces are the terrain where app developers and providers jostle for best advantage (Hesmondhalgh & Lobato, 2019, p. 967). David Hesmondhalgh and Lobato suggest that the visibility or "prominence" of software systems (which in turn feature different algorithmically driven recommendation systems designed to shape and provide discoverability of programs) is "determined by opaque layers of intermediation—platforms within platforms, like a series of Russian dolls" (p. 968). They give the example of a viewer who accesses BBC content via an Apple TV where user choices would be "structured by the differential integration of as many as three different platforms: the iPlayer app, Apple's tvOS and, possibly, the operating system of their smart TV." This leads to implicating apps and their role in video interfaces in what Hesmondhalgh and Amanda Lotz conceptualize as issues of "media circulation power" (Hesmondhalgh & Lotz, 2020).

In some markets and for many groups, this refurbished traditional architecture of television, which has slowly evolved over decades of market reforms, political shifts, cultural changes, and digital transitions, has less sway than others. There are a number of countries where widespread mobile phone ownership and recourse to mobiles for Internet, video, and television have seen apps play an important role in the cultural economy. The situation in China is distinctive because of the sheer multitude, scope, and impact of audiovisual consumption via mobile apps. This is the case with various other markets, including the huge and fast-growing Indian market, where video apps have been adapted by a cornucopia of vibrant regional content creators so as to support new social and digital practices. However, in China, as we saw in chapter 3, there are various video apps that are widely used to make their firms highly capitalized. Thus apps are a fabric for accessing, consuming, adapting, and distributing video content supported by digital platforms. This content and this activity are the "SME [social media entertainment] content on the big platforms" that, Cunningham and Craig suggest, "is able to circle the globe completely independently of standard windowing and territorial licensing, and without standard IP control"; and this, they feel, "suggests a fundamentally different model of extreme spreadability without domination" (Cunningham & Craig, 2019, p. 261).

Sound Media

Sound, audio, and music have been a defining part of mobile media and communication, achieving a certain form and status in the heyday of 2G cell phones. Sounds of the telephone were modified and taken to new heights by mobile phones, ringtones becoming a distinctive signifying activity and a lucrative business in its own right. Mobile phones have been equipped with reasonably high-quality audio recorders, so are widely used for recording conversations and sounds in professional as well as in amateur and everyday contexts. With pre-installed receivers and chips, mobile phones were also able to offer radio audiences a new device for listening. Mobile phones have long had the functionality to play music via digital formats such as MP3 and iTunes, and then via videos with audio recorded in these formats. The personal technology of music listening is already symbolically, technically, via design, and in other ways "baked" into the form of the mobile phone, through the influence of its predecessors in media and mobility—the Sony Walkman and the iPod (Bull, 2007a and 2007b). Many of these aspects of the sound media of mobile phones were further elaborated with smartphones, then elaborated some more and extended via apps.

The music recording industry was already reliant on digital music and on systems such as iTunes. The advent of apps made the process of purchasing and playing digital music easier, and also enhanced its datafication by extending the information on the integration of user interaction with music. The digitalization of the recorded music industry was taken in new directions with the advent of streaming-based subscription services, which are practically synonymous with Spotify. Eventually these services incorporated a wide range of platforms such as Apple Music and came to depend on the cloud (Wikström, 2020). Streaming music via the Internet had already been around for some years, but apps such as Spotify brought together device, broadcasting, transaction, music library, database, and—crucially—algorithm, recommendation, and personalization in one neatly sealed package.

As noted already, radio, too, appears relatively early in the incubation of mobile phones, as a built-in feature of handsets; and the convergence between radio and mobile cultures is something that has continued to be important for many users across the world (Algan, 2013; Hampshire et al., 2015). Here we are reminded of portable radio, for example the famous "transistor radio," and of the habits of people moving around and taking their personal radio receiver with them (Bull, 2000). This practice survives in the present day: in many places one can observe people playing music in public as they move around, via their mobile phone—but choosing not to use their iPods or headphones. This is rather an act of public listening and playing of music associated with walking and other forms of mobility in urban places—music from a potential range of sources encased in the smartphone, and typically played via apps.

Radio was a very interesting feature of Internet cultures; a slew of small or solo radio stations broadcast via the Internet, taking advantage of the absence of requirements to gain access to a typically scarce radio spectrum, or to be licensed). Streaming audio via the Internet had achieved a sizable following. Then dedicated Internet radio sites and programs aggregated stations and programs from around the world for listeners. Established radio broadcasters also got into the act, using their websites to post and archive programs for subsequent download. With the advent of mobile messaging, mobile Internet, and mobile social media, public participation in radio cultures received a boost, as new channels for feedback and interactivity were established (Chiumbu & Ligaga, 2013)—though the exact nature and implications of this participation have been debated (Willems, 2013). With apps, radio—already very much a survivor medium—experienced a renaissance. Radio stations were very often accessed via their dedicated apps and streamed via mobile devices at roughly the same time as the broadcasts themselves.

Among radio apps, the novel phenomenon has been the podcast, which has emerged as an important media form. Podcasts provided a way for people to "disintermediate" the gatekeepers of broadcast and recorded audio, such as radio stations or record stores, and reach listeners directly—a development turbocharged with apps. A relatively inexpensive, ease-to-use form, podcasts can serve a range of purposes and niche audiences. They are increasingly integrated into other apps and services, such as iTunes and Spotify. Podcasts have been integrated into the reconfigured radio and broadcasting industry, but have also been used to offer content in a different way across a wide range of other media organizations—newspapers, magazines, and press, or newer digital, mobile, and social media ventures—and previously non-media-centric organizations—consulting firms, businesses, educational institutions. In the podcast as much as in radio apps, digital music apps, or streaming music apps, the *app* form itself has proven decisive: it brings together the various "moving parts" of hardware, software, content, data, personalization, and portability, flexibly fused into ensembles of computing, mobile, broadcast, and cultural technology. By doing all this, apps have also become an important part of the new cultural assemblages of what Maura Edmond calls "transmedia radio" (Edmond, 2015).

Message Media

Messages are an ancient form of communication and in new ways retain their importance. They are possessed of a deceptively simple character. Often short and to the point (as in a "call to action"), messages are also polyvalent and ambiguous as signs, imparting a larger resonance of an intricately symbolic nature.

We have already noted the function that alerts and notifications have for predecessors of the mobile phone and, afterwards, the highly sophisticated role they play in mobile media cultures. Messages evolve via successive technologies, from the telegraph through early radio communications and pagers. In 2G mobiles, text messaging emerged as a major sociotechnical innovation. Messaging has been a storied feature of the Internet, especially through instant messaging (IM) systems such as MSN messenger and QQ (predecessors of today's Facebook Messenger). These were followed by messaging via a range of social media platforms such as Twitter or LinkedIn. Messaging involves conversational architectures and practices of an enduring and flexible character, captured in the word "chat."

The short message service (SMS) on mobile devices became so regular as to be taken for granted, and fascinating cultures of use and functions developed in different places around the world. SMSs also raised some issues, for example related to cost. There were also problems about messaging across different devices while still using the same program or platform. Then SMSs were underpinned by telecommunications networks and numbering, while Internet-based messaging was not tied to telephone numbers but was underpinned by Internet-based numbers, identifiers, and addresses. Another problem was how to store, retain, and collect one's text messages. Apple provided a partial solution with its iMessage technology, which could send and receive SMSs and messages—at least in communications with users who also had Apple iMessage and iCloud accounts. Many users eschewed these options in favor of messaging via social media platforms such as Facebook, once these became near ubiquitous. Many users persisted with and deeply embraced messaging apps, as these developed into a defining feature of the contemporary digital media landscape—services such as WhatsApp, WeChat, and a babel of other, minor apps—such as Signal, or the Russian-developed Telegram—that skew toward particular locales, taste cultures, or communities, for instance of people who are privacy and security conscious.

Messaging apps are a species of what is called "over-the-top" (OTT) services. OTT got its name from the fact that such services are IP-based and are designed to run on the top of telecommunications and mobile networks, without requiring permissions from their operators. A pioneering and disruptive instance of OTT was that of voice over IP (VOIP) services, represented by Skype, Viber, and others. These services allowed new players to enter and compete for voice telephony services, offering calls at a much cheaper rate than established telecommunications providers. VOIP providers' costs were minimized because they only had to purchase sufficient Internet network and data capability to underpin their voice telephony services—and they banked on their customers not being too fussy about the poor or indifferent quality of connection and service. Before the advent of such OTT services, the alternative had been to pre-purchase long-distance calling cards, which relied upon resellers of telecommunications services and were also characterized, quite often, by poor or unreliable connections and poor-quality calls. The OTT services that attracted significant attention have been the streaming media services—starting with multichannel and Internet TV.

One of the most successful early messaging apps was Kakao Talk. Launched in South Korea in 2010, Kakao Talk included free talk and messages, establishing itself as the default app for chat, communication, and social network, especially in youth cultures. Kakao Talk has been credited with driving smartphone adoption in South Korea—but also mobile gaming, which the app strongly pushed (Jin et al., 2015). Kakao Talk proved successful in other markets too and laid the foundation for the company to become an enduring player in apps.

Another important and pioneering chat messaging and chat app has been LINE, developed by Naver Japan—the Japanese subsidiary of the South Korean search, portal, and technology company Naver (Steinberg, 2020, pp. 3–4). Marc Steinberg describes the LINE app as a "collaborative project between Japanese and South Korean engineers and designers, influenced by both the i-mode model of platform building and the KakaoTalk chat app" (p. 4). LINE has achieved a strong adoption across various markets, especially in East Asia and Southeast Asia, but also in Mexico. Also hailed as a super app, LINE offers a wide range of platform-integrated services and functionalities. More than anything, LINE is synonymous with stickers, which became a craze among young users (Wang, 2016), its dynamics being characterized by what Sun Sun Lim (2015) has described as "communicative fluidities." As Steinberg explains, LINE's stickers have precursors in Japan's long-standing pre-digital visual cultures; specifically, they follow on from emojis, pioneered by i-Mode in 1999—especially i-mode's large emojis called "deco-mail" (Steinberg, 2020, p. 3). LINE has driven the creation of a sticker market; one example is the Creators Market, launched in 2014 within the LINE sticker shop as a site for amateurs to become entrepreneurs. There are some concerning implications for cultural work and production (pp. 5–8). Stickers have spread widely and have become a staple of marketing, communications, and branding (Liu et al., 2019), as well as a resource in intergenerational communication, care, and intimacies (see the discussion of LINE as a form of "digital kinship" in Ohashi et al., 2017). The appeal and profitability of stickers have been featured in various social media platforms and apps; they were established especially in Kakao Talk (Yoon, 2016), then across WeChat, Facebook, and others. Through stickers and through messaging and chat apps, the dynamics of personalization, cute customization, visualities, and gender in Japanese and Korean mobile media charted by Larissa Hjorth (Hjorth, 2009; Hjorth & Arnold, 2013) have moved center stage in global media cultures.

Two apps that have come on the heels of Kakao Talk and LINE and have greatly extended the global reach and influence of messaging apps are WhatsApp and WeChat. Both rely on the mobile phone number as a linchpin of customer ID, just as other messaging apps have come to do. To register an account, the user needs to give a cell phone number, and the confirmation of identity occurs via this number. While inextricably linked in this way to the phone number as ID, the messaging apps otherwise operate through the Internet across networks, platforms, and devices. One can also receive phone calls or video calls via messaging apps. This is, increasingly, a default option, as many prefer it to telecommunicating via the mobile phone network. The quality of calls is captive to the characteristics and capabilities of the Internet connection as well as to the quality of the mobile connectivity.

WhatsApp originated in the United States. Although it was acquired by Facebook, the company has largely left WhatsApp to flourish in its own realm. What is extraordinary about WhatsApp is how it has become a relied-upon, generative, and often extremely powerful tool across many social settings and countries. For many people, WhatsApp has become the reflex option for setting up a group of contacts for information or messages, for sporting groups, tours, family or friendship groups; it has taken over the role of a "phone tree," email list, or Facebook group in earlier times—albeit often with a high noise-to-signal ratio, as users post messages incessantly.

We have already discussed WeChat at some length. WeChat is still largely tied to the geo-linguistic community or diaspora of Chinese users as well as to their many non-Chinese interlocutors. WeChat has many features and social functions similar to those of WhatsApp—messages, voice and video calls, emojis, stickers, and so on—but plays a much more expansive role in the lives of its users than WhatsApp. WeChat Pay, for example, is a mobile payment platform used by a claimed 800 million monthly users. WeChat has features often found in social media platforms like Facebook, such as the Moments section. The Moments section generates commercial analytics that WeChat offers as a service to manufacturers, to help them better target and place their brand. WeChat also offers Official Accounts, that is, mini-websites for merchants, just like Facebook. It provides a wide range of other services, all of which have earned it the qualification of super app, as we saw in chapter 3. In many ways, WeChat is reminiscent of the Japan i-mode system, just like LINE and KakaoTalk. Its wide-ranging and pervasive social role makes it indispensable to many aspects of social participation, in a way that WhatsApp has not yet rivaled. Instead it relies upon Facebook for game-changing innovation in potentially lucrative areas such mobile money and cryptocurrency (as in Facebook's 2020 Libra initiative).

Creative new ways of engaging in protest, intervention, social change, and political struggle have surged in waves associated with technologies such as video cameras, Internet, web, social media, and especially mobile phones and smartphones (Boler, 2008; Meikle, 2018). In the smartphone era, apps have spurred a wide range of activism. The kinds of witnessing and organizing noted in the early phase of mobile phone diffusion have expanded, being associated with powerful new visibilities for groups whose uses of apps have been core to resurgence activism; this is evident in protest movements that have gained global attention, for instance the #RhodesMustFall movement in South Africa (Adomako Ampofo, 2016; Bosch, 2017), #BlackLivesMatter in the United States (Canella, 2018; Richardson, 2020), or the #metoo movement (Mishra, 2020). As various scholars have argued, this kind of global digital politics needs careful examination and attention to contexts, as both old and new exclusions and kinds of violence can coexist with the new affirmative possibilities for change (Udupa et al., 2020). Social media platforms and apps such as Facebook, Twitter, and Weibo have been augmented by and interwoven with messaging apps—a fact highlighted by the uses of WeChat in Chinese activism (Chen et al., 2018) and in the mobile-enabled reconfiguration of political life (Liu, 2020): these developments represent new ways in which chat and messages are involved in redrawing the boundaries between private conversation and public communication. The same goes for the use of Instagram in "discursive activism," as illustrated by the feminist Bye Felipe Instagram campaign, in which screenshots of misogynistic harassment and sexual entitlement on dating apps are collated (Shaw, 2016). We have also seen innovative efforts to appropriate apps in protests against forms of oppression and injustice wrought by the apps themselves. This move is evident in the fight for better work conditions and labor rights in the gig economy, where tactics of "algorithmic activism" have developed through taxi drivers' struggles against the practices of employers and app companies—as seen in the case of the Chinese ride-hailing app Didi (Chen, 2018).

The use of apps for activism is a hallmark of activism across the spectrum, from progressive to conservative, right through left, and is also emblematic of many cross-cutting or hard to categorize movements—especially those that work via messaging apps. In Brazil, for instance, WhatsApps was credited as the platform that helped entrench the radical, national right-wing movement that brought President Bolsonaro to power in the "WhatsApp election" of 2018 (Davis & Straubhaar, 2020). Along with email lists, Facebook groups, and messages, WhatsApp also played a facilitative role in the celebrated progressive Mexican student movement #Yosoy132, through what Emiliano Treré (2015) dubs "social media backstage practices," contrasting them with the publicly much more visible front stage social media of Twitter streams and Facebook posts. As this brief case study of activism shows, messaging apps have become an important zone of experimentation and participation. They draw together various affordances of messaging across analogue and digital communication and media, something that many users have experimented with in civil and political action, as well as in many other areas of their lives.

Quotidian Voice Media

We see many instances of voice communication cropping up in apps. Voice itself is an ancient, embodied, mediated form of communication (Peters, 1999), often seen as defining *humans* in communication. Voice emphasizes the paradigmatic centrality of human communications, both generally and in the discipline of communication studies. Voice was at the core of early mobile phones, which revolved around portability and the reconfiguration of dyadic communication (i.e. between A and B as parties to a telephone call), answering machines, multiparty (i.e. speaker phone or push-to-talk features), and collective communication, as well as around imaginaries of mobile communication (Goggin, 2006). "After" the mobile phone, mobile media are shot through with the reappearance of voice in new digital forms and formats. Telephone answering machines were phased out, as mobiles phones incorporated voice message options into the network. Messages could be forwarded as voice mail or converted, on the fly, into text messages. The diffusion of SMSs excluded many people for whom text is not the preferred mode of communication, so in many parts of the world the availability of text-to-voice options, interactive voice response (Myles, 2013), and other voice-based media became important—as happened for instance in the rural Indian context (Mudliar et al., 2013).

The telephone, the mobile phone, the recording of parts

of conversation, and the message are instances of what I am calling "quotidian voice media." These are predecessors and partners in something emergent in voice mediations in apps. Alongside new communication forms and expressions, this phenomenon has to do with the centrality of voice-enabled apps, which now become common and command ways of operating, navigating, and driving a range of technologies.

There is the rise of voice as a way of operating the smartphone itself. For a long time we have been accustomed to witnessing people talking to the air, into their phones. For some years it has been possible to beckon one's phone to dial a regular contact or undertake an instruction. Now the voice interface on smartphones is far more extensive and powerful. Many people dictate, write, and communicate using the voice commands and features of their mobile devices. Previously the province of specialist programs such as Dragon Dictate or of screen readers used by blind people or by people with vision impairments, or a functionality prized by people with mobility or dexterity impairments, the voice accessibility feature of computer OSs has been ported to mobile devices. Taking notes, composing emails, issuing commands for the device to execute, writing long documents, and generally doing things with mobile technology has become much easier. Apart from the optical character recognition (OCR) technology developed by Ray Kurzweil and many others, there have been dramatic improvements in speech recognition technology. These developments are underpinned by the evolution of data, machine learning, and AI, allowing, for instance, large databases of samples of voice to be gathered and interrogated, in real time, to pattern-match what someone is saying. Translation apps are a special instance of such developments, which nowadays are widely used too. Of course, the computational analysis of voice requires access to servers via network connectivity. As a consequence, poor or no connectivity impairs voice recognition.

The digital assistant is a notable class of voice apps that has both fueled these developments and taken advantage of them. Apple took digital assistants to market with the Siri feature built into its iOs. Siri has subsequently developed in a full-blown digital assistant that can also operate other apps on a user's phone; it can hail a ride via the Uber app, for example. Google Assistant does many similar things, and also has privileged access to capabilities via the Android OS. What Google Assistant also draws upon is the unrivaled store of the data that Google's digital properties across search, maps, docs, mail, and so on collect from their users. To take advantage of these environments, app developers need to incorporate and design interoperability between a particular app and the digital assistant. App developers are mindful, of course, that, given the users' growing reliance on digital assistants, they need to consider the costs of their apps, which are not connected to and woven into this ecosystem. The ubiquity of the human-to-machine communication that voice apps represents has been most dramatically enhanced by the advent of smart home and entertainment devices such as those popularized by Amazon's Echo and Alexa and by Google Home. These are harbingers of the Internet of Things, vividly laid out in Mercedes Bunz and Graham Meikle's eponymous book (Bunz & Meikle, 2018). These devices are activated and driven by users' voices, respond to them, and in turn speak back. The devices are also operated by apps on mobile devices such as smartphones and tablets. In July 2020, for instance, Amazon announced a redesign that allowed Alexa to launch iOS and Android apps: "Amazon clearly wants Alexa to become a platform-agnostic alternative to Google Assistant and Siri, and its mobile app is a key part of making that happen" (Porter, 2020). The deployment of AI-enabled digital voice assistants is a conspicuous feature of the new service landscapes that emerge across many sectors of business, government, and social service provision, which feature such automated technologies at different points of customer service interaction and decision-making processes (Fernandes & Oliveira, 2021).

There is a powerful social and cultural shaping to the imagining, design, and deployment of app-based voice media. Justine Humphry and Chris Chesher remind us, for instance, both of the histories of machinic and robotic voice that constitute the cultural foundation of these voice technologies and of the particular gender, race, and class logics at play in how companies have designed the voices and personae (Humphry & Chesher, 2020). This example underscores voice apps as a key zone of control of the expanding universe of smart devices, and not just of the mobile phone. One of the specters haunting this area is that of surveillance via recording by smartphone devices such as Alexa, as they update their audio. Boundaries of all sorts are being continually crisscrossed by such apps and the systems in which they function. Harking back to the "personal digital assistant" of the 1980s through to the early oos, these devices, as well as mobile phones such as the Blackberry, both raised concerns and generated opportunities: they would confound work–life boundaries or, alternatively, serve as a resource for negotiating them (Golden & Geisler, 2007). With the new, app-based digital assistants that could be addressed via voice inputs, the necessity and scope for such boundary work and debates loom much larger. This is underscored in recent research and debates on the kinds of data collected by digital assistants, the role that technology may play in deepening a "surveillance" society, the cyber and other insecurities of these assistants, the reconfiguring of human–machine communication, and the tendencies to personalization and control directions that this kind of app technology might involve or represent (Stucke & Ezrachi, 2018).

Conclusion

In this chapter I have reviewed, exemplified, and discussed a wide range of ways in which apps extend the media. I am aware that there are other important areas of media where apps have also proved to be a zone of innovation. In news apps, for instance, news notifications and alerts in ambient media have stretched the nature of what we regard as news and the ways in which we consume it. I have courted a distinct risk of skimming over the surface instead of going into the substance and complexity of app media, not only in each of the broad areas I have covered but also with regard to the contributions of particular apps or cultures of use to the identity of apps in media. Nonetheless, I hope that, by bringing together a wide range of instances, the question of app media will come to our attention. I also hope that I have managed to underscore the many and telling ways in which apps are central to the kind of media changes and innovations that have been decisive across digital media and society in recent years.

Apps do remain a species of software. However, they are designed for and work with hardware, with a focus on taking advantage of, amplifying, and curating their affordances. Apps function as a fabric that weaves users, bodies, emotions, senses, contexts, and environments into layered digital infra-structures that societies rely upon.

An app is a kind of "container technology" (Sofia, 2000). Apps are vested with the ability to "call" or "hail" a user as a subject: they have the kind of invocational quality and action that Chris Chesher has associated with computers (Chesher, 2002). Apps also have the ability of an Occam's razor; they are disciplined by the constraints of the device, its computing, sensing, and other powers to marshal a set of resources for a purpose. This underpins the much vaunted design focus of apps, which is buttressed by other OSs: the smartphone, the tablet, the wearables, the car, the home. Through its form and nature, the app forecloses many rich possibilities of wider media, let alone of cultural life and reality itself. Like a pair of glasses, it focuses on some things to the exclusion of others.

On the positive side, the kaleidoscopic step changes that apps instigate in their variety of media incarnations make them privileged nodes in the larger environment of technologies, things, and social life. We will explore this in chapter 5, looking at apps and everyday life and at how apps broaden the realms and functions of the media by promising to serve as social laboratories.

CHAPTER FIVE

Social Laboratories of Apps

In this chapter we look at the ways in which apps anchor us in everyday life. Apps build on and deepen the multilayered processes by which media, communication, and technology play a fundamental role in shaping society, and especially everyday life. However, apps promise to go further than this: they function as what I dub "social laboratories."

"Everyday life" refers to zones of our lives that are associated with mundane, apparently uneventful, taken-for-granted, routinized activities, habits, meanings, and structures whose ensemble constitutes our daily reproduction as individuals in society: "Everyday life always takes place in and relates to the immediate environment of a person" (Heller, 1984, p. 6). These aspects of everyday life have often been seen as standing in opposition to either exceptional things and events or official, formal, proper occurrences in the realm of public life (Highmore, 2002). In a strain of cultural studies especially dedicated to thinking, everyday life is often associated with creativity, innovation through DIY, "making do," and resistance to authorities and power structures (Certeau, 1984; Certeau et al., 2014).

For some decades, media changes have been associated with the deep social changes that are under way across many societies (Couldry, 2012). One signal element is that, with the sociotechnical changes associated with the infiltration of ICTs, which constitute now a large proportion of media and communication (Loos et al., 2008; Silverstone & Hirsch, 1992), digital media have extended the reach of media into everyday life (Meikle, 2012; Schroeder, 2018), in a complex and ongoing process (Haddon, 2004; Haddon et al., 2005; Humphreys, 2018; Ling, 2012). The role played by mobile media in redrawing the boundaries between public and private spheres has been highly significant (Abeele et al., 2018; Beer, 2012; Goggin, 2006; Hjorth & Arnold, 2013). With the advent of smartphones (Barkhuus & Polichar, 2011; Hobbis, 2020), apps have come to the fore as a feature of social practices and digital media in everyday life.

In terms of the salience and presence of apps in everyday life, we could sketch two extremes. One is the position that apps are glaring and novel items, to be placed in the foreground. At the other end is the position that apps should be placed in the background, as they blend in and are taken for granted—just like the mobile phone itself, which Rich Ling characterized as a "social fact," applying to it Émile Durkheim's concept (Ling, 2012). Or the fate of apps might look like that of other shiny objects and technologies—one of weathering: we saw how the SMS went from being a new and exciting feature in the youth cultures of certain Nordic countries to being something obvious and a bit boring. This is what Troels Fibæk Bertel and Rich Ling dubbed the "changing centrality" of such technology (Fibæk Bertel & Ling, 2016).

Another way of looking at it could be to move away from the macro perspective and zoom in on distinct, often small worlds of apps. While apps are global and international in their bearing and intermedial and interdependent with digital ecologies, platforms, and infrastructures, they are also distinct, often self-contained realms that users can inhabit, explore, and use as a base.

We can discern a shift by which some aspects of previous "cultures" associated with various forms of media, communication, and ICT—notably computing, software, mobile phones, Internet, and social media—are reanimated into app cultures. On some pejorative and often reductive accounts, app culture is a serious negative phenomenon. It is often presented as a shrinking or hollowing out of proper culture, which in this scenario appears as the inexorable casualty of the monocultural, commercialized world ruled by apps (Gould, 2014).

This will not do. Hence we need an account that steers away from blaming apps for the proposed woes of the world and comes to grips instead with the actual nature of apps and their implications for everyday life. We can think of a twofold phenomenon called "apps culture": first, the multi-actor creation of an ensemble of habits, meanings, forms, economics, and technologies distinctive to apps; secondly, the quite specific cultures that are associated with particular apps. The usefulness of such an account of the development and dynamics of app culture is that it yields a critical framework for understanding the myriads of apps and their categoriz-ations, contexts, and structural principles. As we have seen, apps form a significant part of the economy and are key to digital media and communication. What we shall now explore further is the wide and deep incorporation of apps into social life through their purchase on and embedding in everyday life. Along the journey, we will often encounter an almost millenarianist, utopian vision associated with apps, in which they offer a kind of laboratory for new social imaginaries and relations.

There is an array of potential single apps to be discussed, many representing rich and influential digital worlds that their users inhabit. We could regard a particular app as token of a type, category, or kind of apps; yet even when we do this there are many different groups of apps, not to mention endless ways to produce taxonomies of them. For the purposes of charting the influence of apps on everyday life, I have chosen four major areas: health and well-being; money; shopping; and intimacies, especially dating and hooking up. As I hope to show, many apps are purely trivial or mundane in their purposes, domestication (or redomestication), use, and abandonment. However, such apparently insignificant, everyday acts and things offer meaning and support in often important, yet unacknowledged ways, as indicated by concepts such as "mundane citizenship" (Bakardjieva, 2012) or "everyday citizenship" (Atton, 2014). This is about understanding "the ordinary" (Corner, 1996) and what media does with it, or at least the "digital ordinary" (Lasén Díaz, 2019), the banal, and the critique of everyday life (Morris, 1998).

Health and Well-Being Apps

As evidenced by the COVID pandemic, health apps form part of the fabric and infrastructure of everyday life and its "horizon of expectations" from technology (Chandler & Murray, 2011; Borup et al., 2006). Health apps are a sustained area of app development, design, and growth. Often produced through co-design efforts of app developers, medical and healthcare professionals, health institutions and industry interests, patients, consumers, and a range of other actors, health apps have also become a major business opportunity for technology companies and the dominant app providers.

The use of mobile phones for health has been in focus for more than fifteen years. The phenomenon came to be referred to as "m-health" in the early 00s. While the rise of 3G networks and developments in health technologies, Internet, data, and other technologies set the scene for expectations that mobile health would become an important factor in health care, the ways in which the future was imagined before smartphones and health apps was qualitatively different (Istepanian et al., 2006). Nearly fifteen years after the launch of the smartphone, it is clear that this type of gadget plays an important role in people's health care around the world. The smartphone's capacity as a sensor medium is a notable aspect of this: "Smartphonebased passive sensing, in particular, has opened new possibilities for health and wellbeing because data recorded by multiple built-in sensors can be combined with behavioral data" (Paglialonga et al., 2018, p. 97).

Apps are often spoken of as an "empowerment tool" that triggers a shift in the privileged locations of health care: "Thanks to the growing number of empowerment tools like apps or portable medical devices, health care is no longer an aspect linked mostly to hospitals, but monitoring also takes place at home, modifying the relation between physicians and patients" (Guarneri et al., 2019, p. 3). Some definitions of m-health revolve now around apps: "mHealth apps and devices hold great promise in terms of potential benefits for the several actors involved (patients, citizens, and professionals)" (Paglialonga et al., 2019, p. 5).

The sheer variety of health apps is staggering. Healthcare apps could be categorized by function: "general solutions for healthcare professionals ... apps for medical education, teaching, and learning; telemedicine support tools; apps for patients and for the general public over wide array of services; and disease-specific apps for patients" (p. 97). But, when it comes to health apps designed for patients or consumers, this category alone can contain a whole range of popular kinds of apps, namely apps designed for the main purpose of providing information, or securing access to health care and services, or monitoring physical and vital signs and indications; and there are also apps for treatment compliance, nutrition and diet apps, and symptom checker apps (pp. 97–98). Each of these types of apps has its own targeted users, affordances and desired responses and behaviors, and intended and unintended effects and influences.

Take the case of symptom monitoring by patients and potential patients, given that it has been in the spotlight during the COVID-19 pandemic. This activity has a long history, as highlighted by the role of daily symptom diaries kept for studies (Larson et al., 2017, p. 259). Symptom monitoring via apps arguably allows faster, near real-time checking and analysis of symptoms; together with crowdsourcing, it can complement—or even threaten to supplant—the traditional role of physicians. The symptom checker app was taken to scale with the arrival of the COVID Symptom app, which was devised by researchers at King's College London and in the health science company ZOE and launched in the United Kingdom and United States in March 2020. Within six weeks, the COVID Symptom app was credited with a take-up of three million users, predominantly in the United Kingdom (Menni et al., 2020). Users reported their symptoms via the app. Then the dataset was analyzed on the fly, to provide and display a daily estimate of people with COVID in the country, disaggregated by area (ZOE, 2020). The study also generated an AI diagnostic, which claimed to predict COVID without patients having to be tested.

Much of the promise of health apps is due to the ways in which they leverage the affordances and social practices associated with mobiles, as extended by smartphones. This includes the role that mobiles play in people's navigation of healthcare systems, as highlighted by a 2012–2014 study of young people in Ghana, Malawi, and South Africa. The study found that "[t]hese young people are not waiting passively for m-health to come to them; they are already ... using mobile phones creatively and strategically to try to secure healthcare" (Hampshire et al., 2015, p. 97). This situation is characterized by a striking and concerning dynamic, marking a shift in the burden of responsibility and risk carried by young people and individuals generally (Hampshire et al., 2015, p. 97). Here the researchers noted the fit between such new kinds of digital, therapeutic citizenship and the "current neoliberal rhetoric that emphasizes and endorses patient 'empowerment,' choice and responsibility" (Hampshire et al., 2015, p. 97). Interestingly, apps are not mentioned in this study. Rather the respondents use their phones for calling, texting, contacts, networks, business and income opportunities, and finding information via mobile Internet-based search. So the mobile Internet plays a role, especially in detecting better health information and options. This is well explained in research on the mobile Internet in the context of the global South, where the ubiquity of apps in resource, bandwidth, data, and handset-constrained features has been slow to manifest itself (Donner, 2015; Donner & Walton, 2013; Goggin, 2018). While there are advocates of mobiles who speak of apps as "the engine for expanded global access to the Internet" (a motto of ITU's Global ICT regulatory outlook report: see ITU, 2017b), it is still unclear where and to what extent apps fit into user practices, despite the spectacular figures of their growth. A skeptical 2012 intervention into the m-health field suggested that m-health should adopt and implement standards already evident in e-health, should aim to be participatory and sustainable, and should promote equity in health, noting: "The very high mobile phone penetration rate of 79 percent in low- and middle-income countries may nevertheless obscure inequities and patterns of exclusion" (Heerden et al., 2012, pp. 393–394). Hence their recommendation that "m-health needs to focus on the health, not on the technology."

These considerations regarding the international diffusion, shaping, and applicability of apps help us understand the transition from a "smartphone-centric" m-health to one dominated by the proliferation of devices and data thematized in developments and imaginaries of the Internet of Things and 5G (Pattnaik et al., 2020; Istepanian & Al-Anzi, 2018). This shift was symbolized by Apple's 2014 announcement of its Health app, included with iOS 8 and later versions. Through this app, Apple embedded health informatics into its core iPhone functionality and its mobile, data, and app ecosystem. Also included was HealthKit, an accompanying application programming interface (API) included in the iOS SDK for Apple devices: "A more personal Health app. For a more informed you." Under the banner of "An app a day keeps the doctor away," Apple suggests that "[t]he Health app can incorporate data from thousands of third-party apps that are designed to promote healthier habits" (Apple, 2020b). It explains that "[d]ata collected from apps is stored alongside data from your Apple Watch and information you've logged directly on your iPhone." The Health app uses "machine learning to determine the metrics that matter most to you, and it automatically creates Highlights to bring that information front and centre."

While Google data and analytics have been widely used in many areas of health, Google has particularly sought to capitalize on its data advantage via its Google Fit app. Google has also fostered close relationships with smart watch and wearables providers. Its Wear OS was designed to work with phones running Android 6.0+ (as well as iPhone 10.0+). In late 2019, Google announced an agreement to partner with Fitbit, one of the most popular veterans of the fitness wearables industry (Osterloh, 2019). The proposed deal raised concerns about Google's privacy policy and the potential use of sensitive personal health information about subscribers to enrich Google's data for targeted advertising. Although Fitbit and Google ruled out this scenario, the deal was likely to be in the frame of the US Justice Department's anti-trust review of Google's search business (Shubber, 2020). For its part, the European Union took a firm interest in 2020 (Espinoza, 2020), reportedly seeking "guarantees that all of Fitbit's data would be open to third parties on equal terms, and a promise that Google would not use the data to improve its search engine business."

The long-term issue here is how to make use of these data in socially appropriate, ethical, and rights-respecting ways, in order to deliver accurate information and make well-conceived interventions. The concerns are heightened when we bear in mind the considerable investments needed to build advanced m-health and health information systems, which countries can afford to do this, and for which groups in their societies:

> [M]any low to middle income countries (LMIC) are expected to be the next fertile grounds for frugal and affordable

mobile health systems to provide better m-health ... The best utilization of big data and machine learning tools in these environments remains another area for future work. (Istepanian & Al-Anzi, 2018, p. 40)

In addition, there are major issues at the core of health apps. They hinge on whether users will download and use apps, whether this use will benefit them or change their behaviors, attitudes, and emotions, and whether the apps will improve health—and, if so, how exactly. These questions preoccupy the people involved in health apps, and especially those among them who work in public health, psychology, health communications, and similar fields. They also underscore the need for requisite modesty and realism about the place of apps in the wider digital health and health ecosystem (Lazakidou et al., 2016). All this is evident from a key source of frustration for app sponsors: complaints that users won't accept or adopt apps. These anxieties featured prominently across many countries, as governments sought to persuade their populations to adopt COVID-19 contact-tracing apps (Bell et al., 2020). A major stumbling block that governments did not wish to highlight was the fact that such apps were largely unproven and their role in the broader suite of public health measures, especially in well-proven systems of contact tracing, was unclear (Goggin, 2020).

A New Zealand study of health app use reveals two other facts that often crop up. First, users experience conflicting emotions as they seek to gain benefits from the many available health apps, for example information and access to free or inexpensive advice and expertise. Typically they try to maintain agency and control while having to cede authority over their data—or, in the words of the study's respondents, while "signing your life away" (Trnka, 2016, p. 253). Secondly, there is a change to the temporalities that health experience and management involve. In part, this change is due to the way in which apps structure and encapsulate time and

desire: "Apps structure particular kinds of affective engage-
ments in health activities, creating a sense of responsibility
and guilt, competition, success or failure" (p. 255). What this
research underscores is that, like other technologies, apps
make demands on us, their users (Johnson, 1988). They add a
new dimension to the kinds of obligations we became accustomed to with the advent of the telephone, then of mobile
phones. From the start, users felt the pressure to answer the
phone when it rang; this was a burden that eased with the
arrival of the answering machine. Mobile communication
brought altered expectations, which Christian Licoppe (2010)
calls the "crisis of the summons." Is there an obligation to
answer the mobile phone, or can we send a message to say
that we will call back later? And with the arrival of the "notifi-
cation culture" of social media, messaging, and chat apps, all
endowed with frequent alerts, pulses, and buzzes that we feel
as well as hear, the obligation intensifies, yet it also attenuates
(Licoppe, 2010). With health and wellness apps, users can
experience a responsibility that goes beyond the communicative level—because such apps pin them down further,
making them feel accountable for their own health in a very
precise and detailed way, in their everyday lives. Here apps
play an important role in materially reinforcing individuals'
increased sense of responsibility in many domains of their
lives, something characteristic of broad political and social
shifts in governance (Rose, 2008, 2009; Trnka & Trundle,
2017).

To understand why health and well-being apps have
become such a feature of everyday life, it is helpful consider
the evolution not just of mobile phones but of wearables,
too. Wearables fit into long histories of social, cultural, and
digital technologies for personal use. Such technologies, as
Lee Humphreys reminds us, involved diaries, letters, and
other objects that established and entrenched our ideas
of self, our sense of identity, and our self-representational
and memorialistic practices (Humphreys, 2018). Humphreys

conceptualizes the formation of all these things as the "accounting of everyday life" associated with social and mobile media; and she dubs the self-tracking processes involved "the qualified self." In the area of wearables, we could consider the connected watch as a remarkable social and technical accomplishment, which draws upon the personal technology of clocks and timekeeping. Self-tracking (Lupton, 2016) reaches an inflection point with the maturation of the smart watch alongside mobile devices, the GPS, sensors, mobile operating systems, and data technology capacity to gather data that can be related to health and well-being. The smart watch is only one part of a potentially joined-up ecosystem in which apps are integral and integrative, a system that connects humans to non-human objects and actors and "quantified self becomes quantified car," as technology theorist Melanie Swan (2015) ironically puts it.

Deborah Lupton offers a helpful perspective on how these developments are framed, suggesting that the "imaginaries invested in health and fitness apps and wearables tend to cohere around the ideas of achieving well-being, optimizing health and improving fitness by motivating the user to take up habits such as regular physical activity, calorie-counting or sleep-tracking" (Lupton, 2019, p. 2). Apps, for instance, may suit some people's bodies, desires, habits, lives, and social contexts but may not work well for others (Lupton, 2020). Then there is the long-standing issue of normality: apps tend to be shaped and designed with powerful ideas of what and who is normal or standard. An illustrative case here is Lupton's study of Australian women's use of health and fitness apps and wearable devices, where efforts toward "achieving the healthy, active, controlled body imagined by these technologies" fly in the face of realities in women's lives (Lupton, 2019, p. 13). Lupton makes the important point that women who cannot afford such expensive devices or who face issues of poor connectivity or digital inclusion probably have experiences that conflict with the ideal encounters suggested by such apps. Not surprisingly, the participants in her study "imagined novel health technologies that would better cater for the diversity of their embodiment and demands of their everyday lives."

Apps and Money

From health apps we will move now to money apps. Finance is another area where apps have been key to social transformation, and where imaginaries and uses have often jostled unproductively. Apps came into the picture at a time when it was accepted that digital media were all about money, or at least had a lot to do with it. This wasn't always the case.

A key feature of apps is their integration of payment systems into a handset, especially by incorporating security and authentication systems; in this way finance meets security (Dieter & Tkacz, 2020). The advent of biometrics and of fingerprint recognition systems such as Apple's Touch ID, together with the adoption of such features by handset vendors and acceptance by users, have seen affordances of mobile phones integrated into payment and commerce (Sathyan et al., 2013). This is because of the relatively high levels of security and assurance that come from users when they log into their phone via tried-and-tested forms of authentication: finger or thumbprint; drawing a particular pattern on screen; a user's touch or swipe patterns; facial recognition; voice recognition; or the old-school, default method of using a password. Once the phone has authenticated the user and she uses an app to make a purchase, if credit card details are stored and called by a payment system run either by a handset vendor (say, Samsung or Apple) or by a digital company (say, Google), the user can click to approve. Or, as we saw in chapter 4 in relation to RFID, a user can place the phone near a suitably equipped terminal to use Apple, Google Pay, or another system to complete a payment. These technologies face various material, technical, and social challenges—whether to do with cultural values and assumptions about faces or with local settings where the hands of different people might have stains or particular features (weathering, scars). During the COVID-19 pandemic, concerns about disease transmission led many users to shun touch-based fingerprinting systems and adopt touchless or face recognition systems instead ("Face ID firms battle," 2020).

Such app-based technologies, as Nathaniel Tkacz suggests in relation to Apple Pay, can be seen as exemplary of important shifts in social life. Tkacz argues that "appification of money" involves a reconceptualization of money:

> The spectrum of money practices, situations, and wider money ecologies richly detailed by anthropologists and sociologists is being carved up into new product niches or features within existing apps. Such specificity is further extended through user personalization. (Tkacz, 2019, p. 270)

Tkacz sees money apps as attempting to capture these particular needs, desires, and rituals. At the same time, apps are involved in a profound abstraction of social life that involves a reworking of the category of experience, a kind of experience turn—prefigured, of course, by discourse on the relatively new concept of experience economy (pp. 280–281).

After some fifteen years of being in the making, apps represent nowadays a new phase in the prosaic realities of how we pay for things, including digital things. At the very least, they have helped entrench mobile money in many nooks and crannies of social life (Maurer, 2011). The history of money is a most human and intriguing topic; it has ancient beginnings and spans many kinds of matter and media (Dodd, 2014; Maurer, 2015). Many kinds of money are portable, be they shells, bars of gold, coins, or notes. So declarations of "real" money are chimerical at best (Wolman, 2012). Money has been relatively reliably despatched around the world via telegraphic transfer systems, whence the question "Can you wire me some money?" Especially as it serves the long-standing remittance economy of migrant and diasporic workers around the world who send money to their families and communities in their home countries (Kunz, 2011; Singh, 2013), this system still thrives; the most famous provider, Western Union, offers services via digital networks to places and countries very poorly served by banks. Western Union is often found in small shops that act as agencies. It is integrated among their other raft of services, so it has been convenient to many people. Mobile money took off with the advent of text messaging and was made famous by money transfer services such as m-pesa, which was a phenomenal success in Kenya (Hughes & Lonie, 2007; Kuriyan et al., 2012; Lashitew et al., 2019)—although slower to attract customers in some other countries, for instance Tanzania and South Africa (Oborn et al., 2019). Supplementing or sometimes supplanting mobile transfer systems, mobile "air time" and data bundles themselves become a form of currency that could be transferred, shared, and used for payment. Other African countries such as Uganda, Tanzania, Cameroon, Benin, and various sub-Saharan countries have also seen intense growth and innovation in mobile money (Apecu et al., 2014; Madise, 2019).

In various contexts, mobile money has proven to be an especially flexible form, which weaves in and is supported by relationships and people's "everyday exchange repertoires," as suggested by Susan Johnson and Froudkje Krijtenburg in their reflections on the rapid, widespread adoption of mobile money in Kenya and other East African countries (Johnson & Krijtenburg, 2018). Mobile money provided forms and systems of money and finance for hundreds of millions, if not billions, of people who are often described as "the unbanked"—that is, the world's populations neglected or underserved by banks and finance because they are seen as unprofitable or as constituting less lucrative markets. Indeed, one great promise of mobiles was the global imaginary of financial inclusion (Singh, 2019), whereby devices would be a catalyst in ending poverty: they would take over the visions often associated with micro-finance—as in the leading instance of Bangladesh's Grameen Bank, for instance—and leverage further technology-enabled income advancement for people "at the bottom of the pyramid" (Agrawal, 2016). As Bill Maurer notes, such an imaginary has profound flaws because it revolves around an "idea of 'the poor' as consumers ... relatively passive, aside from their consumer choices" (Maurer, 2012, p. 590). Instead, Maurer suggests, the reality is that mobile money "complicates the story," given that "people [are] adapting and modifying those systems."

These insights are important to bear in mind as anchoring points in evaluating the move toward full-blown, more elaborate, and more pervasive mobile money ecosystems (Kendall et al., 2011). Consider, for instance, the typical framing of mobile banking apps as serving to "streamline the mobile experience" for customers, via apps that offer the "possibilities of accessing the data of the financial institution anywhere and at any time" (Nicoletti, 2014, pp. 36, 26). While streamlining, integrating, unifying, and smoothing the consumer experience is a laudable and omnipresent business desire, the reality of how the technology and the business environment, the players, and the systems are evolving along with the social practices and cultural understandings of money suggests that things won't go smoothly.

This is evident when we look at the great excitement in the area of FinTech, where apps are center stage in the challenges raised by technology firms and new actors in banking and finance against established players such as bankers and lenders. Among the successful firms so far are those that can leverage off their existing base of loyal customers. For instance, the Chinese technology purveyors have been conspicuous global movers in the money, payment, and FinTech apps. Alibaba's Alipay is widely used in China and around the world, its main competitor being WePay (leveraging WeChat).

In different parts of the world, banks have sought to leverage and extend their existing accounts by offering services through which account holders can instantly transfer money by entering their mobile number. Such services are often specific to a particular bank rather than to a consortium. They offer a way for banks and customers alike to have a workaround, as traditional bank transfer remains slow, owing to interbank agreements and protocols on clearance. Many jurisdictions now allow digital banks and FinTech services, which also provide new ways to ease money matters. TransferWise, for instance, is a Belgian-based digital bank that allows multiple-currency accounts, relatively inexpensive international transfers, and currency exchange; then it penetrates the official banking system of other countries to generate bank account details that can be used by TransferWise customers.

The complex developments in mobile money (Mutambara, 2018) prompted the need for more adequate concepts of financial inclusion and for more responsive and appropriate policy and regulatory frameworks (Madise, 2019). Given that mobile money actors include many small businesses, shops, and agents in many contexts, especially in global South locations, there is a need to look beyond the formal, state-based regulation to older, traditional institutions of law such as the clan, as argued by the policy scholars Nicole Stremlau and Ridwan Osman in a study of Somali territories (Stremlau & Osman, 2015). Mobile money has also been a boon for shadier reaches of the informal economy, such as money laundering, so this topic has exercised the minds of regulators and policy scholars (Kernan, 2018).

Amid hope and hype, it is still not clear to what extent mobile money has enhanced welfare and savings (Aron, 2018) or improved livelihoods for households (Bruhn & Wieser, 2019). There are indications that mobile money in the app era has enhanced financial access for the poor (Munyegera &

Matsumoto, 2018). Also, it can have some positive macroeconomic effects, as shown in a recent study of Uganda, a country where the introduction of mobile money has received considerable attention (Mawejje & Lakuma, 2019). One obstacle lies in the availability of apps and functionality that allow easy and cheap transfer of funds from mobile money wallets to a user's bank account (Acquah-Sam & Bugre, 2018). Another key issue is the sustainability of mobile money ecosystems and value chains (Dong et al., 2018), something highlighted by the lack of accepted or dominant ecosystems in FinTech apps (Dietz et al., 2018). At a deeper level, there are the social and cultural dynamics at play—as is evident, for instance, in the gendered nature of money, "mobie" and other (Singh, 2019; Suri & Jack, 2016).

The area of digital money that continues to attract attention and speculation is cryptocurrency, which works via distributed ledger technology such as a blockchain (Brunton, 2019; Lee & Low, 2018). A leading light here is the currency Bitcoin, but there are many other currencies rivaling it. With the Internet of Things and blockchain systems, a new area has emerged: that of distributed apps (dapps). Muscling in on this scene, Facebook has literally tried to create a new currency with its Libra initiative (Berg, 2020; Brühl, 2020). Libra has had a mixed reception and is seen by many as doomed. However, Facebook soldiers on to gather support and make Libra viable. If successful, Libra does raise the specter of a "gobal monetary system governed by private corporations," as suggested by international relations scholar Iwa Salami (2019). Amid such blue-sky thinking, much of the action in apps and money remains in the innovation of new, smartphone- and app-based mobile payment systems, FinTech, or apps—a key element in a major shift in ecosystems of mobile- and digital-enabled money (Lee & Deng, 2018).

These complex, lucrative, and uneven developments in mobile money raise some concerns. Ironies abound, because the enlistment of users in mobile apps is far from creating a seamless situation for us to shift our transactions to digital systems. While for many consumers mobile money can often feel like a breeze, tap and go (being just that) often doesn't work, leaving one to scrabble around for coins or notes, different kinds of bank account or credit cards, store value cards, quick response (QR) payment apps on one's device, and so on. The situation may well settle down, rather on the model of credit cards; two or three dominant providers may come to reign worldwide, simplifying life for consumers. But right now, at this point in the "creative destruction" of cash, banking, telegraphic, and digital payment and currency systems, consumers are far from being served, while providers make a mint from the mobile app society.

The stakes in the appification of money are high, especially if we look at the implications of this process for social relations. This is something that Adrian Athique theorizes as representing a profound phase of "digital transactions" (Athique, 2020; Athique & Baulch, 2019) underwritten by the platform economy. Athique analyzes India's infamous "demonetization" move in November 2016, when 500 and 100 rupee notes were rendered worthless by government fiat, literally overnight. Billed as a move to address "black money" in the Indian economy, it aimed as much as anything to fastforward the "cashless economy," as part of Prime Minister Narendra Modi's Digital India campaign and policy (Athique, 2019). Around the world, mobile phones and apps are key to the expansion of digital transactions spurred by demonetization (Chaurasia et al., 2019). This was expressed a decade earlier by a leading figure in the India banking and finance sectors:

> The convenience of the mobile phone as an instrument for conduct of financial transactions and the immense potential it has in the process of financial inclusion and financial growth is well recognized ... the benefits of M-Commerce should reach the common man at the remotest locations in the country. (Chakrabarty, 2009, p. 10)

But, for such dreams of financial inclusion to become reality, fundamental shifts are needed in economy, society, and polity. As Athique (2019, p. 1710) contends, "[t]he acquisition of taxation powers by fintech companies and the end of independent value outside the banking sector is an unprecedented shift in the contract between citizens and the state." Given the reliance of the majority of the Indian population on cash, as well as the low proportion of people with bank accounts, flicking the switch to digital in this context is very costly indeed—and this should serve as a cautionary tale elsewhere as well.

Shopping Apps

The changes that money apps represent have parallels in another closely related area of everyday life and consumption: shopping.

A lot of the time, in many parts of the world people are doing their shopping via apps. Yet this app reflex has been a long time in the making. It took a fair while to make digital shopping a thing (Linke, 1992), and the histories of shopping itself stretch back much further (Bowlby, 2002; Furnée & Lesger, 2014). It took a sustained effort to construct e-commerce as a viable area, especially since many of its so-called use cases seemed far-fetched when they emerged in the 1990s, having little anchoring in established social practices (see Tapscott et al., 1998; Westland & Clark, 1999). There were also various policy and regulation issues to be addressed and frameworks to be constructed, starting with the 1992 change to the US National Science Foundation Act, which lifted the ban on commerce on the Internet in its acceptable use policy (Goggin, 2000). Over two or so decades, the deeply social and cultural dynamics of trading, commerce, transactions, and money have changed in concert with digital technology, creating very interesting geographies of e-commerce as it has diffused globally (Warf, 2013).

(E-commerce and digital commerce are often used inter-
changeably. Digital commerce can refer to a wider range of
transactions than e-commerce does.) In the last decade or so,
apps have played an important role in what many societies
now regard as commonplace shopping.

As already discussed, mobile phone payment systems were
vital to stabilizing a key stage of e-commerce: authenticated
payments and transfers of funds. These systems were a
critical factor in underpinning the great potential of what is
now called "click and mortar" retailing. The roll call of great
Internet retailers is long indeed, and certainly would include
the likes of Alibaba, Amazon, Craigslist, eBay, Rakuten,
and Taobao, and other innovative e-commerce behemoths.
Also significant are the technology companies that sell
ICT products and especially digital services, too numerous
to mention here. Among the biggest Internet retailers in
the early 2020s are many long-standing retailers that have
embraced the Internet, such as Walmart, Target, and Ikea.
Search, as a general Internet function, has an extraordinary
potential to combine with web and social media platforms.
This potential, enhanced by advances in logistics, made
shopping one of the earliest, and now one of the most taken-
for-granted and pervasive features of the digital economy.

Apps ushered in new kinds of retail systems and shopping
experiences for consumers. This has made the app the
first port of call—and often the only port of call—for many
shoppers (Einav et al., 2014). Shopping via an app allows the
streamlining, integration, and customization of the online
shopping experience (Cheong & Mohammed-Baksh, 2019).
The app incorporates display and advertising of products by
a retailer and allows shoppers to browse or search for items
and then either purchase them on the spot or leave them
bookmarked or in their shopping cart, so that they can come
back to them later on. After purchase, an item's delivery can
be tracked with the help of the app, through alerts and updates
sent via the app, text message, or the preferred messaging

app. Ultimately, should it be necessary, a retailer can also call the customer via a mobile phone. Usability, which is key to e-commerce and online shopping and purchasing (Konradt et al., 2012), is something that mobile apps sought to specifically enhance.

A more sophisticated and subtle dimension of shopping that became salient with the rise of apps and with the place they came to occupy in the ecology that developed from the Internet, Web 2.0, and social media is the role of consumer expertise, social relationships, and communication on products, services, brands, and experience. This has been captured with the help of a rubric on consumers' roles in "co-design" and "value co-creation." Marketing researchers suggested that firms should focus on fostering consumer expertise, learning, and thus long-term loyalty and engagement with their brands (Barrutia et al., 2016).

Apps also allow retailers and shoppers to blend digital, online, and built environment aspects of the shopping experience. Major retail developments assume and incorporate apps into their architecture, design, and day-to-day operations, and, in many middle- to upper-income contexts, also into the crafting of the all-important experiential aspects of shopping. Despite early prognostications that Internet-based shopping would see the death of brick and mortar, shopping centers as well as all varieties and locales of shops have gone from strength to strength (although, like many other things, they are seriously challenged by the COVID pandemic). Apps have been key to this. From simple things such as QR codes that provide enhanced or basic information on in-store goods and services to photos of desired products taken on mobile phones for comparison shopping and to shopping apps that can be relied upon to collect customer details, apps are vitally important. Apps have also provided a way for small brands to group together in a larger collective or marketplace. A case in point is Etsy, the American e-commerce website that focuses on handmade, vintage, and craft items.

Apps also help address a central and by now long-standing aspect of contemporary shopping. Despite the initial flush of enthusiasm for e-commerce and online shopping and repeated predictions that they would take over the lion's share of retail, they still have only a relatively minor component of the market. Wholly online shopping was experienced only at the worst of the 2020–2021 COVID pandemic, when most shops were closed for a few months (apart from essential services such as local grocery and convenience stores, supermarkets, and petrol stations). Despite the shuttering of the retail landscape, online shopping is only a part of the wider environment of e-commerce, mobile commerce (m-commerce), and shopping in general. What has steadily grown in significance over many years is the role played by online technologies and digital cultures, and especially apps, across the spectrum of shopping experiences. Apps are an important part of an intensive shift toward making the online trip richer in productive information, and above all richer in *experience*, especially when it comes to experiencing the goods themselves.

There are many international contexts in which the rise of apps can be considered in relation to the longer histories of e-commerce and m-commerce. A key location is, of course, the highly publicized US market, which presents case studies of firms such as eBay and Amazon, both pioneers in e-commerce that sought to maintain and extend their positions by adopting apps. But the Chinese context may be especially instructive in this area too, given China's historical intersection with the rise of apps. Because e-commerce emerged in China slightly later than in many western countries, or indeed than in East Asian early movers such as Japan and South Korea, we witness there an especially striking and interesting set of experiments with the smartphone and apps.

By the year 2000, China had the largest number of mobile phone subscriptions in the Asia–Pacific region; and it topped the world in 2001, when, with 144.8 million subscriptions, it overtook the United States (128.5 million). During the period 2000–2007 the range of m-commerce innovations expanded in China (Kshetri et al., 2006). Yet on the cusp of the smartphone and app moment there was skepticism about the potential of China's e-commerce and m-commerce markets for quick or accelerated growth (Martinsons, 2008). As it turned out, China's retail m-commerce market has sustained a phenomenal growth, especially in the 2010s (Chi, 2018). Researchers have pointed to the ways in which online shopping plays into the tensions bound up with the intense social changes in Chinese societies, offering new leverage for some social groups to garner and make use of information in purchasing contexts (Tian, 2018). In June 2020 there were reports that China's "digital retail shift" had "accelerated" during the COVID pandemic (Cheung, 2020). This uptick also dramatized the implications of a deepening reliance on e-commerce for the practicalities of logistics and location (Panova et al., 2019). At the height of the pandemic, the growth in online shopping was frustrated by problems with the fulfillment of orders. Global supply chains were disrupted and regional and local shipping, transportation, and delivery of goods all had to expand, at a time when many workers' capacity was hampered by the impact of the disease, with its changed living, childcare, and other caring arrangements.

The economic and social reconfigurations entailed in app-enabled m-commerce can be demonstrated with the famous case of the Taobao villages (Naughton, 2018). These are poor villages and areas, often located in Chinese cities, that have been designated as e-commerce hubs by Alibaba. Working with local authorities, Alibaba provides training, support, and infrastructure improvements (e.g. in roads, power, and infrastructure) in order to encourage poor farmers to offer produce and local specialities for online sale via the hugely successful Taobao website, which is presented as the "killer app" of online commerce (Ming, 2015, p. 29). Taobao villages have been described as a kind of "hybrid rurality" (Lin et al., 2016), "villages in the City" that contribute to China's "e-urbanism" (Lin, 2019)—especially platform urbanism (Caprotti & Liu, 2020). They are the most highly publicized example of a deliberate national policy shift in China from 2014 on that saw the government turning to e-commerce in order to boost the country's prospects and alleviate poverty (Guohua, 2019). As Guohua points out, especially in the Chinese case we see how "digitization and platformization" with apps and social media "provide new and creative means for the pursuit and guarantee of "naturalness" or "organicness" in relation to food and grocery consumption (p. 288). Consumers can buy products directly from local producers, quality, freshness, and origin being vouchsafed through detailed description and documentation, sometimes through a streaming video of the farming and processing of products, and through direct engagement with farmers via WeChat and other platforms. With the development of the affordances of apps in a wider social and digital media ecosystem have come ways to finesse the long-standing problem of the "fake," but also challenges around ensuring the authentic. Guouhua suggests that such practices can amount to "micro-tactics of everyday life" and "online shopping as everyday resistance" (pp. 287–289).

With these details of shopping apps in mind, we can move back to consider the bigger picture. The market, price information, and competition aspects of the new technology and data developments ushered in by apps have some mixed and uncertain implications. Do consumers benefit from algorithmic, data profiling, personalization of pricing when firms can quickly respond to other firms' prices—which may raise concerns about a possible automatic alignment of price, and hence about anti-competitive conduct, or even collusion (OECD, 2017)? A further worry is that the segmentation of consumers on the basis of perceptions of known behavior may heighten a firm's ability to offer goods and services at a higher price to shoppers whom they know to be prepared to pay (Ezrachi & Stucke, 2019). Further still, in the reworking of shopping that these apps and digital cultures entail, we glimpse the outline of big shifts in the relationships between people, markets, and societies (Cochoy et al., 2020). What are the social relations at stake in the digitalization of consumption, including via devices? Consider, for instance, the forms of sociality and the social relations in new kinds of technology-mediated retail settings, as suggested in a study of young London shoppers:

> The young consumers at the heart of this study conceive their own shopping sociality as tightly connected to their intimacy ... The intensity of this intimacy ... blends with utilitarian conceptions of consumer choice that are implicit, rather than explicit. (Pantano & Gandini, 2017, p. 372)

It seems that the changes in consumption and production that apps represent can have implications on matters of relationships, trust, ethics, and morality no less than they have on choice.

Dating and Hookup Apps

These algorithmic characteristics of apps and the concerns they generate in the shopping world show up in different guises and are even more troubling when it comes to the sensitive area of dating and hookup apps.

Dating and hooking up have long cultural histories. These are two curious categories that converge in the apps: both refer to intimacies, relationships, connections, and pleasures, playing out in various forms across cultures, genders, and sexualities. Internet dating, as a phenomenon distinct from online dating, emerged during the 1990s and by the 2010s had become big business in many countries. Professional introductions agencies, matchmaking agencies, and dating agencies prefigured Internet dating businesses, as had the "personal" columns of magazines. Sexual identities and cultures took a new turn via the layers of pre-Internet network communities such as newsgroups, erotic bulletin board systems (BBS), or sex chat and telephone information lines (e.g. the French Minitel system) (Chaplin, 2014). Then came the Internet and evolving online spaces such as the Internet relay chat (IRC) and other kinds of chatrooms (Campbell, 2004), together with messaging technologies, web cultures, and so on (Berry et al., 2003). Dating websites such as E-Harmony, Match. com, Ashley Madison (a website for married people seeking affairs), or OKCupid established themselves as lucrative businesses from the mid-1990s. Remediated and new forms of self-presentation—the profile, for instance (Ellison et al., 2012)—also emerged with Internet dating, in order to assist with scrutinizing the charms, desirability, and suitability of potential partners and intimate playmates (Ellison et al., 2006). Online dating garnered much attention from publics and researchers alike, as the latter started delving into the implications of such websites and new practices for understanding processes of relationship formation, progress, and ending, processes of communication, processes of social and sexual interplay—and also the interplay of gender, sex, class, race, disability, location, age, and other categories in the appropriation of these digital media technologies.

Early forms of mobile phone communication had explored and experimented with new possibilities. For instance, the Japanese Lovegety was an egg-shaped device for meeting potential partners that gained some currency among young people and caused a stir worldwide in the late 1980s (Crawford, 2008; Humphreys, 2013; Rheingold, 2002). Users could input data about their preferences that reflected their mood or indicated the partner they were seeking. They would set a mode through a button, and the device would beep if it detected a suitable user in a five-meter range (Iwatani, 1998). Lovegety worked by proximity rather than by locality (Humphreys, 2013; Iwatani, 1998). So do many apps that have attempted to use Bluetooth for hookups, sometimes in conjunction with WiFi or location and user data; none has been especially successful. Typically, a more popular use of Bluetooth has been sharing photos (Gye, 2007; Kray et al., 2009), especially as part of the digital sharing of intimacies (Lasén & Gómez-Cruz, 2009; Niknam, 2010). As discussed in the previous chapter, location emerged as a pervasive feature of other technologies, bridging the gap between social software, networking, and media on the one hand and mobile media on the other (Humphreys, 2013; Wilken & Goggin, 2014; Wilken, Goggin, et al., 2019). With the advent of SMS, text messaging cultures incorporated a prominent strand of intimate digital practices, especially when the maturity of camera phones, the explosion of visual digital cultures and platforms, and multimedia messaging (MMS) intersected the emergence of sexting, which triggered considerable social anxieties in many countries. These Internet, mobile, social media (Burgess et al., 2016), and digital cultural histories of sexuality and intimacy, the evolving affective properties of mobile technologies (Lasén, 2004) and of digital intimacies (Hjorth & Lim, 2012), and the changing geographies of sexuality (Nash & Gorman-Murray, 2019; Valentine & Bell, 1995) set the scene for dating and hookup apps.

Owing to their reliance on location technology, hookup apps were called for a while "geosocial" networking or media apps, or "location-aware" dating apps. Existing Internet dating sites retooled for smartphones, adding locality functionality; OKCupid's Local is an example (Slater, 2013a, 2013b). By now there is a wide field of apps adapted to users' preferences, communities, identities, locales, and desired scene. By and large, the apps attract significant usage (see Table 5.1). A Pew Research Center survey conducted in October 2019 found that 30 percent of the adult respondents had used a dating site or app before, and 11 percent had done so in the past year (Anderson et al., 2020). Many countries reported increased usage of dating apps during the lockdowns and social distancing of the COVID-19 pandemic; India reported spikes in first-time users (Chakraborty, 2020).

Table 5.1   Top 10 grossing dating apps worldwide by overall revenue, 2020.
SOURCE   Sensor Tower. (2020). Top grossing dating apps worldwide for May 2020. June 17. https://sensortower.com/blog/top-grossing-dating-apps-worldwide-may-2020.

1	Tinder
2	Bumble
3	Pairs
4	MeetMe
5	Tantan
6	Badoo
7	Tagged
8	Grindr
9	Plenty of Fish
10	Hinge

NOTES   Ranked according to revenue from both App Store and Google Play. Does not include revenue from third-party Android stores in China or other regions. App revenue estimates are from Sensor Tower's Store Intelligence platform.

It is worth noting that 41.5 percent of Tinder's revenue derived from the United States, 5.6 percent from the United Kingdom, and 5.4 percent from Japan (Sensor Tower, 2020). One market with a stark divergence is, again, China, where global leaders such as Tinder and Bumble are absent. Instead Tantan (no. 5 globally) is often referred to as the equivalent of Tinder. However, there are many other Chinese apps that dominate this geolinguistic market, which embraces China's diasporic communities overseas (see Table 5.2).

In various other markets there is, typically, a mix between a range of preferred international dating apps, regional

Table 5.2   Top 9 dating apps in China, 2020.

SOURCE   Chen, W. (2020). The nine most popular Chinese dating apps in 2020 aren't what you would expect [updated]. KrAsia, May 1. https://kr-asia.com/top-nine-chinese-dating-apps-in-2020-to-make-your-best-online-impression.

1	Yidui
2	Tantan
3	Momo
4	Soul
5	Yimu
6	Zhenai
7	Hezi
8	Blued
9	Rela

NOTE   China iOS app store ranking, as of April 27, 2020. Rankings are based on real-time iOS app store downloads per third-party app data tracker Chandashi.

apps, and home-grown apps. In India, for instance, Aisle is a relatively new app, billed as a "dating app with a focus": "We're a community of vibrant Indians from around the world connecting online to go on meaningful offline dates" (Aisle, 2020a). Aisle's LinkedIn profile describes this "curated" app as the "wise middle-path between traditional matrimony websites and casual dating applications" (Aisle, 2020b), which explains its reliance on a freemium model with a relatively expensive VIP subscription option.

The year 2012 is often identified as the one in which mobile dating overtook Internet dating (Sales, 2015). The political economy of dating and hooking up ventures is complex, as laid out in Wilken and colleagues' pioneering study (Wilken, Burgess, et al., 2019). For instance, subscription-based Internet dating sites such as Ashley Madison continued to hold their own for some years, until a widely publicized data leak (Tanner, 2015). From its US headquarters, Match.com parleyed its advantage as one of the first movers into dating app space by acquiring a number of popular dating apps such as Tinder, Hinge, PlentyofFish, OurTime, OKCupid, and its own Match.com, which it styled a "global leader in dating products." In May 2020, Match.com reported US$2.1 billion in revenue and 9.9 million average subscribers and highlighted—with the tag "sparking *meaningful* connections for every *single* person worldwide"—that it offers its products in forty languages to users around the world (MatchGroup, 2020).

The top grossing and most downloaded dating app is Match.com's Tinder. Tinder is predominantly heterosexual, though it is also used by people across genders and sexualities. Started in 2012 by group of friends, it was marketed to US college campuses through 2013, as a way for people to meet and connect with strangers. From there, Tinder quickly attracted a significant base of users. Initially users had to select a photo, then click on a green heart to seek to connect with someone, or alternatively reject that person with a red cross. The feature that underpinned Tinder's extraordinary success was, of course, the "swipe" function. This made it easy and fast to signal one's interest or lack of it to a potential partner. In the hothouse of mobile dating app startups and try-hards, the swipe function became the most copied feature. Tinder's intellectual property office (IPO) on the US Nasdaq in November 2015 realized a market capitalization of some US$3.5 billion (Bertoni, 2016). In 2017, Tinder rolled out a "more genders" update under the banner #alltypesallswipes, allowing users flexibility in describing and displaying their identity. This was part of a policy shift that introduced a set of measures designed to improve diversity and inclusion, and specifically "learning to be a better ally to transgender and gender non-conforming communities" (Tinder, 2016).

While Tinder is the app most often associated with what

has been termed "the hook-up culture" (Sales, 2015), it has many rivals. Bumble is an app generated directly in response to Tinder. Launched in 2015, Bumble requires women to initiate contact with matched males (in the case of same-sex partners, either would-be partner can initiate contact). Bumble was founded by Whitney Wolfe, one of the co-founders of Tinder, after she left the organization and sued it for sexual harassment, settling out of court (Alter, 2015). In her quest to develop Bumble as an avowedly "feminist" app, Wolfe combined forces with Andrey Andreev, the founder of the leading European social media app Badoo (Yashari, 2016). She started with a "swipe" feature similar to Tinder's and experimented with and incorporated various features such as photo authentication and in-app voice calls and messaging. In 2020 Bumble claimed over 100 million users worldwide. It has been criticized for its fixation on narrow norms of gender, inscribed into systems "optimized for straight cisgender women," and for its tendency to simplify the fluidity and diversity of masculinities (Bivens & Hoque, 2018, p. 445).

Another much used and discussed app is Grindr. Grindr preceded Tinder, launching as an iOS app in March 2009. Subsequently it claimed to be the "world's largest social networking app for gay, bi, trans, and queer people," promoting itself as "a safe space where you can discover, navigate, and get zero feet away from the queer world around you" (Grindr, 2020). Like Tinder, Grindr has become an important app for people who want to connect with their communities and feel that they belong in them (Shield, 2019). This approach has underscored its prospects for profitability. Consequently Grindr was acquired in two tranches, in 2016 and 2018, by the Chinese video game and software development firm Kunlun Tech. These attempts on Grindr ran afoul of the growing suspicion against Chinese government access to data on apps, discussed earlier in the book. Such national security concerns in the US government forced Kunlun Tech to divest its ownership of Grindr: "data from the app's some 27 million users could be used by the Chinese government" (Whittaker, 2020). A fix was provided when the US-based company San Vicente Acquisition Partners agreed to buy a 98 percent stake in the company (Reuters, 2020).

Grindr is but one out of many queer dating and hookup apps. These include apps for specific communities such as Scruff, the bear community (Batiste, 2013; Roth, 2014). There is also Jack'd, an app that prides itself on being the "most inclusive dating app for QPOC [queer people of color]." Then there is a range of lesbian dating and hookup apps such as Hong Kong's Butterfly (Choy, 2018). Lesbian dating apps were often considered by various actors to be slow to develop. Sarah Murray and Megan Sapnar Ankerson questioned this assumption in their account of the design of "lesbian contact" in the Dutch app Dattch, where they look at the nuances of the tension between "queer timelines of everyday lived experience" and the placement of an app in a "fast-paced market that necessitates both a distilled message for investors and an inclusive enough product to be scalable" (Murray & Sapnar Ankerson, 2016, p. 67). As is evident, many apps either are implicitly shaped by the geographies of their incubation, use, and circulation or reference explicitly particular sexual and gender communities across countries. China, for instance, has launched a number apps for LGBTQI+ communities. One of them is the Blued app (Wang, 2020a), dubbed the Chinese Grindr, which in English features the tagline "One world. One gay social app." In 2020, Blued claimed over forty million users, most of them in China, but also many diasporic users from around the world (Wang, 2020b).

Dating and hookup apps crystallize questions about changes in the social organization of sexuality, pleasure, and power (Laumann et al., 1994), not to mention the sexual organization, markets, and networks of places and spaces such as cities (Laumann et al., 2004). Overall, there are important questions regarding where apps fit into a deeper understanding of how the social is structured by the sexual (Adkins & Merchant, 1996).

What role apps such as Tinder have in contemporary sexuality and relationships and how they differ from online dating agencies has been widely discussed (see Gatter & Hodkinson, 2016). There has been considerable debate over the meanings, affordances, constraints, and possibilities of what Gaby David and Carolina Cambre term the "swipe logic" of Tinder as an app and as a platform. The two authors contend that, in their Paris study, "users revealed how they work to communicate otherwise through inventive and vernacular uses of the Tinder app" (David & Cambre, 2016, p. 9). In gay male culture, hookup apps take over and extend digital cultures; through dating and sex, they establish websites such as Gaydar, established in 1999 (Mowlabocus, 2010), not to mention earlier sexual cultures. Elija Cassidy sums up this kind of shift as a transition "from the hankie code to the hanky app" (Cassidy, 2018, pp. 23–39); and Sam Miles, in a retrospective of 30 years of queer male spaces and digital technologies, sums it up as "cruising meets locative media"—a notable stage in the "digital takeover" of queer space (Miles, 2018, pp. 6, 2). There has been wide-ranging debate on the extent to which digital technologies, especially apps, have been involved in decisive changes, or even in the skewing of previously valued identities, cultures, and spaces—for instance in the "Grindrization of gay identity" (Samuel, 2016). Discussing apps such as Grindr and Tinder in 2016, the digital anthropologist Freddy Mackee noted that "hook-up apps have now become commonplace and normative, which in turn leads us to the need of revising gay sociality from the perspective of not just one single app or affordance, but as a complex environment of tools and subject positions" (Mackee, 2016, p. 1).

In an Australian study, Kath Albury and Paul Byron suggest that "[m]obile hook-up apps could be seen to perform multiple functions for young same-sex attracted men and women: promoting a sense of belonging within 'queer cartographies'" (Batiste, 2013), facilitating intimacy and friendship, and "serving as a password-protected 'container' for sexual experimentation, picture exchange, and chat" (Albury & Byron, 2016, pp. 1–2). They tell us that "the phone was seen as a means of managing intimate encounters (including messaging and picture exchange) across different settings and contexts" (p. 1).

There are many diverse aspects of the culture of dating apps that have often been submerged in the controversies that the technologies have occasioned, particularly in mainstream society. This is a key point made by researchers of dating apps, especially those who seek to study, acknowledge, and discuss the diverse roles the apps play in people's lives. So, amid the public clamor about dating apps, there is still a fair way to go to understand how these forms of digital media intersect with sexual practices and intimacies, positive as well as negative—that is, to grasp the "new forms of intimacy and relationality associated with digital cultures" (Albury et al., 2020). There has been the novelty of the technologies. There have been the ways in which our practices and notions of the social change along with these technologies and through them and the ways in which these apps and the related technologies bring to the surface aspects of sexuality and sexual culture that are little known and in many cases are contested or curtailed by other groups in societies. This applies especially to non-normative sexualities and genders, but also to non-normative practices in dominant social formations.

Alongside "classic" or clearly labeled hookup apps, there are a wide range of others, used for seeking partners and sexual and other intimacies, for example messaging apps such as LINE, which is popular in Asian cultures, both at home and in the diaspora (Cassidy & Wang, 2018). Various researchers have drawn attention to off-label uses of hookup apps, for instance to deal with issues of visibility and multiple belonging—say, to a queer community and to the rural community one lives in (Gorman-Murray et al., 2012; Gray, 2009)—and especially to "negotiat[e] the perceptions of safety and risk associated with hooking up and dating" (Albury & Byron, 2016, p. 8). As Kath Albury and Paul Byron point out, experiences with hookup apps are not all safe or affirmative: "Both male and female app users negotiated a range of challenges in relation to the risk of being outed, harassed, or physically threatened online" (p. 2). Stefanie Duguay conceptualizes off-label uses in relation to examples from Tinder as "platform appropriations" (Duguay, 2020, pp. 31–33) that extend our understanding of technology and its adoption. Duguay proposes that "off-label use brings into focus the complications that platforms' discursive strategies, commercial imperatives, and responses to user activity— through updates to governance structures, operating models, and infrastructures—pose for users as they respond to these sociotechnical arrangements" (p. 39). In a nutshell, such interactions occur within notable constraints of design and technology as much as of imagination, by reason of an app's signature capabilities and meanings (Duguay, 2020).

These research perspectives on Tinder and a range of other dating and hookup apps show how much people rely on and improvise with these apps and the wider ecology of digital media platforms, devices, and software as they fashion new practices and arrangements in everyday life. These configurations and negotiations can be surprisingly intricate, leveraging on the changing affordances of the apps and their algorithms (Wang, 2020a). For instance, the data cultures of dating and hookup apps represent ubiquitous and much debated facets of the apps phase of digital intimacies (Chambers, 2013; Dobson et al., 2018) and, unsurprisingly, have often been the flashpoint for privacy concerns, as part of a wider set of debates concerning platform and digital media governance (Lutz & Ranzini, 2017). There are also significant ways in which apps fit into, abut, or, alternatively, generate friction within the lives and communities of those who use them. So it is important that issues of inclusion, exclusion, and inequality are brought to the fore. Such discussions embrace the effectiveness, fairness, inclusiveness, and distinctiveness of online dating for various groups, such as people with disabilities (Gavin et al., 2019; Mazur, 2017; Milbrodt, 2019).

Conclusion

In this chapter I have discussed four distinct but often overlapping areas of apps in everyday life. Within each area, there is a considerable range and diversity of apps with specific purposes, design, contexts, and users. Across this span, one meets a recurrent ambition that apps take social life in new directions. This often demands a reworking of relationships among human individuals, non-humans, things, environments, and communities. The "will to apps" across these areas has implications that extend much more widely into social life than previous media and communications did.

This versatility and the interest in apps bring with them some challenges. Apps have often been mentioned in connection with broader anxieties about trends toward antisocial behavior and the attenuation of social connectivity in various societies. This is an area where specific issues are often difficult to pin down. This is largely because antisocial behavior laws and regulations often target marginalized, minority, or less powerful groups in society, as research in Britain has shown (Hall et al., 1978; Pickard, 2014).

Often concerns are raised that particular groups—usually children or young people—are too engrossed in an app. This kind of absorption and immersion may well be music to the ears of app developers, who seek stickiness and continued use because they design apps and tweak them as vital parts of their toolkit of persuasive media. Here a broader approach to what counts as desirable and valued versus deprecated and undesirable social behavior is a must, if we wish to be able to situate actually existing app use, with its effects and consequences, in a wider picture of life course and social norms and relations. Voices in research, policy, and debates on children and young people's media have played a vital role in gathering and dissecting evidence and debunking app myths and moral panics (Goggin, 2006).

The other side of the coin is that apps have also been pressed in the service of documenting, calling out, and guarding against threats to social order and life. Many apps have been devised for users to make complaints to authorities about service or facilities failures, to report crime, to draw attention to breaches of social norms (e.g. anti-environment practices, failures in social distancing or mask wearing in the COVID-19 pandemic), or to advance social progress. These are described as instances of "smartphone apps for good" (Kugler, 2016). Such efforts run the risk of going too far. We have seen it in some cases of overzealous, app-powered "digital vigilantism" where a subject of heated debate generated online naming and shaming (Dunsby & Howes, 2019; Legocki et al., 2020), or where chauvinist and racist mobs committed acts of violence and lynching (Mukherjee, 2020). There are further complexities in seeking to leverage apps and other forms of digital media as tools of empowerment in the effort to address abuses of power, because one should also be mindful of the ways in which apps can be involved in entrenching or extending systems of control and oppression, as demonstrated in the area of domestic violence (Dragiewicz, 2018).

Across their uses and the controversies they occasion, apps play a significant role. They are nodal points in enrolling users, groups, organizations, and publics into digital infrastructures; they help enlisting people and things and making them participate in wide-ranging changes to how economy and society are organized. Apps encapsulate innovations into fine-grained, specific, and often extremely influential sociotechnical systems. They have a box seat for many of the contemporary social changes, as a result of the flexible and powerful ways in which they can concentrate, underpin, and personalize the forces, economies, and extractive capacities of digital platforms. In the process, apps assist with the reorganization of private corporations, governments, and many civil society bodies, reaping benefits from new kinds of goods, services, and infrastructures premised on data and profiling. Accordingly, apps raise many concerns—ancient, traditional, and novel—that require attention, debate, and intervention. We will discuss this range of problems in chapter 6.

CHAPTER SIX

After Apps

Whither apps? It is difficult to imagine a world without apps, or at least a digital society without them. In large part, this is because of our reliance on mobile phones, especially smartphones, across most parts of the world, in the extended shift toward a more mobile Internet and toward a growing range of mobile devices.

Inequality and exclusion go hand in hand with the social evolution of mobile and digital technologies. It is a complex dynamic. There are entrenched inequalities that shape digital participation and inclusion, and new forms and patterns of injustice associated with emerging technologies in which apps are often prominent. There are also many ways in which apps advance social progress, rights, and equalities.

Yet the smartphone-centric period of apps may well be coming to an end, or at least we have passed its high-water mark. Since fairly early on, apps have existed beyond the mobile phone, most obviously and creatively with the rise of the tablet computer, which was popularized through the introduction of the iPad. Apps are designed for a range of other hardware and operating systems and for the capabilities, constraints, environments, and social settings in which they function and take on meaning. Many of these major locations of apps also involve mobilities: laptops, watches and wearables, cars, game consoles, VR headsets, TV sets, radio frequency identification (RFID), drones and air mobility technologies, and home virtual assistant technology.

The meaning and identity of apps vary across these different technology systems. However, software is typically framed as "apps," because the actors and supporters of apps still feel, presumably, that "apps" make a difference to the bridging of digital media and society that they are charged to do.

To speak, design, promote, or use an app likely suggests characteristics that have made apps a part of everyday life of their users: ease of use and attention to user experience (UX); "one-stop shop" quality, or the capacity to integrate aspects of actions, transactions, and human–computer interaction in a way that we now find familiar (as in "learning" to use websites); and reliance on a broad range of senses, especially touch and hearing, and on new media affordances that activate and amplify capacities of hardware.

Yet one can imagine a near future in which apps have moved from being taken for granted and staying in the background to becoming wholly absorbed into technologies and the forms of social relations that go along with them. Apps will be invisible, or minimally visible, because they will revert to being just applications in a realm of software; they will lose their special status of remarkable entities. Apps (taken in this sense) would be succeeded by software that is already running on the myriad of devices imagined with the Internet of Things, as well as by software that is embedded in, and provides the fabric for, the kinds of "smart," connected, intelligent, and ICT-intensive buildings and dwellings, paths and roads, urban, rural, and even planetary geographies that developed in recent years and are being conceived, designed, and built for the future. In this politics of the future in the specific situated here-and-now situations in which we live, the imaginary app will retain its allure and productiveness for some time.

It's impossible to predict the career of any medium, apps included. But, while we wait for times after apps, there is quite a bit to reflect upon and do, as I will suggest by way of conclusion.

What Do We Know about Apps?

First, what do we know about apps, and what priority areas should we consider? Despite the reaches of research, deliberation, and debate on apps, we know surprisingly little. There are many insights into this body of knowledge, yet much of what we glimpse relates to quite specific uses, functions, and settings of apps.

This is understandable, given the kaleidoscope-nature of apps, as I have noted. Apps are bewildering in their forms and applications, and often quite complex in the way each one hooks into, draws down, and curates data, computational power, connectivity, and other capabilities from infrastructures, and also from its host devices. We do now have good studies of many kinds of apps, but there is a great deal more to be done. Especially pressing is the need for studies of apps: of their dynamics, economies, uses and meanings, implications, and effects across a wide range of international, social, and cultural settings. As we have seen from other work on international media such as television, the Internet, or location technologies, key aspects of the definition of a technology can change. This is especially true in the case of technologies as ductile and malleable as software.

We would also benefit greatly from more integrative work and theory on apps, given the various things that they may have in common as a class or that might be shared by groups of apps or by apps associated with a particular social or economic domain. Dating apps, money apps, productivity apps, ride-hailing and sharing apps, and so on target, and insert themselves into, specific areas of social life. Those interested in developing, distributing, promoting, and securing the continuous use of such apps can include a range of different business, technology, governmental, civil society, political, and other groups. However, as we have also seen, because of the commercial nature of the foundations of the system of apps, there are recurring, overlapping, and concentrated capital, financial, and business interests that shape apps.

Living With/out Apps

Must we take apps as we find them? This is a question asked throughout the career of apps that we can no longer ignore and that implicitly orients our will to know more about apps. The question of life in the presence of apps—or how to reconfigure life with or without apps—has many dimensions and is complicated, but has acquired high levels of significance and a rich meaning.

I hasten to say that I am not too convinced that the burning issues lie in the perception that apps are addictive, though clearly aspects of their design, content, milieux, and so on aim to make them persuasive, compelling, frequently used—real must-haves. We have a growing body of research and evidence that seeks to cut through the general matter of reliance upon digital technologies and digital cultures, as well as specific aspects of emerging digital societies. Apps form an important part of this inquiry, but often we do need to be careful about whether they are really "in the frame" for nominated evils and ills, and what their part really is. Similarly, much of the literature discusses, quite rightly, the good that apps might do. This is most evident in the health and medical area, where, before prescribing or receiving an app, the professional, let alone the patient or user, would really like to know whether the app in question is efficacious. We do have a great deal of work in these areas of the benefits and negatives of apps; but less attention has been paid to important realities about the spectrum of connections and disconnections via apps, their qualities, and their subtleties. There is a need now for work that goes against this grain and charts much more accurately the actual use of apps, the amount of effort, work, and value that goes into the maintenance of apps, and where apps fit into digital and social lives.

One obvious area where such an analysis is needed is the study of the environmental implications of apps. Where apps fit into broad discussions of "carbon capitalism" (Brevini & Murdock, 2017), and especially into projects of greening the smartphone and the media (Maxwell & Miller, 2012, 2020), is one topic or great import. Apps are pressed into service to assist with environmental concerns, yet it is clear that they are at the same time a big part of the problem when it comes to achieving sustainable development and just societies; and this is evident also in the area of fair work and labor (Qiu, 2016).

While we would benefit from knowing much more about fundamentals and specifics, as I have just suggested, apps constitute an important media and technology system, on which we rely in culture, economy, and elsewhere. Hence their entrenchment in society raises many more problems and questions that we need to tackle.

Here is one of the first and most crucial. As we have seen, apps rely upon a proprietary and commercial system of provision and control: the app store. There is no particular reason why apps cannot be offered outside the app store regime. However, most apps are downloaded from an app store—typically from one of the two main app stores (the Apple App Store or Google Play), or at best from a select number of them.

As we have seen, the ownership and control of app stores are strikingly concentrated in a few hands. There is some competition across markets and considerable competition at least in one market, where different players (such as local companies) have leading roles. However, there are many markets around the world, and their users depend on apps, producers, software, and ICT developers and companies where the local app stores are skewed toward the big global players, often in partnership with compradors who act for regional and local interests.

Again, a threshold problem is that we have very few

accurate and up-to-date studies of app economies around the world. There is enough indication, however, of concern about the adequacy of these arrangements, and of the need for better and fairer policy and governance arrangements. Four decades have just passed since the MacBride report *Many Voices, One World*, which sounded a clarion call, especially from decolonizing countries and emerging economies. Transnational corporations had a disproportionate role in shaping the world's media and information systems, which were crucial by then (MacBride, 1980). When we look at the current state of things in apps in relation to the goal of achieving democratic global media, we get an uncanny sense that oppressive continuity rather than much needed change is afoot (Rodriguez & Iliadis, 2019). This is resonantly articulated in new calls for global action on digital technologies, as part of the wider project of securing social progress for all (Couldry et al., 2018).

Perhaps in a more subtle, yet also definitive way, apps—in the main form we have come to download, use, and know them—represent a peculiar vision and reality of software, but also of how we enact and imagine media and the culture(s) associated with them. This was a debate that attracted some airtime at the dawn of apps, famously via Jonathan Zittrain's swingeing critique of the advent of the iPhone as a locked down system (Zittrain, 2008). His critique keys into a larger debate about commons, and especially digital commons (Schoonmaker, 2018). A major worry here is that the new kinds of enclosure via appification, for instance, are threatening to curtail the enormous potential benefits that digital technologies can offer for social participation. Such benefits might be captured by digital technology, systems, and practices that better support, or dovetail with, peer production (Franquesa & Navarro, 2017).

More recently, Zittrain has decried the decline of "layered architecture" "and "decentralization" in emerging Internet technologies, suggesting that the creeping "centralization, and exploitation of its [Internet's] users, call for action" (Zittrain, 2018, p. 871). There is greater complexity to this process, given the co-evolution of apps with infrastructures, data, new forms of interactivity, and business models; witness the baroque evolution, the immense investment, the technological capabilities, and the intricate, almost ceaseless reconfiguration of platforms that hinge on apps. All these features are demonstrated by the cases of Facebook, WeChat, TikTok, and many other platforms much less present or noticeable in the public sphere (e.g. enterprise, digital government, and other systems).

As I have noted, apps are the jewel in the crown of many digital platforms, or at least a friendly face as well as the software pivotal to connecting the many sides of digital platform markets. Also, various apps represent new incursions into and reconfigurations of social relations and culture that many people do not like, feel they have no say in or control of, and would like to resist, change, or choose not to use. A house cleaner may be hired by a person who requested his or her services via an app. Ratings, rankings, and feedback can be provided through the app, for the information and action of the app operator, as well as for the service provider. Communications between the two parties, when not occurring at the site of domestic work, are encouraged to occur via the app rather than "off-app" (i.e. directly between the parties).

Governing and Reimagining Apps

At stake in the emergence of the new social relations and politics of super apps are two overarching and entwined imperatives.

First, as emphasized in the literature on digital platforms, there is, along with a groundswell of wider work on and deep rethinking of digital technologies, an epochal call for new systems of governance that should be coordinated at all levels, from global through regional and local to national, but that should also pay heed to the specific communities and publics relevant to specific apps.

Global communication governance is at the crossroads, and apps are at the heart of this. A relatively new area, global media policy has sought over the past two or so decades to capture and address the expanded range of arenas, institutions, and actors involved in contemporary media and technologies. Apps are the paradigm. Existing global institutions—especially the UN system and previously widely supported rule-based organizations such as WTO—are under a major strain. New models of governance—for example the much vaunted multistakeholder model of Internet governance endorsed at the World Summit of the Information Society in 2003 and 2005—are being eclipsed, on the one hand by the complicated, messy evolution of the next wave of techologies and their social coordinates, which are evident in the Internet of Things, 5G, artificial intelligence, automation, and the role of algorithms, and on the other hand by a shifting geopolitics, which is rewarded by and latches onto national sovereignty, law, and policy as a way to veto and regulate apps and digital platforms.

At the level of the small worlds of apps (a level that often involves apps with sizable constitutencies and user bases), there are important issues of design, policy, configuration, price, and affordability that directly affect users. However, the license conditions and contracts that govern app users often give the lion's share of power and rights to the developers, owners, or operators of apps. And yet, as we see in social media apps, for instance, a small change to the features, affordances, design, or user interface of an app can immediately have impacts on its users' livelihood or, at a lower order of magnitude and impact, on how they interact with content, services, and other users and organizations. The treatment of data is one canary in a coal mine for many apps where data and privacy policies can still vary greatly, even after legislators, regulators, and companies have paid a great deal of attention to improving protections. There are also subtle yet large implications about changes to affordances that users feel they should be consulted about yet often are not. Social media platforms frequently provide a quick and highly effective way for users to express concerns and discontent about changes to apps, but this watchdog function tends to have a broad-brush and episodic character and to be exercised after the fact rather than incorporated into a proactive, continuous, and well-supported dialogue between apps and their users.

The bulk of the world's citizens, users, communities, and publics use apps and are deeply invested in them, or are markedly affected by apps even when they don't use them. Yet all these people are rarely invoved in the emerging systems of governance of apps. Those who live at the margins of all our societies and are enjoined to become digital find it especially difficult to have a voice and, although they attempt in many ways to make themselves heard, are rarely listened to and don't expect their interests or views to matter.

And now I come to my second point. These shortcomings and structural problems in communication create the need for a fundamental reconsideration of the peculiar ways in which many such apps are structured and imagined; a search for alternatives is required. Why are apps conceived of narrowly, as commercial or entrepreneurial opportunities? Why are they used to batten down or reduce workers' conditions, or to curtail their rights? Why are they introduced without regard for existing consumer protections, safeguards, or requirements for information and transparency, as many commercially driven digital technologies have been since the rise of the mass Internet in mid-1990s? All too often, the scenario seems to be one of apps versus the rest, or one in which apps are disruptive challengers of the existing order. Many app promoters are none too keen on the idea that the new order might be scrutinized. In consequence, many people disquieted by apps have increasingly raised their voices to ask inconvenient questions. Why can't ride-hailing apps support collectives rather than for-profit companies? In what situations could particular apps be banned? For instance, what force might the calls for bans on the use of facial recognition technologies have?

We need more radical alternatives to apps, at the various scales at which we encounter them and at the sites where they supply the props and create the conditions for our digital lives. This, I feel, is the sense in which we should think beyond apps and live without apps. At its root, this approach would restore the core insight that technology is not inexorable or inevitable, although its sunk costs, cultural scripts, and potential social imaginaries should not be underestimated. Digital technology and software in particular should be liminal zones of great imagination and flexibility.

At the very least, a debate on the futures of apps, carried out without prejudice and without any requirement that we suspend our assumptions, would help us get a clear view of the benefits of apps and apps systems—for instance, of their role in supporting innovation and in channeling its flows (to whom it goes, how, etc.)—or of the role of apps in cultural and creative economies. We may still work toward achieving digital societies in the various ways that are envisaged in the current conjuncture, but do so by decentering apps as one of the preordained pillars of these near-future societies. Rather we should take a pitiless and utterly app-agnostic perspective on what apps offer for nourishing social life, and thus on what digital life might look like at its best.

References

Abeele, M. V., Wolf, R. D., & Ling, R. (2018). Mobile media and social space: How anytime, anyplace connectivity structures everyday life. *Media and Communication*, 6(2), 5–14. doi: 10.17645/mac.v6i2.1399.

Abidin, C. (2018). *Internet celebrity: Understanding fame online*. Emerald.

Abidin, C., & Brown, M. L. (eds.). (2019). *Microcelebrity around the globe: Approaches to cultures of Internet fame*. Emerald.

Ackerman, D. (2016). *The Tetris effect: The game that hypnotized the world*. Public Affairs.

Acquah-Sam, E., & Bugre, D. (2018). Effects of mobile money on Beige Bank, Ghana. *European Scientific Journal*, 14(31), 29–57. doi: 10.19044/esj.2018.v14n31p29.

Adkins, L., & Merchant, V. (eds.). (1996). *Sexualizing the social power and the organization of sexuality*. Palgrave Macmillan.

Adomako Ampofo, A. (2016). Re-viewing studies on Africa, #Black Lives Matter, and envisioning the future of African studies. *African Studies Review*, 59(2), 7–29. https://doi.org/10.1017/asr.2016.34.

Agrawal, R. (2016). Mobile money empowering people living at bottom of pyramid and boosting socio-economic development in a big way. *Economic Analysis*, 49(1–2), 15–23.

Aisle. (2020a). Aisle: Dating app with a focus on romance over flings. https://www.aisle.co/#/home.

Aisle. (2020b). Sign up: LinkedIn. https://www.linkedin.com/company/aisle.

Akhgar, B. (ed.). (2019). *Serious games for enhancing law enforcement agencies from virtual reality to augmented reality*. Springer.

Akrich, M., Callon, M., Latour, B., & Monaghan, A. (2002). The key to success in innovation Part I: The art of interessement. *International Journal of Innovation Management*, 6(2), 187–206. doi: 10.1142/S1363919602000550.

Albergotti, R. (2019). How Apple uses its App Store to copy the best ideas. *Washington Post*, September 5. https://www.washingtonpost.com/technology/2019/09/05/how-apple-uses-its-app-store-copy-best-ideas.

Albury, K., & Byron, P. (2016). Safe on my phone? Same-sex attracted young people's negotiations of intimacy, visibility, and risk on digital hook-up apps. *Social Media + Society*, 2(4). doi: 10.1177/2056305116672887.

Albury, K., McCosker, A., Pym, T., & Byron, P. (2020). Dating apps as public health "problems": Cautionary tales and vernacular pedagogies in news media. *Health Sociology Review*, 29(3), 232–248. doi: 10.1080/14461242.2020.1777885.

Algan, E. (2013). Youth, new media, and radio: Mobile phone and local radio convergence in Turkey. In J. Loviglio & M. Hilmes (eds.), *Radio's new wave: Global sound in the digital era* (pp. 89–100). Routledge.

Alizadeh, T. (2017). An investigation of IBM's Smarter Cities Challenge: What do participating cities want? *Cities*, 63, 70–80. https://doi.org/10.1016/j.cities.2016.12.009.

Almeida, F., & Simoes, J. (2019). The role of serious games, gamification and industry 4.0 tools in the education 4.0 paradigm. *Contemporary Educational Technology*, 10(2), 120–136.

Alter, C. (2015). Whitney Wolfe wants to beat Tinder at its own game. *Time*, May 15. https://time.com/3851583/bumble-whitney-wolfe.

Ambani, M. (2018). Keynote address: Paper presented at the Republic Summit 2018. https://www.youtube.com/watch?v=NcDqx_Q6yfo.

Anders, H., Mark, O., & Mark, B. (2007). Mobile phone-based augmented reality. In H. Michael, B. Mark, & T. Bruce (eds.), *Emerging technologies of augmented reality: Interfaces and design* (pp. 90–109). IGI Global.

Anderson, C. (2004). The long tail. *Wired*, October 1. https://www.wired.com/2004/10/tail.

Anderson, C. (2006). *The long tail: Why the future of business is selling less of more.* Hyperion.

Anderson, M., Vogels, E. A., & Turner, E. (2020). The virtues and downsides of online dating. Pew Research Centre. https://www.pewresearch.org/internet/2020/02/06/the-virtues-and-downsides-of-online-dating.

Andreessen, M. (2007). The three kinds of platform you meet on the Internet. Pmarchive.com, September 16. https://pmarchive.com/three_kinds_of_platforms_you_meet_on_the_internet.html.

Andrews, T. M. (2020). Did TikTokers and K-pop fans foil Trump's Tulsa rally? It's complicated. *Washington Post*, June 22. https://www.washingtonpost.com/technology/2020/06/21/tiktok-kpop-trump-tulsa-rally.

Android. (2020a). About the platform. May 7. https://developer. android.com/guide/platform.

Android. (2020b). Android compatibility program overview. April 27. https://source.android.com/compatibility/overview.

Apecu, J., Sewankambo, I. K., & Abdalla, Y. A. (2014). Mobile money services provision in East Africa: The Ugandan experience. In A. H. Lim & B. De Meester (eds.), *WTO domestic regulation and services trade: Putting principles into practice* (pp. 201–220). Cambridge University Press.

App Annie. (2019). A look back at the top apps and games of the decade. App Annie Blog, December 16. https://www.appannie.com/en/insights/market-data/a-look-back-at-the-top-apps-games-of-the-decade.

App Annie. (2021). App Store Rankings: Index. https://www.appannie.com/indexes

App spots signs of disease in photos. (2019). *New Scientist, 244*(3251), 17. doi: 10.1016/S0262-4079(19)31905-0.

Appel, G., Libai, B., Muller, E., & Shachar, R. (2020). On the monetization of mobile apps. *International Journal of Research in Marketing, 37*(1), 93–107. doi: 10.1016/j.ijresmar.2019.07.007.

AppInChina. (2020). The AppInChina app store index. July 8. https://www.appinchina.co/market/app-stores.

Apple. (2008a). iPhone SDK downloads top 100,000. https://www.apple.com/newsroom/2008/03/12iPhone-SDK-Downloads-Top-100-000.

Apple. (2008b). iPhone SDK downloads top 250,000. https://www.apple.com/au/newsroom/2008/06/09iPhone-SDK-Downloads-Top-250-000.

Apple. (2020a). Apple and Google partner on COVID-19 contact tracing technology. https://www.apple.com/newsroom/2020/04/apple-and-google-partner-on-covid-19-contact-tracing-technology.

Apple. (2020b). A more personal health app. https://www.apple.com/sg/ios/health.

Apple & AT&T (2009). iPhone 3g commercial "There's an app for that" [video]. https://www.youtube.com/watch?time_continue=25&v=szrsfeyLzyg&feature=emb_logo.

AppLovin. (2020). Entertaining people everywhere with the world's best mobile games. https://www.applovin.com.

Aron, J. (2018). Mobile money and the economy: A review of evidence. *World Bank Research Observer, 33*(2), 135–188. https://doi.org/10.1093/wbro/lky001.

Arora, S., Ter Hofstede, F., & Mahajan, V. (2017). The implications of offering free versions for the performance of paid mobile apps. *Journal of Marketing, 81*(6), 62–78. doi: 10.1509/jm.15.0205.

Arthur, C. (2014). *Digital wars: Apple, Google, Microsoft and the battle for the Internet* (2nd edn.). Kogan Page.

Ash, J. (2015). *The interface envelope gaming and the logics of affective design*. Bloomsbury.

Ash, J. (2018). *Phase media: Space, time and the politics of smart objects*. Bloomsbury.

Ashlin, L., Adrian, M., Gavin, J. D. S., & Paul, B. (2020). Mapping platform urbanism: Charting the nuance of the platform pivot. *Urban Planning*, 5(1), 116–128. doi: 10.17645/up.v5i1.2545.

Athique, A. (2016). *Transnational audiences: Media reception on a global scale*. Polity.

Athique, A. (2019). A great leap of faith: The cashless agenda in digital India. *New Media & Society*, 21(8), 1697–1713. doi: 10.1177/1461444819831324.

Athique, A. (2020). Integrated commodities in the digital economy. *Media, Culture & Society*, 42(4), 554–570. doi: 10.1177/0163443719861815.

Athique, A., & Baulch, E. (eds.). (2019). *Digital transactions in Asia: Economic, informational, and social exchanges*. Routledge.

Atkins, B. (2019). Are super apps the future? *Forbes*, September 3.

Atton, C. (2014). Alternative media, the mundane, and "everyday citizenship." In M. Ratto & M. Boler (eds.), *DIY citizenship: Critical making and social media* (pp. 343–357). MIT Press.

Avle, S. (2020). Radio via mobile phones: The intersecting logics of media technologies in Ghana. *Media, Culture & Society*, 42(5), 789–799. https://doi.org/10.1177/0163443720923490.

Bakardjieva, M. (2012). Mundane citizenship: New media and civil society in Bulgaria. *Europe–Asia Studies*, 64(8), 1356–1374. doi: 10.1080/09668136.2012.712247.

Ball, J. (2014). Angry Birds and "leaky" phone apps targeted by NSA and GCHQ for user data. *Guardian*, January 28. https://www.theguardian.com/world/2014/jan/27/nsa-gchq-smartphone-app-angry-birds-personal-data.

Banaji, S. (2015). Behind the high-tech fetish: Children, work and media use across classes in India. *International Communication Gazette*, 77(6), 519–532. https://doi.org/10.1177/1748048515597874.

Bangwayo-Skeete, P. F., & Skeete, R. W. (2015). Can Google data improve the forecasting performance of tourist arrivals? Mixed-data sampling approach. *Tourism Management*, 46, 454–464.

Barkhuus, L., & Polichar, V. (2011). Empowerment through seamfulness: Smart phones in everyday life. *Personal and Ubiquitous Computing*, 15(6), 629–639. doi: 10.1007/s00779-010-0342-4.

Barnett, I., Torous, J., Staples, P., et al. (2018). Beyond smartphones and sensors: Choosing appropriate statistical methods for the analysis of longitudinal data. *Journal of the American Medical Informatics Association*, 25(12), 1669–1674. doi: 10.1093/jamia/ocy121.

Barns, S. (2020). *Platform urbanism: Negotiating platform ecosystems in connected cities*. Palgrave Macmillan.

Barrutia, J. M., Echebarria, C., & Paredes, M. R. (2016). Value co-creation in e-commerce contexts: Does product type matter? *European Journal of Marketing*, 50(3–4). doi: 10.1108/EJM-10-2014-0603.

Batiste, D. P. (2013). "o feet away": The queer cartography of French gay men's geo-social media use. *Anthropological Journal of European Cultures*, 22(2), 111. doi: 10.3167/ajec.2013.220207.

Beer, D. (2012). The comfort of mobile media: Uncovering personal attachments with everyday devices. *Convergence*, 18(4), 361–367. doi: 10.1177/1354856512449571.

Bell, G., & Andrejevic, M., & Barry, C., et al. (2020). What motivates people to download and continue to use the COVIDSafe app? https://www.chiefscientist.gov.au/RRIF.

Bell, K. (2018). *Game on! Gamification, gameful design, and the rise of the gamer educator*. Johns Hopkins University Press.

Benjamin, R. (2019). *Race after technology: Abolitionist tools for the new Jim code*. Polity.

Berg, A. (2020). The identity, fungibility and anonymity of money. *Economic Papers: A Journal of Applied Economics and Policy*, 39(2), 104–117. doi: 10.1111/1759-3441.12273.

Berry, C., Martin, F., & Yue, A. (eds.). (2003). *Mobile cultures: New media in queer Asia*. Duke University Press.

Berry, D. M. (2019). *Against infrasomatization: Towards a critical theory of algorithms*. Routledge.

Bertoni, S. (2016). Sean Rad. *Forbes*, January 18, p. 80.

Birkinbine, B. J., Gómez, R., & Wasko, J. (2017). *Global media giants*. Routledge.

Bivens, R., & Hoque, A. (2018). Programming sex, gender, and sexuality: Infrastructural failures in the "feminist" dating app bumble. *Canadian Journal of Communication*, 43(3), 441–459. doi: 10.22230/cjc.2018v43n3a3375.

Bogost, I., & Monfort, N. (2009). Platform studies: Frequently questioned answers. *Digital Arts and Culture 2019*, Irvine, California, December 12–19. https://escholarship.org/uc/item/01rok9br.

Boler, M. (ed.). (2008). *Digital media and democracy: Tactics in hard times*. MIT Press.

Borup, M., Brown, N., Konrad, K., & van Lente, H. (2006). The sociology of expectations in science and technology. *Technology Analysis & Strategic Management*, 18(3–4), 285–298.

Bosch, T. (2017). Twitter activism and youth in South Africa: The case of #RhodesMustFall. *Information, Communication & Society*, 20(2), 221–232. https://doi.org/10.1080/1369118X.2016.1162829.

Boudreau, K. (2010). Open platform strategies and innovation: Granting access vs. devolving control. *Management Science*, 56(10), 1849–1872. doi: 10.1287/mnsc.1100.1215.

Bourdon, J., & Méadel, C. (eds.). (2014). *Television audiences across the world: Deconstructing the ratings machine*. Palgrave Macmillan.

Bowlby, R. (2002). *Carried away: The invention of modern shopping*. Columbia University Press.

Brevini, B., & Murdock, G. (eds.). (2017). *Carbon capitalism and communication: Confronting climate crisis*. Palgrave Macmillan.

Brookshaw, C., Talley, B., & Garza, V. (1997). The Palm Pilot cult, anthropomorphic solutions, and other unfortunate trends. *InfoWorld*, 19(25), June 23, p. 64J.

Brown, D. (2020). Byte, video app from creator of Vine, is here and it's overrun with spam comments. *USA Today*, January 27. https://www.usatoday.com/story/tech/2020/01/27/byte-app-vine-creator-launches-new-short-form-video-app/4586454002.

Brühl, V. (2020). Libra: A differentiated view on Facebook's virtual currency project. *Intereconomics*, 55(1), 54–61. doi: 10.1007/s10272-020-0869-1.

Brühlmann, F. (2016). *The effects of framing in gamification: A study of failure*. Springer.

Brugger, N. (2015). A brief history of Facebook as a media text: The development of an empty structure. *First Monday*, 20(5). doi: http://dx.doi.org/10.5210/fm.v20i5.5423.

Bruhn, M., & Wieser, C. (2019). Does mobile money improve livelihoods for households in poor and remote areas? Finance and PSD Impact series, no. 55. World Bank. http://hdl.handle.net/10986/32605.

Bruno, A. (2008). Whither the widget? As social networks prep their music services, mini-apps could fall by the wayside. *Billboard*, 120, April 26, p. 18.

Brunton, F. (2013). *Spam: A shadow history of the Internet*. MIT Press.

Brunton, F. (2019). *Digital cash: The unknown history of the anarchists, utopians, and technologists who created cryptocurrency*. Princeton University Press.

Bull, M. (2000). *Sounding out the city: Personal stereos and the management of everyday life*. Berg.

Bull, M. (2007). *Sound moves: iPod culture and urban experience.* Routledge.

Bunz, M., & Meikle, G. (2018). *The Internet of Things.* Polity.

Burgess, J. (2010). Remediating vernacular creativity: Photography and cultural citizenship in the Flickr photo-sharing network. In D. Leslie, T. Edensor, N. Rantisi, & S. Millington (eds.), *Spaces of vernacular creativity: Rethinking the cultural economy* (pp. 116–125). Routledge.

Burgess, J. (2015). From "broadcast yourself" to "follow your interests": Making over social media. *International Journal of Cultural Studies,* 18(3), 281–285.

Burgess, J., Cassidy, E., Duguay, S., & Light, B. (2016). Making digital cultures of gender and sexuality with social media. *Social Media + Society,* 2(4). doi: 10.1177/2056305116672487.

Burgess, J., & Green, J. (2009). *YouTube: Online video and participatory culture.* Polity.

Butcher, L., Tucker, O., & Young, J. (2020). Path to discontinuance of pervasive mobile games: The case of Pokémon Go in Australia. *Asia Pacific Journal of Marketing and Logistics.* doi:https://doi.org/10.1108/APJML-12-2019-0710.

Cadwalladr, C., & Graham-Harrison, E. (2014). Revealed: 50 million Facebook profiles harvested for Cambridge Analytica in major data breach. *Guardian,* March 17.

Campbell, J. E. (2004). *Getting it on online: Cyberspace, gay male sexuality, and embodied identity.* Harrington Park Press.

Campbell-Kelly, M. (2003). *From airline reservations to Sonic the Hedgehog: A history of the software industry.* MIT Press.

Campbell-Kelly, M., Garcia Swartz, D., Lam, R., & Yang, Y. (2015). Economic and business perspectives on smartphones as multi-sided platforms. *Telecommunications Policy,* 39(8), 717–734. https://doi.org/10.1016/j.telpol.2014.11.001.

Canella, G. (2018). Racialized surveillance: Activist media and the policing of Black bodies. *Communication, Culture & Critique,* 11(3), 378–398. https://doi.org/10.1093/ccc/tcy013C.

Caprotti, F., & Liu, D. (2020). Emerging platform urbanism in China: Reconfigurations of data, citizenship and materialities. *Technological Forecasting & Social Change,* 151, 1196903. doi: 10.1016/j.techfore.2019.06.016.

Cassidy, E. (2018). *Gay men, identity, and social media: A culture of participatory reluctance.* Routledge.

Cassidy, E., & Wang, W. Y. (2018). Gay men's digital cultures beyond Gaydar and Grindr: LINE use in the gay Chinese diaspora of

Australia. *Information, Communication & Society* (AoIR special issue), 21(6), 851–865. doi: 10.1080/1369118X.2018.1437201.

Cavazos-Rehg, P., Krauss, M., Spitznagel, E., et al. (2015). Monitoring marijuana use and risk perceptions with Google Trends data. *Drug and Alcohol Dependence*, 146, e242–e243. doi: 10.1016/j.drugalcdep.2014.09.126.

Cavusoglu, H., Cavusoglu, H., & Geng, X. (2020). Bloatware and jailbreaking: Strategic impacts of consumer-initiated modification of technology products. *Information Systems Research*, 31(1), 240–257. doi: 10.1287/isre.2019.0883.

Certeau, M. de. (1984). *The practice of everyday life*, trans. S. Rendall. University of California Press.

Certeau, M. de, Giard, L., & Mayol, P. (2014). *Practice of everyday life*, vol. 2: *Living and cooking*, trans. T. J. Tomasik. University of Minnesota Press.

Ceruzzi, P. E. (2003). *A history of modern computing* (2nd edn.). MIT Press.

Ceruzzi, P. E. (2012). *Computing: A concise history*. MIT Press.

Chakrabarty, K. (2009). Mobile commerce, mobile banking. IDEAS Working Paper Series from RePEc. https://ideas.repec.org/p/ess/wpaper/id2338.html.

Chakraborty, D. (2020). Why Indians are flocking to dating apps to "beat" the lockdown. *Huffington Post*, May 24. https://www.huffingtonpost.in/entry/indians-dating-app-lockdown_in_5ec9796dc5b607a94dedb946.

Chambers, D. (2013). *Social media and personal relationships: Online intimacies and networked friendship*. Palgrave Macmillan.

Chambers, D. (2017). Networked intimacy: Algorithmic friendship and scalable sociality. *European Journal of Communication*, 32(1), 26–36. doi: 10.1177/0267323116682792.

Chan, M. (2014). *Virtual reality: Representations in contemporary media*. Bloomsbury .

Chandler, D., & Murray, R. (2011). Horizon of expectations. In D. Chandler & R. Murray (eds.), *A dictionary of media and communication* (p. 190). Oxford University Press.

Chaplin, T. (2014). Lesbians online: Queer identity and community formation on the French Minitel. *Journal of the History of Sexuality*, 23(3), 451–472. doi: 10.7560/JHS23305.

Chaston, I. (2016). *Entrepreneurial management in small firms*. SAGE.

Chaurasia, S. S., Verma, S., & Singh, V. (2019). Exploring the intention to use M-payment in India. *Transforming Government: People, Process and Policy*, 13(3/4), 276–305. doi: 10.1108/TG-09-2018-0060.

Chen, J. Y. (2018). Thrown under the bus and outrunning it! The logic of Didi and taxi drivers' labour and activism in the on-demand economy. *New Media & Society*, 20(8), 2691–2711. https://doi.org/10.1177/1461444817729149.

Chen, J., & Hu, X. (2013). Smartphone market in China: Challenges, opportunities, and promises. In I. Lee (ed.), *Mobile services industries, technologies, and applications in the global economy* (pp. 120–132). IGI Global.

Chen, W. (2020). The nine most popular Chinese dating apps in 2020 aren't what you would expect. KrAsia, May 1. https://kr-asia.com/top-nine-chinese-dating-apps-in-2020-to-make-your-best-online-impression.

Chen, Y., Mao, Z., & Qiu, J. L. (2018). *Super-sticky WeChat and Chinese society*. Emerald.

Cheng, A., Ren, G., Hong, T., et al. (2019). An exploratory analysis of travel-related WeChat Mini program usage: Affordance theory perspective. In J. Pesonen & J. Neidhardt (eds.), *Proceedings of information and communication technologies in tourism 2019* (pp. 333–343). Springer.

Cheng, K., Schreieck, M., Wiesche, M., & Krcmar, H. (2020). Emergence of a post-app era: An exploratory case study of the WeChat Mini-Program ecosystem. Paper presented at the 15th International Conference on Wirtschaftsinformatik, Potsdam. https://www.researchgate.net/publication/337623024_Emergence_of_a_Post-App_Era_-_An_Exploratory_Case_Study_of_the_WeChat_Mini-Program_Ecosystem.

Cheong, H. J., & Mohammed-Baksh, S. (2019). US consumer m-commerce involvement: Using in-depth interviews to propose an acceptance model of shopping apps-based m-commerce. *Cogent Business & Management*, 6(1). doi: 10.1080/23311975.2019.1674077.

Chesher, C. (2002). Why the digital computer is dead. CTHEORY. https://journals.uvic.ca/index.php/ctheory/article/view/14581.

Chess, S. (2014). Augmented regionalism: Ingress as geomediated gaming narrative. *Information, Communication & Society*, 17(9), 1105–1117. doi: 10.1080/1369118X.2014.881903.

Chess, S., & Paul, C. A. (2018). The end of casual: Long live casual. *Games and Culture*, 14(2), 107–118. doi: 10.1177/1555412018786652.

Cheung, M.-C. (2020). China's digital retail shift has accelerated in the past few months. eMarketer, June 2. https://www.emarketer.com/content/china-s-digital-retail-shift-has-accelerated-in-the-past-few-months.

Chi, T. (2018). Understanding Chinese consumer adoption of apparel mobile commerce: An extended TAM approach. *Journal of Retailing and Consumer Services*, 44, 274–284. doi: 10.1016/j. jretconser.2018.07.019.

Chih-Wen, C. (2012). The system and self-reference of the app economy: The case of Angry Birds. *Westminster Papers in Communication and Culture*, 9(1), 47–66. doi: 10.16997/wpcc.148.

Chiumbu, S. H., & Ligaga, D. (2013). "Communities of stranger-hoods?": Internet, mobile phones and the changing nature of radio cultures in South Africa. *Telematics and Informatics*, 30(3), 242–251. https://doi.org/10.1016/j.tele.2012.02.004.

Chow, K. K. N. (2013). *Animation, embodiment, and digital media: Human experience of technological liveliness*. Palgrave Macmillan.

Choy, C. H. Y. (2018). Smartphone apps as cosituated closets: A lesbian app, public–private spaces, mobile intimacy, and collapsing contexts. *Mobile Media & Communication*, 6(1), 88–107. doi: 10.1177/2050157917727803.

Chun, W. (2016). *Updating to remain the same: Habitual new media*. MIT Press.

Claburn, T. (2007). Google phone: Revolutionary or evolutionary? Google's acquisitions and patents support the suggestion that there's phone work going on. *Information Week*, August 24. https://www. informationweek.com/google-phone-revolutionary-or-evolutionary/ d/d-id/1058501?piddl_msgorder=thrd.

Clark, L. S. (2013). *The parent app: Understanding families in the digital age*. Oxford University Press.

Clayton Antitrust Act and Sherman Antitrust Act: Antitrust Trade and Regulation: Antitrust Standing: *Apple Inc. v. Pepper*. (2009). *Harvard Law Review*, 131(1), 382–391.

Cochoy, F., Licoppe, C., McIntyre, M. P., & Sörum, N. (2020). Digitalizing consumer society: Equipment and devices of digital consumption. *Journal of Cultural Economy*, 13(1), 1–11. doi: 10.1080/17530350.2019.1702576.

Collins, K. (2014). A history of handheld and mobile video game sound. In S. Gopinath & J. Stanyek (eds.), *The Oxford Handbook of Mobile Music Studies* (pp. 383–401). Oxford University Press.

Cooke, T. (2020). Metadata, jailbreaking, and the cybernetic govern-mentality of iOS: Or, the need to distinguish Digital Privacy from digital privacy. *Surveillance & Society*, 18(1), 90–103. https://doi. org/10.24908/ss.v18i1.13118 .

Copland, R., & Higgins, T. (2020). Google's exclusive search deals with Apple at the heart of US lawsuit. *Wall Street Journal*, 21 October. https://www.wsj.com/articles/googles-exclusive-search-deals-with-apple-at-heart-of-u-s-lawsuit-11603221146.

Corner, J. (1996). Mediating the ordinary: The "access" idea and television form. In J. Corner & S. Harvey (eds.), *Television times: A reader* (pp. 165–174). Arnold.

Couldry, N. (2012). *Media, society, world: Social theory and digital media practice*. Polity.

Couldry, N., & Mejias, U. A. (2019). *The costs of connection: How data is colonizing human life and appropriating it for capitalism*. Stanford University Press.

Couldry, N., Rodriguez, C., Bolin, G., et al. (2018). Media, communication and the struggle for social progress. *Global Media and Communication*, 14(2), 173–191. doi: 10.1177/1742766518776679.

Craig, A. (2013). *Understanding augmented reality*. Morgan Kaufmann.

Crawford, A. (2008). Taking social software to the streets: Mobile cocooning and the (an-) erotic city. *Journal of Urban Technology*, 15(3), 79–97. doi: 10.1080/10630730802677970.

Cunningham, S., & Craig, D. (2019). *Social media entertainment: The new intersection of Hollywood and Silicon Valley*. NYU Press.

Curwen, P., & Whalley, J. (2009). *The internationalisation of mobile telecommunications: Strategic challenges in a global market*. Edward Elgar.

Curwen, P., & Whalley, J. (2010). *Mobile telecommunications in a high-speed world: Industry structure, strategic behaviour, and socio-economic impact*. Ashgate.

Curwen, P., Whalley, J., & Vialle, P. (2019). *Disruptive activity in a regulated environment: The case of telecommunications*. Emerald.

Cusumano, M. (2011). Platform wars come to social media. *Communications of the ACM*, 54(4), 31–33. doi: 10.1145/1924421.1924433.

Cuthbertson, R., Furseth, P. I., & Ezell, S. J. (2015). Apple and Nokia: The transformation from products to services. In R. Cuthbertson, P. I. Furseth, & S. J. Ezell (eds.), *Innovating in a service-driven economy: Insights, application, and practice* (pp. 111–129). Palgrave Macmillan.

Dai, S., & Chau, K. H. (2018). China's Sogou banks on AI-powered answers to your questions in battle for search lead. *South China Morning Post*, May 28. https://www.scmp.com/tech/tech-leaders-and-founders/article/2147838/chinas-sogou-banks-ai-powered-answers-your-questions.

Daly, A. (2016). *Socio-legal aspects of the 3D printing revolution*. Palgrave Macmillan.

David, G., & Cambre, C. (2016). Screened intimacies: Tinder and the swipe logic. *Social Media + Society*, 2(2). doi: 10.1177/2056305116641976.

Davis, S. & Straubhaar, J. (2020). Producing antipetismo: Media activism and the rise of the radical, nationalist right in contemporary Brazil. *International Communication Gazette*, 82(1), 82–100. https://doi.org/10.1177/1748048519880731.

de Looper, C. (2019). From Android 1.0 to Android 10, here's how Google's OS evolved over a decade. Digital Trends, October 25. https://www.digitaltrends.com/mobile/android-version-history.

de Souza e Silva, A. (2009). Hybrid reality and location-based gaming: Redefining mobility and game spaces in urban environments. *Simulation & Gaming*, 40(3), 404–424. doi: 10.1177/1046878108314643.

de Souza e Silva, A., & Frith, J. (2012). *Mobile interfaces in public spaces: Locational privacy, control, and urban sociability*. Routledge.

Desai, K. (2020). United Kingdom: The CMA's report, online platforms and digital advertising, in context. *CoRe*, 4(3), 210–222. https://doi.org/10.21552/core/2020/3/9.

Di Ionno, M., & Mandel, M. (2016). Tracking Colombia's apps economy. https://www.progressivepolicy.org/wp-content/uploads/2016/10/Colombia-ENGLISH.pdf.

Dieter, M., Gerlitz, C., Helmond, A., et al. (2019). Multi-situated app studies: Methods and propositions. *Social Media + Society*, 5(2), 1–15. doi: 10.1177/2056305119846486.

Dieter, M., & Tkacz, N. (2020). The patterning of finance/security: A designerly walkthrough of challenger banking apps. Computational Culture, 7. http://computationalculture.net/the-patterning-of-finance-security.

Dietz, M., Sengupta, J., & Zhou, N. (2018). Banking needs an ecosystem play. *McKinsey Quarterly*, 1, 88–91.

Dillon, R. (2011). *The golden age of video games: The birth of a multibillion dollar industry*. A. K. Peters and CRC Press.

Dobson, A. S., Robards, B., & Carah, N. (eds.). (2018). *Digital intimate publics and social media*. Palgrave Macmillan.

Dodd, N. (2014). *The social life of money*. Princeton University Press.

Dong, Y., Chung, M., Zhou, C., & Venkataraman, S. (2018). Banking on "mobile money": The implications of mobile money services on the value chain. *Manufacturing & Service Operations Management*, 21(2). doi: 10.1287/msom.2018.0717.

Donner, J. (2015). *After access: Inclusion, development, and a more mobile Internet*. MIT Press.

Donner, J., & Walton, M. (2013). Your phone has Internet: Why are you at a library PC? Re-imagining public access in the mobile internet era. In H. Ifip (ed.), *Proceedings of Human-Computer Interaction: INTERACT 2013* (pp. 347–364). Springer.

Dragiewicz, M. (2018). Technology facilitated coercive control: Domestic violence and the competing roles of digital media platforms. *Feminist Media Studies*, 18(4), 609–625. https://doi.org/1 0.1080/14680777.2018.1447341.

Dubbels, B. R. (ed.). (2017). *Transforming gaming and computer simulation technologies across industries*. IGI Global.

Duguay, S. (2016). Lesbian, gay, bisexual, trans, and queer visibility through selfies: Comparing patform mediators across Ruby Rose's Instagram and Vine presence. *Social Media + Society*, 2(2). doi: 10.1177/2056305116641975.

Duguay, S. (2020). You can't use this app for that: Exploring off-label use through an investigation of Tinder. *Information Society*, 36(1), 30–42. doi: 10.1080/01972243.2019.1685036.

Dunsby, R., & Howes, L. M. (2019). The NEW adventures of the digital vigilante! Facebook users' views on online naming and shaming. *Australian & New Zealand Journal of Criminology*, 52(1), 41–59. https://doi.org/10.1177/0004865818778736.

Economic Times. (2018). Mukesh Ambani says "data colonisation" as bad as physical colonisation. December 19. https://economictimes. indiatimes.com/news/company/corporate-trends/mukesh-ambani-says-data-colonisation-as-bad-as-physical-colonisation/articleshow/ 67164810.cms.

Edmond, M. (2015). All platforms considered: Contemporary radio and transmedia engagement. *New Media & Society*, 17(9), 1566–1582. https://doi.org/10.1177/1461444814530245.

Ehrenhard, M., Wijnhoven, F., van den Broek, T., & Stagno, M. Z. (2017). Unlocking how start-ups create business value with mobile applications: Development of an app-enabled business innovation cycle. *Technological Forecasting & Social Change*, 115, 26–36. doi: 10.1016/j.techfore.2016.09.011.

Einav, L., Levin, J., Popov, I., & Sundaresan, N. (2014). Growth, adoption, and use of mobile e-commerce. *American Economic Review*, 104(5), 489–494. doi: 10.1257/aer.104.5.489.

Elkins, E. (2019). Algorithmic cosmopolitanism: On the global claims of digital entertainment platforms. *Critical Studies in Media Communication*, 36(4), 376–389. doi: 10.1080/15295036. 2019.1630743.

Ellis, K., & Goggin, G. (2016). Disability, locative media, and complex ubiquity. In U. Ekman, J. D. Bolter, L. Díaz, et al. (eds.), *Ubiquitous computing, complexity, and culture* (pp. 270–285). Routledge.

Ellison, N. B., Hancock, J. T., & Toma, C. L. (2012). Profile as promise: A framework for conceptualizing veracity in online dating self-presentations. *New Media & Society*, 14(1), 45–62. doi: 10.1177/1461444811410395.

Ellison, N. B, Heino, R., & Gibbs, J. (2006). Managing impressions online: Self-presentation processes in the online dating environment. *Journal of Computer-Mediated Communication*, 11(2), 415–441. doi: 10.1111/j.1083-6101.2006.00020.x.

Espinoza, J. (2020). Google's $2bn Fitbit deal faces longer EU probe. *Financial Times*, July 30. https://www.ft.com/content/6b29015d-af2b-4c85-b2c3-14eb5f40c929 (available on subscription).

Estrada-Jiménez, J. (2019). On the regulation of personal data distribution in online advertising platforms. *Engineering Applications of Artificial Intelligence*, 82, 13–29. https://doi.org/10.1016/j.engappai.2019.03.013.

Evans, L. (2015). *Locative social media: Place in the digital age*. Palgrave Macmillan.

Evans, L., & Saker, M. (2017). *Location-based social media: Space, time and identity*. Palgrave Macmillan.

Ezrachi, A., & Stucke, M. E. (2019). *Virtual competition: The promise and perils of the algorithm-driven economy*. Harvard University Press.

Face ID firms battle Covid-19 as users shun fingerprinting. (2020). *Biometric Technology Today*, 4(1–2). doi: 10.1016/S0969-4765(20)30042-4.

Fantazzini, D., & Toktamysova, Z. (2015). Forecasting German car sales using Google data and multivariate models. *International Journal of Production Economics*, 170, 97–135. doi: 10.1016/j.ijpe.2015.09.010.

Farman, J. (2012). *Mobile interface theory: Embodied space and locative media*. Routledge.

Farman, J. (ed.). (2014). *The mobile story: Narrative practices with locative technologies*. Routledge.

Feldman, B. (2018). Agency and governance: Pokémon-Go and contested fun in public space. *Geoforum*, 96, 289–297. doi: 10.1016/j.geoforum.2018.08.025.

Fernandes, T., & Oliveria, E. (2021). Understanding consumers' acceptance of automated technologies in service encounters: Drivers of digital voice assistants adoption. *Journal of Business Research*, 122, 180–191. https://doi.org/10.1016/j.jbusres.2020.08.05.

Fernandez, M. D. M., Hernandez, J. D. S., Gutierrez, J. M., et al. (2017). Using communication and visualization technologies with senior citizens to facilitate cultural access and self-improvement. *Computers in Human Behavior*, 66, 329–344. doi: 10.1016/j.chb.2016.10.001.

Fibæk Bertel, T., & Ling, R. (2016). "It's just not that exciting anymore": The changing centrality of SMS in the everyday lives of young Danes. *New Media & Society*, 18(7), 1293–1309. doi: 10.1177/1461444814555267.

Fischer, D. (2020). Facebook invests $5.7 billion in India's Jio platforms. April 21. https://about.fb.com/news/2020/04/facebook-invests-in-jio.

Fitzek, F. H. P., & Reichert, F. (2007). Introduction to mobile phone programming. In F. H. P. Fitzek & F. Reichert (eds.), *Mobile phone programming and its application to wireless networking* (pp. 3–20). Springer.

Foley, P. (2000). Internet editorial. *European Business Review*, 12(6). https://doi.org/10.1108/ebr.2000.05412fag.001.

Fondeur, Y., & Karame, F. (2013). Can Google data help predict French youth unemployment? *Economic Modelling*, 30(C), 117–125.

Forsyth, E. (2011). Ar u feeling appy? Augmented reality, apps and mobile access to local studies information. *Australasian Public Libraries and Information Services*, 24(3), 125, n.p.

Franquesa, D., & Navarro, L. (2017). Sustainability and participation in the digital commons. *Interactions*, 24(3), 66–69. doi: 10.1145/3058139.

Frissen, V. (ed.). (2015). *Playful identities: The ludification of digital media cultures*. Amsterdam University Press.

Frith, J. (2014). Communicating through location: The understood meaning of the Foursquare check-in. *Journal of Computer-Mediated Communication*, 19(4), 890–905. doi: 10.1111/jcc4.12087.

Frith, J. (2015a). Communicating behind the scenes: A primer on radio frequency identification (RFID). *Mobile Media & Communication*, 3(1), 91–105. doi: 10.1177/2050157914554728.

Frith, J. (2015b). *Smartphones as locative media*. Polity.

Frith, J. (2019). *A billion little pieces: RFID and the structures of identification*. MIT Press.

Frith, J., & Wilken, R. (2019). Social shaping of mobile geomedia services: An analysis of Yelp and Foursquare. *Communication and the Public*, 4(2), 133–149. doi: 10.1177/2057047319850200.

Fröhlich, M. (2014). The smartphone patent wars saga: Availability of injunctive relief for standard essential patents. *Journal of Intellectual Property Law & Practice*, 9(2), 156–159. doi: 10.1093/jiplp/jpt231.

Fung, B. (2019). The app-store war between Netflix and Apple is heating up. *Washington Post*, January 5. https://www.washingtonpost.com/technology/2019/01/04/app-store-war-between-netflix-apple-is-heating-up.

Funk, J. L. (2001). *The mobile Internet: How Japan dialed up and the West disconnected.* ISI.

Funk, J. L. (2002). *Global competition between and within standards: The case of mobile phones.* Palgrave.

Furnée, J. H., & Lesger, C. (eds.). (2014). *The landscape of consumption: Shopping streets and cultures in Western Europe, 1600–1900.* Palgrave Macmillan.

Fussell, S. (2020). The Apple–Google contact tracing plan won't stop Covid alone. *Wired*, April 14. https://www.wired.com/story/apple-google-contact-tracing-wont-stop-covid-alone.

Galetovic, A., Haber, S., & Zaretzki, L. (2018). Is there an anticommons tragedy in the world smartphone industry? *Berkeley Technology Law Journal*, 32(4), 1527–1557.

Galloway, A. R. (2006). *Gaming: Essays on algorithmic culture.* University of Minnesota Press.

García Canclini, N. (1989). *Hybrid cultures: Strategies for entering and leaving modernity.* University of Minnesota Press.

García Canclini, N. (2014). *Imagined globalization.* Duke University Press.

Gardner, H., & Davis, K. (2013). *The app generation: How today's youth navigate identity, intimacy, and imagination in a digital world.* Yale University Press.

Gase, M. (2014). Super apps: Superintendents tell us which apps they can't live without, and how they utilize them on the course. *Golfdom*, 70(9), 36, 38.

Gatter, K., & Hodkinson, K. (2016). On the differences between Tinder™ versus online dating agencies: Questioning a myth: An exploratory study. *Cogent Psychology*, 3(1), 1–12. doi: 10.1080/23311908.2016.1162414.

Gaudin, S. (2010). Google, China play game of cat and mouse: Google's end run around censorship rules draws a subdued response from China. *Computerworld*, 44(7), April 5, p. 8. https://www.computerworld.com/article/2550610/google--china-play-game-of-cat-and-mouse.html.

Gavin, J., Rees-Evans, D., Duckett, A., & Brosnan, M. (2019). The attractiveness, trustworthiness and desirability of autistic males' online dating profiles. *Computers in Human Behavior*, 98, 189–195. doi: 10.1016/j.chb.2019.04.016.

Gehl, R. W. (2014). *Reverse engineering social media: Software, culture, and political economy in new media capitalism.* Temple University Press.

Geissinger, A., Laurell, C., & Sandström, C. (2020). Digital disruption beyond Uber and Airbnb: Tracking the long tail of the sharing economy. *Technological Forecasting & Social Change*, 155, 119323. doi: 10.1016/j.techfore.2018.06.012.

Gerber, B. (1995). Messaging: Are you prepared for the super apps of tomorrow? *Network Computing*, 6 (12), Oct. 1, p. 74. https://ntu-sp.primo.exlibrisgroup.com/permalink/65NTU_INST/iuhkic/cdi_proquest_reports_215440674.

Geroimenko, V. (ed.). (2019). *Augmented reality games: Understanding the Pokémon GO phenomenon*. Springer.

Gervasio, D. (2019). Apps, AI, and automated fake news detection. *Information Outlook*, 23(2), 9–12.

Gilder, G. (2018). *Life after Google: The fall of big data and the rise of the blockchain economy*. Regnery Gateay.

Gillespie, T. (2010). The politics of "platforms." *New Media & Society*, 12(3), 347–364. doi: 10.1177/1461444809342738.

Gillespie, T. (2014). The relevance of algorithms. In P. Boczkowski & K. Foot (eds.), *Media technologies: Essays on communication, materiality, and society* (pp. 167–193). MIT Press.

Gillespie, T. (2018). *Custodians of the Internet: Platforms, content moderation, and the hidden decisions that shape social media*. Yale University Press.

Glazer, R., Asirvatham, B. J., Mai, T., et al. (2017). *Palm computing in 1994*. Haas School of Business, University of California. http://dx.doi.org/10.4135/9781526410788.

Global mobile apps [report]. (2019). MarketLine, December. https://store.marketline.com/report/ohmf8279--global-mobile-apps-6.

Goethe, O. (2019). *Gamification mindset*. Springer.

Goggin, G. (2000). Pay per browse? The web's commercial futures. In D. Gauntlett (ed.), *Web.studies: Rewiring media studies for the digital age* (pp. 103–112). Arnold.

Goggin, G. (2006). *Cell phone culture: Mobile technology in everyday life*. Routledge.

Goggin, G. (2008). Cultural studies of mobile communication. In J. E. Katz (ed.), *Handbook of mobile communication studies* (pp. 353–366). MIT Press.

Goggin, G. (2009). Adapting the mobile phone: The iPhone and its consumption. *Continuum*, 23(2), 231–244. doi: 10.1080/10304310802710546.

Goggin, G. (2011). *Global mobile media*. Routledge.

Goggin, G. (2012). Google phone rising: The Android and the politics of open source. *Continuum*, 26(5), 741–752. doi: 10.1080/10304312.2012.706462.

Goggin, G. (2014). Facebook's mobile career. *New Media & Society*, 16(7), 1068–1086. doi: 10.1177/1461444814543996.

Goggin, G. (2017). Locating mobile media audiences: In plain view with Pokémon GO. In C. Hight & R. Harindranath (eds.), *Studying digital media audiences: Perspectives from Australasia* (pp. 1–19). Routledge.

Goggin, G. (2018). Emergence of the mobile web. In N. Brügger & I. Milligan (eds.), *SAGE handbook of web history* (pp. 297–312). SAGE.

Goggin, G. (2020). COVID-19 apps in Singapore and Australia: Reimagining healthy nations with digital technology. *Media International Australia*, 177(1), 61–75.

Goggin, G., & Crawford, K. (2011). Generation disconnections: Youth culture and mobile media. In R. Ling & S. Campbell (eds.), *Mobile communication: Bringing us together or tearing us apart?* (pp. 249–270). Transaction.

Goggin, G., & McLelland, M. (eds.). (2017). *Routledge companion to global Internet histories.* Routledge.

Goggin, G., & Spurgeon, C. (2007). Premium rate culture: The new business of mobile interactivity. *New Media & Society*, 9(5), 753–770. doi: 10.1177/1461444807080340.

Golden, A. G., & Geisler, C. (2007). Work–life boundary management and the personal digital assistant. *Human Relations*, 60(3), 519–551. doi: 10.1177/0018726707076698.

Golder, P. N., Shacham, R., & Mitra, D. (2009). Findings: Innovations' origins: When, by whom, and how are radical innovations developed? *Marketing Science*, 28(1), 166–179. doi: 10.1287/mksc.1080.0384.

Goodyear, V. (2019). Young people learning about health: The role of apps and wearable devices. *Learning, Media and Technology*, 44(2), 193–210. https://doi.org/10.1080/17439884.2019.153901.

Google. (2020). About the Android Open Source project. https://source.android.com.

Gorman-Murray, A., Pini, B., & Bryant, L. (eds.). (2012). *Sexuality, rurality, and geography.* Lexington Books.

Gould, T. (2014). I'd like to buy the world a Coke: One culture via apps and global advertising. *Publishing Research Quarterly*, 30(3), 282–294. doi: 10.1007/s12109-014-9371-6.

Graham, M. (ed.). (2019). *Digital economies at global margins.* MIT Press.

Gray, M. L. (2009). *Out in the country: Youth, media, and queer visibility in rural America.* NYU Press.

Green, B. (2019). *The smart enough city: Putting technology in its place to reclaim our urban future.* MIT Press.

Gregg, M. (2015). Hack for good: Speculative labour, app development and the burden of austerity. *Fibreculture Journal* 25, 183–201. doi: 10.15307/fcj.25.186.2015.

Grindr. (2020). About: Zero feet away. https://www.grindr.com/about.

Grundy, Q., Chiu, K., Held, F., et al. (2019). Data sharing practices of medicines related apps and the mobile ecosystem: Traffic, content, and network analysis. *BMJ*, 364. doi: 10.1136/bmj.l920.

Guarneri, M. R., Sironi, R., & Perego, P. (2019). Introduction. In G. Andreoni, P. Perego, & E. Frumento (eds.), *Health: Current and future applications* (pp. 1–4). Springer.

Guo, H., Zhao, X., Hao, L., & Liu, D. (2019). Economic analysis of reward advertising. *Production and Operations Management*, 28(10), 2413–2430. doi: 10.1111/poms.13015.

Guohua, Z. (2019). Shopping "natural" and "local" food as everyday resistance: Digitisation, platformisation, and online retail of rural products. In L. Scheen, Y. Fai Chow, & J. De Kloet (eds.), *Boredom, shanzhai, and digitisation in the time of creative China* (pp. 283–290). Amsterdam University Press.

Gye, L. (2007). Picture this: The impact of mobile camera phones on personal photographic practices. *Continuum*, 21(2), 279–288. https://doi.org/10.1080/10304310701269107.

Haas, M. (2006). *Management of innovation in network industries: The mobile Internet in Japan and Europe.* Deutscher Universitätsverlag.

Haddon, L. (2004). *Information and communication technologies in everyday life: A concise introduction and research guide.* Berg.

Haddon, L., Fortunati, L., Kant, A., et al. (eds.). (2005). *Everyday innovators: Researching the role of users in shaping ICTs.* Springer.

Haddon, L., & Vincent, J. (eds.). (2018). *Smartphone cultures.* Routledge.

Haiyan, H., & Yuan, G. (2015). Phone firms dial into smarter world. *China Daily*, May 29. http://www.chinadaily.com.cn/a/201507/10/WS5a2b5597a310eefe3e99fdc7.html.

Hall, S., Critcher, C., Jefferson, T., Clarke, J., & Roberts, B., et al. (1978). *Policing the crisis: Mugging, the state, and law and order.* Macmillan.

Hampshire, K., Porter, G., Owusu, S. A. et al. (2015). Informal m-health: How are young people using mobile phones to bridge healthcare gaps in Sub-Saharan Africa? *Social Science & Medicine*, 142, 90–99. doi: 10.1016/j.socscimed.2015.07.033.

Hamrick, K. B. (1996). The history of the hand-held electronic calculator. *American Mathematical Monthly*, 103(8), 633–639. doi: 10.2307/2974875.

Hao, L., Guo, H., & Easley, R. F. (2017). A mobile platform's in-app advertising contract under agency pricing for app sales. *Production and Operations Management*, 26(2), 189–202. doi: 10.1111/poms.12647.

Heerden, A. v., Tomlinson, M., & Swartz, L. (2012). Point of care in your pocket: A research agenda for the field of m-health. *Bulletin of the World Health Organization*, 90(5), 393–394. doi: 10.2471/BLT.11.099788.

Heller, A. (1984). *Everyday life*, trans. G. L. Campbell. Routledge.

Helmond, A., Nieborg, D. B., & van Der Vlist, F. N. (2019). Facebook's evolution: Development of a platform-as-infrastructure. *Internet Histories*, 3(2), 123–146. doi: 10.1080/24701475.2019.1593667.

Henman, P. (2019). Of algorithms, apps and advice: Digital social policy and service delivery. *Journal of Asian Public Policy*, 12(1), 71–89. doi: 10.1080/17516234.2018.1495885.

Henthorn, J., Kulak, A., Purzycki, K., & Vie, S. (eds.). (2019). *The Pokémon Go phenomenon: Essays on public play in contested spaces*. McFarland.

Hern, A. (2020a). Digital contact tracing will fail unless privacy is respected, experts warn. *Guardian*, April 20. https://www.theguardian.com/world/2020/apr/20/coronavirus-digital-contact-tracing-will-fail-unless-privacy-is-respected-experts-warn.

Hern, A. (2020b). France urges Apple and Google to ease privacy rules on contact tracing. *Guardian*, April 21. https://www.theguardian.com/world/2020/apr/21/france-apple-google-privacy-contact-tracing-coronavirus.

Hern, A. (2020c). New vulnerability allows users to "jailbreak" iPhones. *Guardian*, May 26. https://www.theguardian.com/technology/2020/may/26/first-iphone-jailbreak-in-four-years-released.

Hern, A. (2020d). NHS in standoff with Apple and Google over coronavirus tracing. *Guardian*, April 16. https://www.theguardian.com/technology/2020/apr/16/nhs-in-standoff-with-apple-and-google-over-coronavirus-tracing.

Hesmondhalgh, D., & Lobato, R. (2019). Television device ecologies, prominence and datafication: The neglected importance of the set-top box. *Media, Culture & Society*, 41(7), 958–974. doi: 10.1177/0163443719857615.

Hesmondhalgh, D., & Lotz, A. (2020). Video screen interfaces as new sites of media circulation power. *International Journal of Communication*, 14, 386–409. https://ijoc.org/index.php/ijoc/article/view/13261/2913.

Hesselberth, P. (2018). Discourses on disconnectivity and the right to disconnect. *New Media & Society*, 20(5), 1994–2010.

Highmore, B. (2002). *Everyday life and cultural theory: An introduction*. Routledge.

Hillebrand, F. (ed.). (2002). *GSM and UMTS: The creation of global mobile communication*. Wiley.

Hjorth, L. (2009). *Mobile media in the Asia–Pacific: Gender and the art of being mobile*. Routledge.

Hjorth, L., & Arnold, M. (2013). *Online @ AsiaPacific: Mobile, social, and locative media in the Asia–Pacific*. Routledge.

Hjorth, L., & Lim, S. S. (2012). Mobile intimacy in an age of affective mobile media. *Feminist Media Studies*, 12(4), 477–484. doi: 10.1080/14680777.2012.741860.

Hjorth, L., & Richardson, I. (2014). *Gaming in social, locative, and mobile media*. Palgrave Macmillan.

Hjorth, L., & Richardson, I. (2017). Pokémon GO: Mobile media play, place-making, and the digital wayfarer. *Mobile Media & Communication*, 5(1), 3–14. doi: 10.1177/2050157916680015.

Hobbis, G. (2020). *The digitizing family: An ethnography of Melanesian smartphones*. Springer.

Hodson, H. (2012). Google's Ingress game is a gold mine for augmented reality. *New Scientist*, 216(2893), 19. doi: 10.1016/S0262-4079(12)63058-9.

Hoefflinger, M. (2017). *Becoming Facebook*. AMACOM.

Hu, S., & Tanner, D. (2018). Solving the antenna paradox: Adding more antennas to your smartphone creates more noise, but 3D manufacturing will fix the problem. *IEEE Spectrum*, 55(11), 40–45. doi: 10.1109/MSPEC.2018.8513783.

Hudson, S. (2013). The app store trademark wars: New year's installment. *Trademark and Copyright Law*, January 14. https://www.trademarkandcopyrightlawblog.com/2013/01/the-app-store-trademark-wars-new-years-installment.

Hughes, N., & Lonie, S. (2007). M-PESA: Mobile money for the "unbanked" turning cellphones into 24-hour tellers in Kenya. *Innovations: Technology, Governance, Globalization*, 2(1–2), 63–81. doi: 10.1162/itgg.2007.2.1-2.63.

Hulsey, N., & Reeves, J. (2014). The gift that keeps on giving: Google, Ingress, and the gift of surveillance. *Surveillance & Society*, 12(3), 389–400. doi: 10.24908/ss.v12i3.4957.

Humphreys, L. (2013). Mobile social media: Future challenges and opportunities. *Mobile Media & Communication*, 1(1), 20–25. doi: 10.1177/2050157912459499.

Humphreys, L. (2017). Involvement shield or social catalyst: Thoughts on sociospatial practice of Pokémon GO. *Mobile Media & Communication*, 5(1), 15–19. doi: 10.1177/2050157916677864.

Humphreys, L. (2018). *The qualified self: Social media and the accounting of everyday life*. MIT Press.

Humphry, J., & Chesher, C. (2020). Preparing for smart voice assistants: Cultural histories and media innovations. *New Media & Society*. doi: 10.1177/1461444820923679.

Hyunjin, K., & Matthew, P. M. (2011). Selling you and your clicks: Examining the audience commodification of Google. *tripleC: Communication, Capitalism & Critique*, 9(2), 141–153. doi: 10.31269/triplec.v9i2.255.

IBIS World. (2020a). App development in the UK: Market research report. March. https://www.ibisworld.com/united-kingdom/market-research-reports/app-development-industry.

IBIS World. (2020b). Smartphone app developers in the US market size 2007–2025. July 21. https://www.ibisworld.com/industry-statistics/market-size/smartphone-app-developers-united-states.

Ioannides, M., Magnenat-Thalmann, N., & Papagiannakis, G. (eds.). (2017). *Mixed reality and gamification for cultural heritage*. Springer.

Irani, L. (2015). Hackathons and the making of entrepreneurial citizenship. *Science, Technology, & Human Values*, 40(5), 799–824. doi: 10.1177/0162243915578486.

Irani, L. (2019). *Chasing innovation: Making entrepreneurial citizens in modern India*. Princeton University Press.

Isaacson, W. (2011). *Steve Jobs: The exclusive biography*. Simon & Schuster.

Ishii, K. (2004). Internet use via mobile phone in Japan. *Telecommunications Policy*, 28(1), 43–58. doi: 10.1016/j.telpol.2003.07.001.

Istepanian, R. S. H., & Al-Anzi, T. (2018). m-Health 2.0: New perspectives on mobile health, machine learning and big data analytics. *Methods*, 151, 34–40. doi: 10.1016/j.ymeth.2018.05.015.

Istepanian, R. S. H., Laxminarayan, S., & Pattichis, C. S. (2006). *M-health: Emerging mobile health systems*. Springer.

ITU. (2017a). The app economy in Africa: Economic benefits and regulatory directions. http://handle.itu.int/11.1002/pub/810b386e-en.

ITU. (2017b). Global ICT regulatory outlook 2017. https://www.itu.int/pub/D-PREF-BB.REG_OUT01-2017.

Ive, J., & Zuckerman, A. (2016). *Designed by Apple in California*. Apple.

Iwatani, Y. (1998). Love: Japanese style. *Wired,*, June 11. https://www.wired.com/1998/06/love-japanese-style.

James, J. (2020). The smart feature phone revolution in developing countries: Bringing the Internet to the bottom of the pyramid. *Information Society*, 36(4), 226–235. doi: 10.1080/019 72243.2020.1761497.

Javornik, A. (2016). Augmented reality: Research agenda for studying the impact of its media characteristics on consumer behaviour. *Journal of Retailing and Consumer Services*, 30, 252–261. doi: 10.1016/j.jretconser.2016.02.004.

Ji, Y., Wang, R., & Gou, Q. (2019). Monetization on mobile platforms: Balancing in-app advertising and user base growth. *Production and Operations Management*, 28(9), 2202–2220. doi: 10.1111/poms.13035.

Jin, D. Y. (2017). *Smartland Korea: Mobile communication, culture, and society*. University of Michigan Press.

Jin, D. Y., Chee, F., & Kim, S. (2015). Transformative mobile game culture: A sociocultural analysis of Korean mobile gaming in the era of smartphones. *International Journal of Cultural Studies*, 18(4), 413–429.

Jin, D. Y., & Yoon, K. (2016). Reimagining smartphones in a local mediascape: A cultural analysis of young KakaoTalk users in Korea. *Convergence*, 22(5), 510–523. https://doi.org/10.1177/1354856 514560316.

Jing, M. (2016). Alibaba said to pay $200m for Wandoujia app store. *China Daily*, July 6. http://usa.chinadaily.com.cn/epaper/2016-07/06/content_25989439.htm.

Jobs, S. (2008). Steve Jobs introduces the App store. March 18. https://www.youtube.com/watch?v=xo9cKe_Fch8.

Jobs, S. (2010). Steve Jobs introducing the iPhone at MacWorld 2007. December 2. https://www.youtube.com/watch?v=x7qPAY9JqE4.

Johnson, J. (1988). Mixing humans and nonhumans together: The sociology of a door-closer. *Social Problems*, 35(3), 298–310. doi: 10.2307/800624.

Johnson, M. R. (2018). Casual games before casual games: Historicizing paper puzzle games in an era of digital play. *Games and Culture*, 14(2), 119–138. doi: 10.1177/1555412018790423.

Johnson, S., & Krijtenburg, F. (2018). "Upliftment," friends and finance: Everyday exchange repertoires and mobile money transfer in Kenya. *Journal of Modern African Studies*, 56(4), 569–594. doi: 10.1017/S0022278X18000435.

Alison & Co. (2015). Google's Niantic labs launches field trip for wearable devices. Niantic, April 16. https://invisioncommunity.co.uk/googles-niantic-labs-launches-field-trip-for-wearable-devices.

Juhász, L., & Hochmair, H. H. (2017). Where to catch 'em all? A geographic analysis of Pokémon Go locations. *Geo-Spatial Information Science*, 20(3), 241–251. doi: 10.1080/10095020.2017.1368200.

Jun, S.-P., Yoo, H. S., & Choi, S. (2018). Ten years of research change using Google Trends: From the perspective of big data utilizations and applications. *Technological Forecasting & Social Change*, 130, 69–87. doi: 10.1016/j.techfore.2017.11.009.

Jung-a, S., Yang, Y., & Bradshaw, T. (2019). Samsung's departure is new blow to Chinese manufacturing. *Financial Times*, October 18. https://www.ft.com/content/4d8285a2-effo-11e9-ad1e-4367d8281195.

Juul, J. (2010). *A casual revolution: Reinventing video games and their players*. MIT Press.

Kang, C., McCabe, D., & Wakabayashi, D. (2020). US accuses Google of illegally protecting monopoly. *New York Times*, October 20. https://www.nytimes.com/2020/10/20/technology/google-antitrust.html.

Katz, J. E., & Aakhus, M. (eds.). (2002). *Perpetual contact: Mobile communication, private talk, public performance*. Cambridge University Press.

Kay, A. (2008). *Oral History of Alan Kay*, interviewed by D. Spicer, recorded on November 5. Computer History Museum, Mountain View, CA. https://archive.computerhistory.org/resources/access/text/2016/08/102658340-05-01-acc.pdf.

Kelty, C. M. (2008). *Two bits: The cultural significance of free software*. Duke University Press.

Kendall, J., Machoka, P., Veniard, C. & Maurer, B. (2011). An emerging platform: From money transfer system to mobile money ecosystem. UC Irvine School of Law, Research Paper No. 2011–14. http://dx.doi.org/10.2139/ssrn.1830704.

Kennedy, M. (2020). "If the rise of the Tiktok dance and e-girl aesthetic has taught us anything, it's that teenage girls rule the Internet right now": Tiktok celebrity, girls, and the coronavirus crisis. *European Journal of Cultural Studies*, 23(6), 1069–1076.

Keogh, B., & Richardson, I. (2018). Waiting to play: The labour of background games. *European Journal of Cultural Studies*, 21(1), 13–25. doi: 10.1177/1367549417705603.

Kernan, A. B. (2018). Sustaining the growth of mobile money services in developing nations: Lessons from overregulation in the United States. *Vanderbilt Journal of Transnational Law*, 51(4), 1109–1151.

King, D. L., Delfabbro, P. H., Gainsbury, S. M., et al. (2019). Unfair play? Video games as exploitative monetized services: An examination of game patents from a consumer protection perspective. *Computers in Human Behavior*, 101, 131–143. doi:https://doi.org/10.1016/j.chb.2019.07.017.

Konradt, U., Held, G., Christophersen, T., & Nerdinger, F. W. (2012). The role of usability in e-commerce services. *International Journal of E-Business Research*, 8(4), 57–76. doi: 10.4018/jebr.2012100104.

Kolakowski, N. (2010). Nokia's Apple lawsuit deepens long-running conflict. *eWeek*, May 9. https://www.eweek.com/mobile/nokia-s-apple-lawsuit-deepens-long-running-conflict.

Kray, C., Rohs, M., Hook, J., & Kratz, S. (2009). Bridging the gap between the Kodak and the Flickr generations: A novel interaction technique for collocated photo sharing [report]. *International Journal of Human-Computer Studies*, 67(12), 1060–1072. https://doi.org/10.1016/j.ijhcs.2009.09.00.

Krieg, J.-G., Jakllari, G., Toma, H., & Beylot, A.-L. (2018). Unlocking the smartphone's sensors for smart city parking. *Pervasive and Mobile Computing*, 43, 78–95. doi: 10.1016/j.pmcj.2017.12.002.

Krill, P. (2007). JBoss adds Google Gadgets to portal software. *InfoWorld*, July 2. https://www.infoworld.com/article/2663562/jboss-adds-google-gadgets-to-portal-software.html.

Kshetri, N., Williamson, N., & Bourgoin, D. L. (2006). China: M-commerce in world's largest mobile market. In N. Dholakia, M. Rask, & R. R. Dholakia (eds.), *M-commerce global experiences and perspectives* (pp. 34–46). IGI Global.

Kugler, L. (2016). Smartphone apps for social good. *Communications of the ACM*, 59(8), 18–20. https://doi.org/10.1145/2949664.

Kunz, R. (2011). *The political economy of global remittances: Gender, governmentality and neoliberalism*. Routledge.

Kunze, P. (2014). Kidding around: Children, comedy, and social media. *Comedy Studies*, 5(1), 2–11. doi: 10.1080/2040610X.2014.905091.

Kuriyan, R., Nafus, D., & Mainwaring, S. (2012). Consumption, technology, and development: The "poor" as "consumer." *Information Technologies & International Development*, 8(1), 1–12.

Larson, E. C., Saba, E., Kaiser, S., et al. (2017). Pulmonary monitoring using smartphones. In J. M. Rehg, S. A. Murphy, & S. Kumar (eds.), *Mobile health: Sensors, analytic methods, and applications* (pp. 239–264). Springer.

Lasén, A. (2004). Affective technologies: Emotions and mobile phones. *Receiver*, 14. https://www.academia.edu/472410/Affective_Technologies._Emotions_and_Mobile_Phones.

Lasén, A., & Gómez-Cruz, E. (2009). Digital photography and picture sharing: Redefining the public/private divide. *Knowledge, Technology, & Policy*, 22(3), 205–215. https://doi.org/10.1007/s12130-009-9086-8.

Lasén Díaz, A. (2019). Lo ordinario digital: Digitalización de la vida cotidiana como forma de trabajo. *Cuadernos de Relaciones Laborales*, 37(2), 313–330. doi: 10.5209/crla.66040.

Lashitew, A. A., van Tulder, R., & Liasse, Y. (2019). Mobile phones for financial inclusion: What explains the diffusion of mobile money innovations? *Research Policy*, 48(5), 1201–1205. doi: 10.1016/j.respol.2018.12.010.

Latino Comedy Project. (2009). There's an app for that: Part 2 (iPhone parody). YouTube, August 24. https://www.youtube.com/watch?v=Ca6O8FRorbQ.

Latour, B. (1996). *Aramis, or The love of technology*, trans. C. Porter. Harvard University Press.

Latzer, M., & Festic, N. (2019). A guideline for understanding and measuring algorithmic governance in everyday life. *Internet Policy Review*, 8(2). doi: 10.14763/2019.2.1415.

Laumann, E. O., Ellingson, S., Mahay, J., et al. (2004). *The sexual organization of the city*. University of Chicago Press.

Laumann, E. O., Gagnon, J. H., Michael, R. T., & Michaels, S. (1994). *The social organization of sexuality: Sexual practices in the United States*. University of Chicago Press.

Lazakidou, A. A., Zimeras, S., Iliopoulou, D., & Koutsouris, D.-D. (eds.). (2016). *M-health ecosystems and social networks in healthcare*. Springer.

Lazer, D., Kennedy, R., King, G., & Vespignani, A. (2014). Big data: The parable of Google Flu: Traps in big data analysis. *Science*, 343(6176), 1203–1205. doi: 10.1126/science.1248506.

Leaver, T., Highfield, T., & Abidin, C. (2020). *Instagram: Visual social media cultures*. Polity.

Leaver, T., & Willson, M. (2016). Social networks, casual games and mobile devices: The shifting contexts of gamers and gaming. In T. Leaver & M. Willson (eds.), *Social, casual and mobile games: The changing gaming landscape* (pp. 1–11). Bloomsbury.

Lee, D., & Deng, R. H. (eds.). (2018). *Handbook of blockchain, digital finance, and inclusion*, vol. 2: *ChinaTech, mobile security, and distributed ledger*. Academic Press.

Lee, D., & Low, L. (2018). *Inclusive fintech: Blockchain, cryptocurrency, and ICO*. World Scientific.

Lee, J., & Shin, D.-H. (2016). Targeting potential active users for mobile app install advertising: An exploratory study. *International Journal of Human–Computer Interaction*, 32(11), 827–834. doi: 10.1080/10447318.2016.1198547.

Lee, M. S., & Soon, I. (2017). Taking a bite out of Apple: Jailbreaking and the confluence of brand loyalty, consumer resistance and the co-creation of value. *Journal of Product & Brand Management*, 26(4), 351–364. doi: 10.1108/JPBM-11-2015-1045.

Lee, W.-H., & Lin, Y-H.(2019). Online communication of visual information. *Online Information Review*, 44(1), 43–61. https://doi.org/10.1108/OIR-08-2018-0235.

Legocki, K., Walker, K., & Kiesler, T. (2020). Sound and fury: Digital vigilantism as a form of consumer voice. *Journal of Public Policy & Marketing*, 39(2), 169–187. https://doi.org/10.1177/0743915620902403.

Lehdonvirta, V. (2009). Virtual item sales as a revenue model: Identifying attributes that drive purchase decisions. *Electronic Commerce Research*, 9(1–2), 97–113. doi: 10.1007/s10660-009-9028-2.

Leorke, D. (2015). Location-based gaming apps and the commercialization of locative media. In A. de Souza e Silva & M. Sheller (eds.), *Mobility and locative media* (pp. 152–168). Routledge.

Lessig, L. (2005). *Free culture: The nature and future of creativity*. Penguin.

Li, M., Chris, K. K., & Yang, Y. (2020). Shehui Ren: Cultural production and rural youths' use of the Kuaishou video-sharing app in Eastern China. *Information, Communication & Society*, 23(10), 1499–1514. https://doi.org/10.1080/1369118X.2019.1585469.

Li, N. (2018). Tencent MyApp (Yingyong Bao): Android app stores and the appification of everything. In J. W. Morris & S. Murray (eds.), *Appified: Culture in the age of apps* (pp. 42–50). University of Michigan Press.

Liao, R. (2019). Alibaba's alternative to the app store reaches 230M daily users. Techcrunch.com, January 29. https://techcrunch.com/2019/01/29/alibaba-alipay-mini-programs-230m-users.

Liao, T. (2016). Is it "augmented reality"? Contesting boundary work over the definitions and organizing visions for an emerging technology across field-configuring events. *Information and Organization*, 26(3), 45–62. doi: 10.1016/j.infoandorg.2016.05.001.

Liao, T., & Humphreys, L. (2015). Layar-ed places: Using mobile augmented reality to tactically reengage, reproduce, and reappropriate public space. *New Media & Society*, 17(9), 1418–1435. doi: 10.1177/1461444814527734.

Licoppe, C. (2010). The "crisis of the summons": A transformation in the pragmatics of "notifications," from phone rings to instant messaging. *Information Society*, 26(4), 288–302. doi: 10.1080/01972243.2010.489859.

Light, B., Burgess, B., Duguay, S. (2018). The walkthrough method: An approach to the study of apps. *New Media & Society*, 20(3), 881–900.

Lim, S. S. (2015). On stickers and communicative fluidity in social media. *Social Media + Society*, 1, 1. https://doi.org/10.1177/2056305115578137.

Lim, S. S. (2020). *Transcendental parenting: Raising children in the digital age*. Oxford University Press.

Lin, G., Xie, X., & Lv, Z. (2016). Taobao practices, everyday life and emerging hybrid rurality in contemporary China. *Journal of Rural Studies*, 47, 514–523. doi: 10.1016/j.jrurstud.2016.05.012.

Lin, Y. (2019). E-urbanism: E-commerce, migration, and the transformation of Taobao villages in urban China. *Cities*, 91, 202–212. doi: 10.1016/j.cities.2018.11.020.

Ling, R. (2012). *Taken for grantedness: The embedding of mobile communication into society*. MIT Press.

Linke, E. (1992). New home-shopping technologies. *OECD Observer*, 178, 17–20.

Liu, J. (2020). *Shifting dynamics of contention in the digital age*. Oxford University Press.

Liu, N., & Shepherd, C. (2019). Baidu, ByteDance and the perilous business of Chinese search. *Financial Times*, October 21. https://www.ft.com/content/aff3c012-f184-11e9-ad1e-4367d8281195.

Liu, S.-F., Liu, H.-H., Chang, J.-H., & Chou, H.-N. (2019). Analysis of a new visual marketing craze: The effect of LINE sticker features and user characteristics on download willingness and product purchase intention. *Asia Pacific Management Review*, 24(3), 263–277. https://doi.org/10.1016/j.apmrv.2018.10.001.

Livingstone, S., & Blum-Ross, A. (2020). *Parenting for a digital future: How hopes and fears about technology shape children's lives*. Oxford University Press.

Lobato, R. (2019). *Netflix nations: The geography of digital distribution*. NYU Press.

Long, E. (2019). The app economy in Canada. Progressive Policy Institute. https://www.progressivepolicy.org/wp-content/uploads/2019/04/PPI_CandianAppEconomy_V7.pdf.

Loos, E., Haddon, L., & Mante-Meijer, E. A. (eds.). (2008). *The social dynamics of information and communication technology*. Ashgate.

Lotz, A. (2017). *Portals: A treatise on Internet-distributed television*. Maize Books. http://dx.doi.org/10.3998/mpub.9699689.

Lotz, A. (2019). The multifaceted policy challenges of transnational Internet-distributed television. *Journal of Digital Media & Policy*, 10(1), 27–31. doi: 10.1386/jdmp.10.1.27_1.

Lovink, G. (2011). *Networks without a cause: A critique of social media*. Polity.

Lucas, L. (2017). China tightens app store regulations. *Financial*

Times, January 16. https://www.ft.com/content/783aad54-dbc8-11e6-86ac-f253db7791c6.

Luna, U., Rivero, P., & Vicent, N. (2019). Augmented reality in heritage apps: Current trends in Europe. *Applied Sciences*, 9(13), 2756. doi: 10.3390/app9132756.

Lupton, D. (2016). *The quantified self: A sociology of self-tracking*. Polity.

Lupton, D. (2019). Australian women's use of health and fitness apps and wearable devices: A feminist new materialism analysis. *Feminist Media Studies*, 20(7), 983–998. doi: https://doi.org/10.1080/14680 777.2019.1637916.

Lupton, D. (2020). *Data selves: More-than-human perspectives*. Polity.

Lutz, C., & Ranzini, G. (2017). Where dating meets data: Investigating social and institutional privacy concerns on Tinder. *Social Media + Society*, 3(1). doi: 10.1177/2056305117697735.

Ma, B. D., Ng, S. L., Schwanen, T., et al. (2018). Pokémon GO and physical activity in Asia: Multilevel study. *Journal of Medical Internet Research*, 20(6), e217. doi: 10.2196/jmir.9670.

Ma, X. (2019). App store killer? The storm of WeChat Mini Programs swept over the mobile app ecosystem. New Media MA Research Blog, University of Amsterdam. https://mastersofmedia.hum.uva. nl/blog/20 19/09/23/app-store-killer-the-storm-ofwechat-mini-pro grams-swept-over-themobile-app-ecosystem.

MacBride, S. (1980). *Many voices, one world: Towards a new more just and more efficient world information and communication order*. Kogan Page.

Mackee, F. (2016). Social media in gay London: Tinder as an alternative to hook-up apps. *Social Media + Society*, 2(3). doi: 10.1177/2056305116662186.

Madise, S. (2019). *The regulation of mobile money law and practice in Sub-Saharan Africa*. Springer.

Madison, N., & Klang, M. (2020). The case for digital activism: Refuting the fallacies of slacktivism. *Journal of Digital Social Research*, 2, 2, 28–47. https://jdsr.se/ojs/index.php/jdsr/article/view/25/23.

Madrigal, A. C. (2012). The world is not enough: Google and the future of augmented reality. *Atlantic*, October 25. https://www.theatlantic. com/technology/archive/2012/10/the-world-is-not-enough-google-and-the-future-of-augmented-reality/264059/#.

Magaudda, P. (2010). Hacking practices and their relevance for consumer studies: The example of the "jailbreaking" of the iPhone. *Consumers, Commodities & Consumption: A Newsletter of the Consumer Studies Network*, 12(1). https://csrn.camden.rutgers.edu/pdf/12-1_ magaudda.pdf.

Magaudda, P. (2012). How to make a "hackintosh": A journey into the "consumerization" of hacking practices and culture. *Journal of Peer Production*, 2, 1–8. http://peerproduction.net/issues/issue-2/peer-reviewed-papers/how-to-make-a-hackintosh.

Mandel, M., & Long, E. (2019). The app economy in India. Progressive Policy Institute, Washington, DC. https://www.progressivepolicy.org/wp-content/uploads/2019/09/PPI_IndianAppEconomy_V3-1.pdf.

Mansell, R. (2012). *Imagining the Internet: Communication, innovation, and governance*. Oxford University Press.

Mansell, R., & Steinmuller, W. E. (2020). *Advanced introduction to platform economics*. Edward Elgar.

Martinsons, M. G. (2008). Relationship-based e-commerce: Theory and evidence from China. *Information Systems Journal*, 18(4), 331–358. doi: 10.1111/j.1365-2575.2008.00302.x.

Marwick, A. (2013). *Status update: Celebrity, publicity, and branding in the social media age*. Yale University Press.

Marwick, A. (2015). Instafame: Luxury selfies in the attention economy. *Public Culture*, 27(1), 137–160. doi: 10.1215/08992363-2798379.

Marwick, A. (2019). The algorithmic celebrity. In C. Abidin & M. L. Brown (eds.), *Microcelebrity around the globe: Approaches to cultures of Internet fame* (pp. 161–169). Emerald.

MatchGroup. (2020). Business overview. MatchGroup, May. https://s22.q4cdn.com/279430125/files/doc_downloads/2020/05/Match-Group-Business-Overview-May-2020.pdf.

Matviyenko, S., Mellamphy, N. B., Dyer-Witheford, N., & Hearn, A. (2015). Editorial: Apps and affect. *Fibreculture Journal*, 25, 1–9. http://twentyfive.fibreculturejournal.org.

Maurer, B. (2011). Afterword: Mobile money, money magic, purse limits and pins: Tracing monetary pragmatics. *Journal of Cultural Economy*, 4(3), 349–359. doi: 10.1080/17530350.2011.586857.

Maurer, B. (2012). Mobile money: Communication, consumption and change in the payments space. *Journal of Development Studies*, 48(5), 589–604. doi: 10.1080/00220388.2011.621944.

Maurer, B. (2015). *How would you like to pay? How technology is changing the future of money*. Duke University Press.

Mawejje, J., & Lakuma, P. (2019). Macroeconomic effects of mobile money: Evidence from Uganda. *Financial Innovation*, 5(1), 1–20. doi: 10.1186/s40854-019-0141-5.

Maxwell, R., & Miller, T. (2012). *Greening the media*. Oxford University Press.

Maxwell, R., & Miller, T. (2020). *How green in your smartphone?* Polity.

Mazur, E. (2017). Diverse disabilities and dating online. In M. F. Wright (ed.), *Identity, sexuality, and relationships among emerging adults in the digital age* (pp. 150–167). IGI Global.

McGee, P. (2019). Uber's quest to become the west's first super-app. *Financial Times*, October 24. https://www.ft.com/content/c5241924-f421-11e9-b018-3ef8794b17c6.

McGovern, M. F. (2019). Stacks, "pacs," and user hacks: A handheld history of personal computing. In F. Willmoth, J. Nall, & L. Taub (eds.), *Whipple Museum of the History of Science: Objects and investigations, to celebrate the 75th anniversary of R. S. Whipple's gift to the University of Cambridge* (pp. 291–231). Cambridge University Press.

McQuail, D., & Deuze, M. (2020). *McQuail's media and mass communication theory* (7th edn.). SAGE.

Meikle, G. (2012). *Media convergence: Networked digital media in everyday life*. Palgrave Macmillan.

Meikle, G. (ed.). (2018). *Routledge companion to media and activism*. Routledge.

Menni, C., Valdes, A. M., Freidin, M. B., et al. (2020). Real-time tracking of self-reported symptoms to predict potential COVID-19. *Nature Medicine, 26, 1037–1040.* doi: 10.1038/s41591-020-0916-2.

Meyer, M. M., Adkins, M. V., Yuan, M. N., et al. (2019). Advertising in young children's apps: A content analysis. *Journal of Developmental & Behavioral Pediatrics*, 40(1), 32–39. doi: 10.1097/DBP.0000000000000622.

Mihailidis, P. (2014). A tethered generation: Exploring the role of mobile phones in the daily life of young people. *Mobile Media & Communication*, 2(1), 58–72. https://doi.org/10.1177/2050157913505558.

Milbrodt, T. (2019). Dating websites and disability identity: Presentations of the disabled self in online dating. *Western Folklore*, 78(1), 68–100.

Miles, S. (2018). Still getting it on online: Thirty years of queer male spaces brokered through digital technologies. *Geography Compass*, 12(11). doi: 10.1111/gec3.12407.

Miller, A. S., Cafazzo, J. A., & Seto, E. (2016). A game plan: Gamification design principles in mHealth applications for chronic disease management. *Health Informatics Journal*, 22(2), 184–193. doi: 10.1177/1460458214537511.

Miller, C. (2012). *iOS hacker's handbook*. Wiley Blackwell.

Miller, C. C. (2012). A new Google app gives you local information: Before you ask for it. *New York Times*, September 27. https://bits.blogs.nytimes.com/2012/09/27/a-new-google-app-gives-you-local-information-before-you-ask-for-it.

Miller, D. (2013). The history of Facebook. In P. N. Miller (ed.), *Cultural histories of the material world* (pp. 81–91). University of Michigan Press Press.

Miller, P. D., & Matviyenko, S. (eds.). (2014). *The imaginary app*. MIT Press.

Milne, E. (2010). *Letters, postcards, mail: Technologies of presence*. Routledge.

Ming, Z. (2015). Three paradoxes of building platforms. *Communications of the ACM*, 58(2), 27–29. doi: 10.1145/2700343.

Mishra, A. (2018). *Amazon Web Services for mobile developers: Building Apps with AWS*. Sybex.

Mishra, D. (2019). Data storage: WhatsApp plans third-party audit. *Times of India*, April 10. https://timesofindia.indiatimes.com/business/india-business/data-storage-whatsapp-plans-third-party-audit/articleshow/68803057.cms.

Mishra, S. (2020). From #MeToo to #MeTooIndia: News domestication in Indian English language newspapers. *Journalism Studies*, 21(5), 659-677. doi: 10.1080/1461670X.2019.1709882.

Mobile apps in Europe [report]. (2019). MarketLine, December. https://www.marketresearch.com/MarketLine-v3883/Mobile-Apps-Europe-12938159.

Mobile apps in North America [report]. (2019). MarketLine, December. https://store.marketline.com/report/ohmf8291--mobile-apps-in-north-america-3.

The Mobile Internet Community. (2000). Symbian releases its first fully integrated software platform for next generation mobile phones. Canadian Corporate News, November 7.

Mojica Ruiz, I. J., Nagappan, M., Adams, B., et al. (2016). Analyzing ad library updates in Android apps. *IEEE Software*, 33(2), 74–80. doi: 10.1109/MS.2014.81.

Montgomery, J., & Roscoe, S. (2013). Owning the consumer: Getting to the core of the Apple business model. *Accounting Forum*, 37(4), 290–299.

Moore, C. (2004). Mobile apps on the rise. *Inforworld*, September 13, p. 20.

Moore, K. (2018). *Situating play: An ethnography of locative play in urban environments*. Doctoral thesis, University of Sydney. http://hdl.handle.net/2123/18603.

Morley, D. (2000). *Home territories: Media, mobility and identity*. Routledge.

Morris, J. W., & Murray, S. (eds.). (2018). *Appified: Culture in the age of apps*. University of Michigan Press.

Morris, M. (1998). Banality in cultural studies. *Discourse*, 10(2), 3–29.

Moutinho, L. (2016). Google phone (the US). In L. Moutinho (ed.), *Worldwide casebook in marketing management* (pp. 297–340). World Scientific Publishing. https://doi.org/10.1142/9789814689 618_0008.

Mowlabocus, S. (2010). *Gaydar culture: Gay men, technology and embodiment in the digital age.* Ashgate.

Mudliar, P., Donner, J., & Thies, W. (2013). Emergent practices around CGNet Swara: A voice forum for citizen journalism in rural India. *Information Technologies & International Development*, 9(2), 65–79.

Mukherjee, R. (2020). Mobile witnessing on WhatsApp: Vigilante virality and the anatomy of mob lynching. *South Asian Popular Culture*, 18(1), 79–101. https://doi.org/10.1080/14746689.2020.17 36810.

Mundy, M.-A., Hernandez, J., & Green, M. (2019). Perceptions of the effects of augmented reality in the classroom. *Journal of Instructional Pedagogies*, 22. https://www.aabri.com/manuscripts/193028.pdf.

Muñiz, A. M., & Schau, H. J. (2005). Religiosity in the abandoned Apple Newton brand community. *Journal of Consumer Research*, 31(4), 737–747.

Munyegera, G. K., & Matsumoto, T. (2018). ICT for financial access: Mobile money and the financial behavior of rural households in Uganda. *Review of Development Economics*, 22(1), 45–66. doi: 10.1111/rode.12327.

Murphy, A., Tucker, H., Coyne, M., & Touryalai, H. (2020). Global 2000: The world's largest public companies. *Forbes*, May 13. https://www.forbes.com/global2000/#4611972d335d.

Murray, S., & Sapnar Ankerson, M. (2016). Lez takes time: Designing lesbian contact in geosocial networking apps. *Critical Studies in Media Communication: Queer Technologies*, 33(1), 53–69. doi: 10.1080/15295036.2015.1133921.

Mutambara, E. (2018). Financial inclusion: Disrupted liquidity and redundancy of mobile money agents in Zimbabwe. *Investment Management & Financial Innovations*, 15(3), 131–142. doi: 10.21511/imfi.15(3).2018.11.

Mutsvairo, B. (2016). *Digital activism in the social media era: Critical reflections on emerging trends in sub-Saharan Africa.* Springer.

Myles, J. (2013). Instrumentalizing voice: Applying Bakhtin and Bourdieu to analyze interactive voice response services. *Journal of Communication Inquiry*, 37(3), 233–248. https://doi.org/10.1177/0196859913491765.

Nagpal, P., & Lyytinen, K. (2013). Key actors in the mobile telephone industry: Feature phone years and the rise of Nokia. *Review of Business Information Systems*, 17(4), 171–178. doi: 10.19030/rbis.v17i4.8239.

Nakamura, Y., & Furukawa, Y. (2018). Japanese tech CEO behind popular "Monster Strike" in search of new hit. *Japan Times*, October 14. https://www.japantimes.co.jp/news/2018/10/14/business/japanese-tech-ceo-behind-popular-monster-strike-search-new-hit.

Nam, S., Nam, C., & Seongcheol, K. (2015). The impact of patent litigation on shareholder value in the smartphone industry. *Technological Forecasting & Social Change*, 95, 182–190.

Nash, C. J., & Gorman-Murray, A. (eds.). (2019). *The geographies of digital sexuality*. Palgrave Macmillan.

Natsuno, T. (2003a). *I-mode strategy*. Wiley.

Natsuno, T. (2003b). *The i-Mode Wireless Ecosystem*. Wiley.

Naughton, B. (2018). *The Chinese economy: Adaptation and growth* (2nd edn.). MIT Press.

NDEMIC Creations. (2020). Statement on the removal of Plague Inc. from the China app store and Steam, March 2. https://www.ndemiccreations.com/en/news/173-statement-on-the-removal-of-plague-inc-from-the-china-app-store.

Newton, C. (2016). Why Vine died. *The Verge*, October 28. https://www.theverge.com/2016/10/28/13456208/why-vine-died-twitter-shutdown.

Neyland, D. (2019). *The everyday life of an algorithm*. Springer.

Nguyen, H., Ganapathy, V., Srivastava, A., & Vaidyanathan, S. (2016). Exploring infrastructure support for app-based services on cloud platforms. *Computers & Security*, 62(C), 177–192. doi: 10.1016/j.cose.2016.07.009.

Niantic Team. (2019). Thanks for the adventure, Field Trip users! Niantic Blog, July 12. https://nianticlabs.com/en/blog/fieldtrip.

Nicoletti, B. (2014). *Mobile banking evolution or revolution?* Palgrave Macmillan.

Nieborg, D. B. (2015). Crushing candy: The free-to-play game in its connective commodity form. *Social Media + Society*, 1(2). doi: 10.1177/2056305115621932.

Nieborg, D. B., Young, C., & Joseph, D. (2019). Lost in the app store: The state of the Canadian game app economy. *Canadian Journal of Communication*, 44(2), 57–62. doi: 10.22230/cjc.2019v44n2a3505.

Niknam, N. (2010). Hidden media: The mobile phone in an Iranian cultural context with a focus on Bluetooth messaging. *Information, Communication & Society*, 13(8), 1172–1190. https://doi.org/10.1080/13691181003639874.

Noam, E., & Steinbock, D. (eds.). (2003). *Competition for the mobile Internet*. Kluwer.

Nolan, J., & McBride, M. (2014). Beyond gamification: Reconceptualizing game-based learning in early childhood environments. *Information, Communication & Society*, 17(5), 594–608. doi: 10.1080/1369118X.2013.808365.

Nothias, T. (2020). Access granted: Facebook's free basics in Africa. *Media, Culture & Society*, 42(3), 329–348. doi: 10.1177/0163443719890530.

Oborn, E., Barrett, M., Orlikowski, W., & Kim, A. (2019). Trajectory dynamics in innovation: Developing and transforming a mobile money service across time and place. *Organization Science*, 30(5), 1097–1123. doi: 10.1287/orsc.2018.1281.

OECD. (2017). *Algorithms and collusion: Competition policy in the digital age*. Paris: http://www.oecd.org/daf/competition/Algorithms-and-colllusion-competition-policy-in-the-digital-age.pdf.

OED. (2020). *The Oxford English dictionary online*. Oxford University Press.

Oestreicher-Singer, G., & Sundararajan, A. (2012). Recommendation networks and the long tail of electronic commerce. *MIS Quarterly*, 36(1), 65. doi: 10.2307/41410406.

Ohashi, K., Kato, F., & Hjorth, L. (2017). Digital genealogies: Understanding social mobile media LINE in the role of Japanese families. *Social Media + Society*, 3(2). https://doi.org/10.1177/2056305117703815.

O'Regan, T., Balnaves, M., & Sternberg, J. (2002). *Mobilising the audience*. University of Queensland Press.

Osterloh, R. (2019). Helping more people with wearables: Google to acquire Fitbit. https://www.blog.google/products/hardware/agreement-with-fitbit.

Paasonen, S., Jarrett, K., & Light, B. (2019). *NSFW: Sex, humor, and risk in social media*. MIT Press.

Paasonen, S., Light, B., & Jarrett, K. (2019). The dick pic: Harassment, curation, and desire. *Social Media + Society*, 5(2). doi: 10.1177/2056305119826126.

Paglialonga, A., Lugo, A., & Santoro, E. (2018). An overview on the emerging area of identification, characterization, and assessment of health apps. *Journal of Biomedical Informatics*, 83, 97–102. doi: 10.1016/j.jbi.2018.05.017.

Paglialonga, A., Mastropietro, A., Scalco, E., & Rizzo, G. (2019). The mhealth. In G. Andreoni, P. Perego, & E. Frumento (eds.), *m_Health current and future applications* (pp. 5–17). Springer.

Paik, Y., & Zhu, F. (2016). The impact of patent wars on firm strategy: Evidence from the global smartphone industry. *Organization Science*, 27, 1397–1416. http://dx.doi.org/10.2139/ssrn.2340899 .

Palmer, K. (2014). *The economy of you*. AMACOM.

Panova, Y., Tan, A., Hilmola, O.-P., et al. (2019). Evaluation of e-commerce location and entry to China: Implications on shipping and trade. *Journal of Shipping and Trade*, 4(1), 1–25. doi: 10.1186/s41072-019-0045-6.

Pantano, E., & Gandini, A. (2017). Exploring the forms of sociality mediated by innovative technologies in retail settings. *Computers in Human Behavior*, 77, 367–373. doi: 10.1016/j.chb.2017.02.036.

Parkin, B., & Murphy, H. (2020). Facebook and Jio deal creates huge lake of Indian data. *Financial Times*, April 23.

Pattnaik, P. K., Mohanty, S., & Mohanty, S. (eds.). (2020). *Smart healthcare analytics in IoT enabled environment*. Springer.

Pau, G., Bazzi, A., Campista, M. E. M., & Balador, A. (2019). Towards 5G and beyond for the Internet of UAVs, vehicles, smartphones, sensors and smart objects. *Journal of Network and Computer Applications*, 135, 108–109. doi: 10.1016/j.jnca.2019.03.003.

Perez, B. (2010). App stores fight for space in mainland mobile marketplace. *South China Morning Post*, November 22.

Peters, J. D. (1999). *Speaking into the air: A history of the idea of communication*. University of Chicago Press.

Peters, J. D. (2015). *The marvelous clouds: Toward a philosophy of elemental media*. University of Chicago Press.

Petrovčič, A., Taipale, S., Rogelj, A., & Dolničar, V. (2018). Design of mobile phones for older adults: An empirical analysis of design guidelines and checklists for feature phones and smartphones. *International Journal of Human-Computer Interaction*, 34(3), 251–264. doi: 10.1080/10447318.2017.1345142.

Pfanner, E. (2013). Baidu deal may reduce app piracy in China. *New York Times*, August 18. https://www.nytimes.com/2013/08/19/business/global/baidu-deal-may-reduce-app-piracy-in-china.html.

Phadnis, S. (2014). WhatsApp: India's preferred messaging application. *Economic Times*, February 22. https://economictimes.indiatimes.com/tech/internet/whatsapp-indias-preferred-mobile-messaging-application/articleshow/30775328.cms?from=mdr.

Phua, J., & Kim, J. (2018). Starring in your own Snapchat advertisement: Influence of self-brand congruity, self-referencing, and perceived humor on brand attitude and purchase intention of advertised brands. *Telematics and Informatics*, 35(5), 1524–1533. doi: 10.1016/j.tele.2018.03.020.

Pickard, S. (ed.). (2014). *Anti-social behaviour in Britain: Victorian and contemporary perspectives.* Palgrave Macmillan.

Pogue, D. (2014). A look at Google's first phone. *New York Times,* October 16. https://www.nytimes.com/2008/10/16/technology/personaltech/16pogue.html.

Pon, B. (2016). Winners & losers in the global app economy. https://www.cariboudigital.net/wp-content/uploads/2019/01/Caribou-Digital-Winners-and-Losers-in-the-Global-App-Economy-2016.pdf.

Pon, B., Seppälä, T., & Kenney, M. (2014). Android and the demise of operating system-based power: Firm strategy and platform control in the post-PC world. *Telecommunications Policy,* 38(11), 979–991. doi: 10.1016/j.telpol.2014.05.001.

Porter, J. (2020, July 28). Amazon's Alexa app redesigned to focus on the bits people actually use. The Verge. https://www.theverge.com/2020/7/28/21344777/amazon-alexa-app-redesign-ios-android-fire-os-skills-routines-weather-reminders.

Poster, W. R. (2019). Racialized surveillance in the digital service economy. In R. Benjamin (ed.), *Captivating technology: Race, carceral technoscience, and liberatory imagination in everyday life* (pp. 133–169). Duke University Press.

Pourmand, A., Lombardi, K., Kuhl, E., & O'Connell, F. (2017). Videogame-related illness and injury: A review of the literature and predictions for Pokémon GO. *Games for Health Journal,* 6(1), 9–18. doi: 10.1089/g4h.2016.0090.

Prasad, R. (2018). Ascendant India, digital India: How net neutrality advocates defeated Facebook's Free Basics. *Media, Culture & Society,* 40(3), 415–431. doi: 10.1177/0163443717736117.

Progressive Policy Institute. (2020). About PPI [website]. August 3. https://www.progressivepolicy.org/about.

Purnell, N. (2019). The hottest phones for the next billion users aren't smartphones. *Wall Street Journal,* July 23. https://www.wsj.com/articles/the-hottest-phones-for-the-next-billion-users-arent-smart-phones-11563879608.

Richardson, A. V. (2020). *Bearing witness while black: African Americans, smartphones, and the new protest #journalism.* Oxford University Press.

Qian, Y. (2018). 2000 个违规微信小程序封停 监管审核尚需合力 [2,000 violating WeChat mini-programs suspended: Their regulation and review still requires a concerted effort]. People.cn, February 2018. http://media.people.com.cn/n1/2018/0222/c14677-29827484.html.

Qiao, X., Ren, P., Dustdar, S., et al. (2019). Web AR: A promising future for mobile augmented reality: State of the art, challenges, and insights. In S. Giannluca (ed.), *Proceedings of the IEEE*, 107(4), 651–666. doi: 10.1109/JPROC.2019.2895105.

Qin, A. (2017). China casts a wary eye at an iPhone cash cow, the app store. *New York Times*, August 10. https://www.nytimes.com/2017/08/10/business/china-apple-app-store.html.

Qiu, J. L. (2016). *Goodbye iSlave: A manifesto for digital abolition.* University of Illinois Press.

Qualcomm. (2020). Snapdragon XR2 5G Platform. https://www.qualcomm.com/products/snapdragon-xr2-5g-platform.

Quirce García, J. (2011). A study on PDAs for onboard applications and technologies and methodologies. *Personal and Ubiquitous Computing*, 15(5), 457–478. doi: 10.1007/s00779-010-0318-4.

Rao, R. (2020). India may have banned TikTok but the app's users have democratised stardom forever. ZDNet, July 16. https://www.zdnet.com/article/india-may-have-banned-tiktok-but-the-apps-users-have-democratized-stardom-forever.

Reiners, T., & Wood, L. C. (eds.). (2015). *Gamification in education and business.* Springer.

Reuters. (2020). Winning bidder for dating app Grindr has ties to Chinese owner Kunlun. *South China Morning Post*, June 2. https://www.scmp.com/tech/apps-social/article/3087219/winning-bidder-grindr-has-ties-chinese-owner-kunlun.

Reynolds, M. (2017). AI artist paints reality by numbers. *New Scientist*, 235(3139), 14. doi: 10.1016/S0262-4079(17)31605-6.

Rheingold, H. (1991). *Virtual reality.* Martin Secker & Warburg.

Rheingold, H. (2002). *Smart mobs: The next social revolution.* Perseus.

Rhodes, G. A. (2019). Waiting for the augmented reality "killer app": Pokémon GO 2016. In V. Geroimenko (ed.), *Augmented reality games: Understanding the Pokémon GO phenomenon* (pp. 3–14). Springer.

Rich, L., Fortunati, L., Goggin, G., et al. (2020). The smartphone decade: An introduction. In L. Rich, L. Fortunati, G. Goggin, et al. (eds.), *Oxford handbook of mobile communication and society* (pp. 3–12). Oxford University Press.

Richardson, I. (2011). The hybrid ontology of mobile gaming. *Convergence*, 17(4), 419–430. doi: 10.1177/1354856511414797.

Rodriguez, A. (2012). Super apps! *PC World*, 30(8), 66–74.

Rodriguez, C., & Iliadis, A. (2019). The MacBride Report legacy and media democracy today. World Association for Christian Communication (WACC), August 11. http://wacc-global.live.publishwithagility.com/articles/the-macbride-report-legacy-and-media-democracy-today.

Rogers, R. (2018). Aestheticizing Google critique: A 20-year retrospective. *Big Data & Society*, 5(1). doi: 10.1177/2053951718768626.

Roma, P., & Ragaglia, D. (2016). Revenue models, in-app purchase, and the app performance: Evidence from Apple's App Store and Google Play. *Electronic Commerce Research and Applications*, 17, 173–190.

Roma, P., & Vasi, M. (2019). Diversification and performance in the mobile app market: The role of the platform ecosystem. *Technological Forecasting and Social Change*, 147, 123–139. doi:https://doi.org/10.1016/j.techfore.2019.07.003.

Rose, N. (2008). *Governing the present: Administering economic, social and personal life*. Polity.

Rose, N. (2009). *The politics of life itself: Biomedicine, power, and subjectivity in the twenty-first century*. Princeton University Press.

Roth, Y. (2014). Locating the Scruff guy. *International Journal of Communication*, 8, 2113–2133. https://ijoc.org/index.php/ijoc/article/view/2286/1192.

Rushkoff, D. (2016). *Throwing rocks at the Google bus: How growth became the enemy of prosperity*. Portfolio/Penguin.

Russell, J. (2017). Google makes its Translate mobile apps available for users in China. TechCrunch, March 28. https://techcrunch.com/2017/03/28/google-translate-china.

Rutkin, A. (2016). Tiny camera lets blind people read with their fingers. *New Scientist*, 232(3100), 25. doi: 10.1016/S0262-4079(16)32120-0.

Sakakibara, K., Lindholm, C., & Ainamo, A. (1995). Product development strategies in emerging markets: The case of personal digital assistants. *Business Strategy Review*, 6(4), 23. doi: 10.1111/j.1467-8616.1995.tb00104.x.

Salami, I. (2019). Facebook's Libra: A global monetary system governed by private corporations? *E-international Relations*, October 9. https://www.e-ir.info/2019/10/08/facebook-libra-a-global-monetary-system-governed-by-private-corporations.

Sales, N. J. (2015). Tinder and the dawn of the "dating apocalypse." *Vanity Fair*, August 6.

Samuel, K. (2016). The grindrization of gay identity. *Gay & Lesbian Review Worldwide*, 23(6), https://glreview.org/article/the-grindrization-of-gay-identity.

Sathyan, J., Narayanan, A., Narayan, N., & Shibu, K. V. (2013). Device capabilities leveraged in apps location, magnetometer, motion sensor, touch, and scanner. In J. Sathyan, A. Narayanan, N. Narayan, & K. V. Shibu (eds.), *A comprehensive guide to enterprise mobility* (pp. 387–404). CRC Press.

Savov, V. (2020). The new Vine successor Byte is already beating TikTok in the app store. *Time*, January 27. https://time.com/5772227/vine-creator-tiktok.

SC issues notice to Govt, TRAI, Facebook, WhatsApp over data privacy. (2017). *Governance Now*, January 16. https://www.governancenow.com/news/regular-story/sc-issues-notice-govt-trai-facebook-whatsapp-data-privacy.

Schoonmaker, S. (2018). *Free software, the Internet, and global communities of resistance.* Taylor & Francis.

Schrock, A. (2015). Communicative affordances of mobile media: Portability, availability, locatability, and multimediality. *International Journal of Communication*, 9, 1229–1246.

Schroeder, R. (2018). Towards a theory of digital media. *Information, Communication & Society*, 21(3), 323–339. doi: 10.1080/1369911 8X.2017.1289231.

Selwyn, L. L., & Golding, H. E. (2010). Revisiting the regulatory status of broadband Internet access: A policy framework for net neutrality and an open competitive Internet. *Federal Communications Law Journal*, 63(1), 91–139.

Senft, T. M. (2008). *Camgirls: Celebrity and community in the age of social networks.* Peter Lang.

Senft, T. M. (2013). Microcelebrity and the branded self. In John Hartley, J. Burgess, & A. Bruns (eds.), *A companion to new media dynamics* (pp. 346–354). Wiley Blackwell.

Senft, T. M., & Baym, N. (2015). Selfies introduction: What does the selfie say? Investigating a global phenomenon. *International Journal of Communication*, 9, 19–33.

Sensor Tower. (2020). Top grossing dating apps worldwide for May 2020. June 17. https://sensortower.com/blog/top-grossing-dating-apps-worldwide-may-2020.

Shaw, A., & Chess, S. (2016). Reflection on the casual games market in a post-GamerGate world. In T. Leaver & M. Willson (eds.), *Social, casual and mobile games: The changing gaming landscape* (pp. 277–289). Bloomsbury.

Shaw, F. (2016). "Bitch I said hi": The Bye Felipe campaign and discursive activism in mobile dating apps. *Social Media + Society*, 2(4). https://doi.org/10.1177/2056305116672889.

Sheller, M., & de Souza e Silva, A. (eds.). (2015). *Mobility and locative media: Mobile communication in hybrid spaces.* Routledge.

Shield, A. D. J. (2019). *Immigrants on Grindr race, sexuality and belonging online.* Springer.

Shklovski, I., & de Souza e Silva, A. (2013). An urban encounter: Realizing online connectedness through local urban play.

Information, Communication & Society (AoIR special issue), 16(3), 340–361. doi: 10.1080/1369118X.2012.756049.

Shubber, K. (2020). US justice department prepares Google antitrust probe. *Financial Times*, June 2. https://www.ft.com/content/92cd496e-8487-11e9-a028-86cea8523dc2.

Silverstone, R., & Hirsch, E. (1992). *Consuming technologies: Media and information in domestic spaces.* Routledge.

Singh, S. (2013). *Globalization and money: A global South perspective.* Rowman & Littlefield.

Singh, S. (2019). Global imaginaries beyond markets: The globalization of money, family, and financial inclusion. In C. Hudson & E. K. Wilson (eds.), *Revisiting the global imaginary: Theories, ideologies, subjectivities: Essays in honor of Manfred Steger* (pp. 85–103). Palgrave Macmillan.

Sitaram, D., & Manjunath, G. (2012). *Moving to the cloud: Developing apps in the new world of cloud computing.* Syngress.

Slater, D. (2013a). *Love in the time of algorithms.* Penguin.

Slater, D. (2013b). A million first dates. *Atlantic.* https://www.theatlantic.com/magazine/archive/2013/01/a-million-first-dates/309195.

Smith, M. (2020). An army of app developers pushes back on Apple's power. *Barron's*, 100(12), 30–31.

Snickars, P., & Vonderau, P. (eds.). (2012). *Moving data: The iPhone and the future of media.* Columbia University Press.

Sofia, Z. (2000). Container technologies. *Hypatia*, 15(2), 181–201.

Sogou. (2020). Q4 2019 Sogou Inc earnings call – final. http://ir.sogou.com/index.php?s=19&item=16.

Sohu.com. (2018). 微信小程序是用什么语言开发的呢 [Which language is used to develop WeChat mini-programs?]. September 25. https://www.sohu.com/a/255969229_100145122.

Srnicek, N. (2019). *Platform capitalism.* Polity.

Staff, N. (2020). Alexa will soon be able to launch Android and iOS apps using voice commands. *The Verge*, July 22. https://www.theverge.com/2020/7/22/21333548/amazon-alexa-for-apps-android-ios-open-launch-skill-app-data-information.

Stald, G. (2008). Mobile identity: Youth, identity, and mobile communication media. In D. Buckingham (ed.), *Youth, identity, and digital media* (pp. 143-164). MIT Press.

Stawski, S. (2015). *Inflection point: How the convergence of cloud, mobility, apps, and data will shape the future of business.* Pearson.

Steinberg, M. (2020). LINE as super app: Platformization in East Asia. *Social Media + Society*, 6(2). https://doi.org/10.1177/2056305120933285.

Steinbock, D. (2007). *The mobile revolution: The making of mobile services worldwide*. Kogan Page.

Steinbock, D. (2013). *Wireless horizon: Strategy and competition in the worldwide mobile marketplace*. AMACON.

Stephenson, M., Renz, J., & Ge, X. (2020). The computational complexity of Angry Birds. *Artificial Intelligence*, 280. doi: 10.1016/j.artint.2019.103232.

Stewart, J., & Misuraca, G. (2013). The industry and policy context for digital games for empowerment and inclusion. Institute for Prospective Technological Studies, European Commission. https://publications.jrc.ec.europa.eu/repository/bitstream/JRC77656/jrc77656.pdf.

Stieglitz, S., Lattemann, C., Robra-Bissantz, S., et al. (2017). *Gamification: Using game elements in serious contexts*. Springer.

Stremlau, N., & Osman, R. (2015). Courts, clans and companies: Mobile money and dispute resolution in Somaliland. *Stability: International Journal of Security and Development*, 4(1). doi: 10.5334/sta.gh.

Striphas, T. (2015). Algorithmic culture. *European Journal of Cultural Studies*, 18(4–5), 395–412. doi: 10.1177/1367549415577392.

Strzelecki, A. (2020). The second worldwide wave of interest in Coronavirus since the COVID-19 outbreaks in South Korea, Italy and Iran: A Google Trends study. *Brain Behavior and Immunity*, 950–951. doi:10.1016/j.bbi.2020.04.042.

Stucke, M., & Ezrachi, A. (2018). How digital assistants can harm our economy, privacy, and democracy. *Berkeley Technology Law Journal*, 32(3), 1239–1299. https://doi.org/10.15779/Z383B5W79M.

Suchman, L. A. (2007). *Human-machine reconfigurations: Plans and situated actions* (2nd edn.). Cambridge University Press.

Suellentrop, C. (2014). Where virtual meets real. *New York Times*, July 14. https://www.nytimes.com/2014/07/15/arts/video-games/ingress-a-mobile-game-from-google.html.

Sun, L. (2019). Is Baidu losing China's voice search market to Sogou? The Motley Fool, August 27. https://www.fool.com/investing/2019/08/27/is-baidu-losing-chinas-voice-search-market-to-sogo.aspx.

Suri, T., & Jack, W. (2016). The long-run poverty and gender impacts of mobile money. *Science*, 354(6317), 1288–1292. doi: 10.1126/science.aah5309.

Swalwell, M. (2012). Questions about the usefulness of microcomputers in 1980s Australia. *Media International Australia 143*, 63–77.

Swan, M. (2015). Connected car: Quantified self becomes quantified car. *Journal of Sensor and Actuator Networks*, 4(1), 2–29. doi: 10.3390/jsan4010002.

Swanson, S. D. (2010). The Digital Millennium Copyright Act and the iphone: An unnecessary proceeding. *Journal of Internet Law*, 14(2), 3–6.

Takahashi, T. (2010). MySpace or Mixi? Japanese engagement with SNS (social networking sites) in the global age. *New Media & Society*, 12(3), 453–475. doi: 10.1177/1461444809343462.

Tanner, A. (2015). Even in the Tinder era, adultery site Ashley Madison keeps making money hand over fist. *Forbes*. https://www.forbes.com/sites/adamtanner/2015/01/21/profiting-from-cheating.

Tapscott, D., Lowy, A., Ticoll, D., & Klym, N. (1998). *Blueprint to the digital economy: Creating wealth in the era of e-business*. McGraw-Hill.

Taylor, K., & Silver, L. (2019). Smartphone ownership is growing rapidly around the world, but not always equally. Pew Research, February 5. https://www.pewresearch.org/global/2019/02/05/smartphone-ownership-is-growing-rapidly-around-the-world-but-not-always-equally.

Taylor, T. L. (2018). *Watch me play: Twitch and the rise of game live streaming*. Princeton University Press.

Telecom Regulatory Authority of India (TRAI). (2020). Highlights of Telecom subscription data as on 30th June, 2020 [press release]. September 24. https://www.trai.gov.in/sites/default/files/PR_No.79of2020_0.pdf.

Teo, T. S. H., & Pok, S. H. (2003). Adoption of the Internet and WAP-enabled phones in Singapore. *Behaviour & Information Technology*, 22(4), 281–289. doi: 10.1080/0144929031000119385.

Thiel, D. (2016). *iOS application security: The definitive guide for hackers and developers*. No Starch Press.

Thurman, N. (2018). Social media, surveillance, and news work: On the apps promising journalists a "crystal ball." *Digital Journalism*, 6(1), 76–97. doi: 10.1080/21670811.2017.1345318.

Tian, X. (2018). Escaping the interpersonal power game: Online shopping in China. *Qualitative Sociology*, 41(4), 545–568. doi: 10.1007/s11133-018-9397-8.

Timberg, C. (2013). "Jailbreaking" Apple devices is becoming a hot underground industry. *Washington Post*, December 31. https://www.washingtonpost.com/business/technology/jailbreaking-apple-devices-is-becoming-a-hot-underground-industry/2013/12/31/0dc3aade-723a-11e3-8def-a33011492df2_story.html.

Tinder. (2016). Introducing more genders on Tinder. November 15. https://www.tinderpressroom.com/genders.

Tkacz, N. (2019). Money's new abstractions: Apple Pay and the economy of experience. *Distinktion: Journal of Social Theory*, 20(3), 264–283. doi: 10.1080/1600910X.2019.1653348.

Trabucchi, D., & Buganza, T. (2020). Fostering digital platform innovation: From two to multi-sided platforms. *Creativity and Innovation Management*, 29(2), 345–358. https://doi.org/10.1111/caim.12320.

Treré, E. (2015). Reclaiming, proclaiming, and maintaining collective identity in the #YoSoy132 movement in Mexico: An examination of digital frontstage and backstage activism through social media and instant messaging platforms. *Information, Communication & Society*, 18(8), 901–915. https://doi.org/10.1080/1369118X.2015.1043744.

Trnka, S. (2016). Digital care: Agency and temporality in young people's use of health apps. *Engaging Science, Technology, and Society*, 2. doi: 10.17351/ests2016.119.

Trnka, S., & Trundle, C. (eds.). (2017). *Competing responsibilities: The ethics and politics of contemporary life*. Duke University Press.

Tsotsis, A. (2013). Apple's flashlight is why we can't fund nice dumb things. *TechCrunch*, June 10. https://techcrunch.com/2013/06/10/apples-flashlight-is-why-we-cant-fund-nice-dumb-things.

Tulloch, R., & Randell-Moon, H. E. K. (2018). The politics of gamification: Education, neoliberalism and the knowledge economy. *Review of Education, Pedagogy & Cultural Studies*, 40(3), 204. doi: 10.1080/10714413.2018.1472484.

Tuunainen, V. K., Tuunanen, T., & Piispanen, J. (2011). Mobile service platforms: Comparing Nokia OVI and Apple App Store with the IISI^n model. In A. Rangone & K. Lyytinen (eds.), *Proceedings of 10th International Conference on Mobile Business, Como, Italy*. https://ieeexplore.ieee.org/document/6047056.

Udupa, S., Venkatraman, S., & Khan, A. (2020). "Millennial India": Global digital politics in context. *Television & New Media*, 21(4), 343–359. https://doi.org/10.1177/1527476419870516.

United Nations (UN). (2019). World population prospects 2019 (online edn.). https://population.un.org/wpp/Download/Standard/Population.

United Nations Conference on Trade and Development (UNCTAD). (2019). Digital economy report 2019. https://unctad.org/en/PublicationsLibrary/der2019_en.pdf.

Vaidhyanathan, S. (2011). *The googlization of everything (and why we should worry)*. University of California Press.

Valentine, G., & Bell, D. (eds.). (1995). *Mapping desire: Geographies of sexualities*. Routledge.

van Dijck, J. (2013). *The culture of connectivity: A critical history of social media*. Oxford University Press.

van Dijck, J., Poell, T., & de Waal, M. (2018). *The platform society*. Oxford University Press.

Vogelstein, F. (2013). *Dogfight: How Apple and Google went to war and started a revolution*. Sarah Crichton Books/Farrar, Straus and Giroux.

Wachter-Boettcher, S. (2017). *Technically wrong: Sexist apps, biased algorithms, and other threats of toxic tech*. W. W. Norton.

Wafa, S. N., & Hashim, E. (2016). Adoption of mobile augmented reality advertisements by brands in Malaysia. *Procedia – Social and Behavioral Sciences*, 219, 762–768. doi: 10.1016/j.sbspro.2016.05.077.

Wagner, S., & Fernández-Ardèvol, M. (2016). Local content production and the political economy of the mobile app industries in Argentina and Bolivia. *New Media & Society*, 18(8), 1768–1786. doi:https://doi.org/10.1177/1461444481557112.

Wake, N., Alexander, A., & Christensen, A., et al. (2019). Creating patient-specific anatomical models for 3D printing and AR/VR. *3D Printing in Medicine*, 5(1), 1–10. doi: 10.1186/s41205-019-0054-y.

Walz, S., & Deterding, S. (eds.). (2014). *The gameful world: Approaches, issues, applications*. MIT Press.

Wan, R. (ed.). (2016). *Mobile media, civic engagement and civic activism in Asia: Private chat to public communication*. Springer.

Wang, H., Liu, Z., & Liang, J., et al. (2018). Beyond Google Play: A large-scale comparative study of Chinese Android app markets. In B. Y. Zhao & E. Katz-Bassett (eds.), *IMC '18: Proceedings of the Internet Measurement Conference* (pp. 293–307). ACM. https://doi.org/10.1145/3278532.3278558.

Wang, S. (2020a). Calculating dating goals: Data gaming and algorithmic sociality on Blued, a Chinese gay dating app. *Information, Communication & Society*, 23(2), 181–197. doi: 10.1080/1369118X.2018.1490796.

Wang, S. (2020b). Chinese affective platform economies: Dating, live streaming, and performative labor on Blued. *Media, Culture & Society*, 42(4), 502–520. doi: 10.1177/0163443719867283.

Wang, S. S. (2016). More than words? The effect of Line character sticker use on intimacy in the mobile communication environment. *Social Science Computer Review*, 34(4), 456–478. https://doi.org/10.1177/0894439315590209.

Wang, W. Y., & Lobato, R. (2019). Chinese video streaming services in the context of global platform studies. *Chinese Journal of Communication: The Platformization of Chinese Society*, 12(3), 356–371. doi: 10.1080/17544750.2019.1584119.

Want, R. (2006). An introduction to RFID Technology. *Pervasive Computing*, 5, 25–33. doi: 10.1109/MPRV.2006.2.

Warf, B. (2013). *Global geographies of the Internet*. Springer.

Wassom, B. (2014). *Augmented reality law, privacy, and ethics*. Syngress/ Elsevier.

Weber, M. S., & Kosterich, A. (2018). Coding the news: The role of computer code in filtering and distributing news. *Digital Journalism*, 6(3), 310–329. doi: 10.1080/21670811.2017.1366865.

Westland, J. C., & Clark, T. H. (eds.). (1999). *Global electronic commerce: Theory and case studies*. MIT Press.

Wetsman, N. (2020). Google and Apple's COVID-19 tracking system can't save lives all on its own. *The Verge*, April 15. https://www. theverge.com/2020/4/15/21222161/apple-google-bluetooth-contact-tracing-system-coronavirus-health.

Whitney, L. (2012). A spotlight on flashlight apps for the iPhone. *Cnet*, October 29. https://www.cnet.com/news/a-spotlight-on-flash light-apps-for-the-iphone.

Whittaker, Z. (2020). Grindr sold by Chinese owner after US raised national security concerns. *TechCrunch*, March 6. https:// techcrunch.com/2020/03/06/grindr-sold-china-national-security.

Wikström, P. (2020). *The music industry* (3rd edn.). Polity.

Wilken, R. (2014). Places nearby: Facebook as a location-based social media platform. *New Media & Society*, 16(7), 1087–1103. doi: 10.1177/1461444814543997.

Wilken, R. (2017). Social media apps economies. In J. Burgess, A. E. Marwick, & T. Poell (eds.), *SAGE handbook of social media* (pp. 279–296). SAGE.

Wilken, R. (2019). *Cultural economies of locative media*. Oxford University Press.

Wilken, R., Burgess, J., & Albury, J. (2019). Dating apps and data markets: A political economy of communication approach. *Computational Culture*, 7, 1–36.

Wilken, R., & Goggin, G. (eds.). (2012). *Mobile technology and place*. Routledge.

Wilken, R., & Goggin, G. (eds.). (2014). *Locative media*. Routledge.

Wilken, R., Goggin, G., & Horst, H. A. (eds.). (2019). *Location technologies in international context*. Routledge.

Wilken, R., & Humphreys, L. (2019). Constructing the check-in: Reflections on photo-taking among Foursquare users. *Communication and the Public*, 4(2), 100–117. doi: 10.1177/2057047319853328.

Wilken, R., & Sinclair, J. (2009). "Waiting for the kiss of life": Mobile media and advertising. *Convergence*, 15(4), 427–445. doi: 10.1177/1354856509342343.

Willems, W. (2013). Participation: In what? Radio, convergence and the corporate logic of audience input through new media in Zambia. *Telematics and Informatics*, 30(3), 223–231. https://doi.org/10.1016/j.tele.2012.02.006.

Wilmott, C. (2016). Small moments in spatial big data: Calculability, authority and interoperability in everyday mobile mapping. *Big Data & Society*, 3(2). doi: 10.1177/2053951716661364.

Winseck, D. (2017). The geopolitical economy of the global Internet infrastructure. *Journal of Information Policy*, 7, 228–267. doi: 10.5325/jinfopoli.7.2017.0228.

Winseck, D. (2019). Internet infrastructure and the persistent myth of US hegemony. In B. Haggart, K. Henne, & N. Tusikov (eds.), *Information, technology and control in a changing world: Understanding power structures in the 21st century* (pp. 93–120). Palgrave Macmillan.

Wolman, D. (2012). *The end of money: Counterfeiters, preachers, techies, dreamers—and the coming cashless society*. Da Capo Press.

Woodward, B. (2016). m-Health computing: m-Health 2.0, social networks, health apps, cloud, and big health data. In R. S. H. Istepanian & B. Woodward (eds.), *m-Health: Fundamentals and Applications* (pp. 67–117). Wiley Blackwell.

Xi, L. (2018). Central government launches new platform to hear from public. *Xinhua*, September 20. http://www.xinhuanet.com/english/2018-09/20/c_137481879.htm.

Xue, K., & Yu, M. (2017). Introduction: New media in China. In K. Xue & M. Yu (eds.), *New media and Chinese society* (pp. xi–xvii). Springer.

Yashari, L. (2016). Meet the Tinder co-founder trying to change online dating forever. *Vanity Fair*, August 7. https://www.vanityfair.com/culture/2015/08/bumble-app-whitney-wolfe.

Yim, K. S., Malchev, I., Hsieh, A., & Burke, D. (2019). Treble: Fast software updates by creating an equilibrium in an active software ecosystem of globally distributed stakeholders. *ACM Transactions on Embedded Computing Systems*, 18(5s), 1–23. doi: 10.1145/3358237.

Yoon, K. (2016). The media practice of "KaTalk" in the face of Facebook: Young Koreans' use of mobile app platforms in a trans-national context. *Critical Arts*, 30(2), 217–232. https://doi.org/10.1080/02560046.2016.1187797.

Zheng, J., Qi, Z., Dou, Y., & Tan, Y. (2019). How mega is the mega? Exploring the spillover effects of WeChat using graphical model. *Information Systems Research*, 30(4), 1343–1362. doi: 10.1287/isre.2019.0865.

Zichermann, G. (2011). *Gamification by design: Implementing game mechanics in web and mobile apps*. O'Reilly Media.

Zittrain, J. (2008). *The future of the Internet: And how to stop it*. Harvard University Press.

Zittrain, J. (2018). Fixing the Internet. *Science*, 362(6417), 871. doi: 10.1126/science.aaw0798.

ZOE. (2020). COVID symptom study: About this research. https://covid.joinzoe.com/about.

Index